Rinna Kullaa is a Postdoctoral Fellow  the Harriman Institute for Russian, Eu at Columbia University. She holds a University of Maryland and an MPhil in Russian and Eastern European Studies from the University of Oxford.

NON-ALIGNMENT AND ITS ORIGINS IN COLD WAR EUROPE

Yugoslavia, Finland and the Soviet Challenge

RINNA KULLAA

BLOOMSBURY ACADEMIC
LONDON • NEW YORK • OXFORD • NEW DELHI • SYDNEY

BLOOMSBURY ACADEMIC
Bloomsbury Publishing Plc
50 Bedford Square, London, WC1B 3DP, UK
1385 Broadway, New York, NY 10018, USA

BLOOMSBURY, BLOOMSBURY ACADEMIC and the Diana
logo are trademarks of Bloomsbury Publishing Plc

First published in Great Britain by I.B. Tauris 2011
Paperback edition published by Bloomsbury Academic 2020

Copyright © Rinna Kullaa, 2011

Rinna Kullaa has asserted her right under the Copyright,
Designs and Patents Act, 1988, to be identified as Author of this work.

For legal purposes the Acknowledgements on p. xi constitute
an extension of this copyright page.

All rights reserved. No part of this publication may be reproduced or
transmitted in any form or by any means, electronic or mechanical,
including photocopying, recording, or any information storage or retrieval
system, without prior permission in writing from the publishers.

Bloomsbury Publishing Plc does not have any control over, or responsibility for,
any third-party websites referred to or in this book. All internet addresses given
in this book were correct at the time of going to press. The author and publisher
regret any inconvenience caused if addresses have changed or sites have
ceased to exist, but can accept no responsibility for any such changes.

A catalogue record for this book is available from the British Library.

A catalog record for this book is available from the Library of Congress.

ISBN: HB: 978-1-8488-5624-0
PB: 978-1-3501-6343-0
ePDF: 978-0-8577-2138-9
ePub: 978-0-7556-3089-9

Series: International Library of Twentieth Century History, vol. 33

To find out more about our authors and books visit
www.bloomsbury.com and sign up for our newsletters.

CONTENTS

List of Abbreviations vii
Acknowledgements xi
Preface xiii

1. Introduction 1

2. 1948: The Soviet test for Yugoslavia and the Tito-Stalin split 25

3. 1948: The Soviet test for Finland and the compromise on neutralism 53

4. The death of Stalin and the beginning of a beautiful Yugoslav-Finnish friendship 81

5. Khrushchev, Tito and Yugoslav/Finnish neutralism: surviving Hungary 1956 109

6. Freezing out Finland and Yugoslavia: the Soviet rifts of 1957–58 145

7. Conclusion and afterword: from neutralism to non-alignment 173

Notes 183
Bibliography 211
Index 223

LIST OF ABBREVIATIONS

	Original	Translation (if non-English)
ASCG	Arhiv Srbije Crne Gore	Archive of Serbia and Montenegro
AP	Maalaisliitto	Agrarians' Party
APR	Arhiv Predsednika Republike	Archive of the Office of the President Josip Broz 'Tito'
AVP RF	Arkhiv Vneshnei Politiki Rossiiskoi Federatsii	Archive of Foreign Policy of the Russian Federation
BRP	Bulgarska rabotnicheska partiia	Bulgarian Workers' Party
Cominform	Informbiro	Communist Information Bureau
CPY	Komunistička partija Jugoslavije	Communist Party of Yugoslavia
DASMIP	Diplomatski arhiv Saveznog ministarstva za inostrane poslove	Archive of the Yugoslav Foreign Ministry
EDES	Ethnikos Dimokratikos Ellinikos Syndesmos	National Democratic Greek League

EFTA	European Free Trade Association	
EK	Etsivä Keskuspoliisi	Investigatory Central Police of Finland
ELAS	Ethnikos Laicos Apeleftherotikos Stratos	National Popular Liberation Army
EU	European Union	
FPRY	Federativna Narodna Republika Jugoslavija	Federal People's Republic of Yugoslavia
FTT	Free Territory of Trieste	
JAT	Jugoslovenski Aerotransport	Yugoslav Airlines
JNA	Jugoslovenska narodna armija	Yugoslav Peoples' Army
JUSTA	Jugoslovenske Sovjet Transport Aviacija	Soviet-Yugoslav Civil Air Transport Company
KGB	Komitet Gosudarstvennoi bezopasnosti	Committee of State Security
KKE	Kommounistikó Kómma Elládas	Communist Party of Greece
LCY	Savez komunista Jugoslavije	League of Communists of Yugoslavia
NATO	North Atlantic Treaty Organization	
NCP	Kokoomus	National Conservative Party
OSCE	Organization on Security and Cooperation in Europe	

LIST OF ABBREVIATIONS

RGASPI	Rossiiskii gosudarstvennyi arkhiv sotsial'no-politicheskoi istorii	Russian State Archive of Socio-Political History
RTsKhIDNI	Rossiiskii Tsentr Khraneniia i Izucheniia Dokumentov Noveishei Istorii	Russian Centre for the Preservation and Study of Documents of Modern History
SDP	Sosialidemokraattinen Puolue	Finnish Social Democratic Party
SKDL	Suomen Kansan Liitto	Finnish People's Democratic League
SKP	Suomen Kommunistinen Puolue	Finnish Communist Party
SUPO	Suojelupoliisi	Finnish Protection Police
UDBa	Uprava državne bezbednosti	Yugoslav Administration for State Security
UKK	Urho Kekkosen arkisto	Presidential Archive of Urho Kekkonen
UM	Ulkoministeriön arkisto	Archive of the Foreign Ministry of Finland
VP	Valtiollinen Poliisi	State Police of Finland
YLE	Yleisradio	Finnish Broadcasting Company

ACKNOWLEDGEMENTS

I owe a special debt of gratitude to my adviser and mentor Professor John R. Lampe, and I wish to thank for their advice and instruction Professor Michael David-Fox, Professor Jeffrey Herf, Professor Ivo Visković, Assistant Professor Peter Wien and Professor Madeline C. Zilfi. I would like to express my gratitude to Maria Marsh and Joanna Godfrey of the Editorial Department at I.B.Tauris together with Nicola Denny. I also wish to thank for their support and guidance Gordon N. Bardos, Professor Victoria de Grazia, Kevin P. Hallinan, Professor John S. Micgiel, and Minister Counsellor Leena Ritola. I would like to thank for their advice Assistant Professor Tvrtko Jakovina, Professor Silvio Pons, Professor Alfred Rieber, Professor Robert Vitalis and Professor Marilyn Young.

I dedicate this book to John and Kevin.

PREFACE

The study of the Cold War initially focused on the examination of the superpower confrontation in Europe: the subsequent rise of Euro-Atlantic interconnection in the west and the Soviet bloc in the east. The original geographic focus was Europe. In the wake of the Cold War, and as a result of the transformative effects of the two World Wars, social science research gained prominence in academia. Disciplines such as economics, political science, sociology and anthropology promised to explain the unpredictable future with scientific and quantitative methods from the perspective of the individual. In the post-Second World War period historians also sought causes and effects in history. In no other area of historical writing did the influences of the emerging social science trends appear more clearly than in the study of the Cold War. Model-building had a strong effect on the scholarship of the conflict as it was increasingly applied to the Soviet Union.

Despite the two-pronged nature of the confrontation, the Cold War was an experience that was international and multinational in nature. The study of international history indeed emerged as a strong influence and reinvigorated the examination of the Cold War after the break-up of the Soviet Union. The study of the conflict became refocused in Africa, Asia and Latin America.

This book brings back the attention to the Cold War in Europe. It approaches the question of the fundamental nature of the conflict from the perspective of two states at the political borders of the Soviet Union: Finland and Yugoslavia. The book addresses the foreign relations of Yugoslavia and Finland with the Soviet Union between 1948 and 1958 as two separate case studies. It narrates their separate yet comparable and, to an extent, coordinated contests with the Soviet Union and their relations with each other. The Tito-Stalin split of 1948 ended the forecast partnership with the Soviet Union. It launched Yugoslavia on a search for an alternative foreign policy. Finnish-Soviet relations between 1944 and 1948 showed an example according to which, in order to avoid invasion, Yugoslavia would have to demonstrate a commitment to minimizing security risks to the Soviet Union along its European political border and to not interfering in the Soviet domination of domestic politics elsewhere in Eastern Europe. The Finnish model of neutralism offered a solution to the Yugoslav security dilemma. Yugoslavia came to abandon that example in favor of the Non-Aligned Movement after 1958, when it became clear that relations between Yugoslav and Soviet parties would not be harmonious, even after an initial rapprochement in the mid-1950s.

This volume argues that the Non-Aligned Movement was born in the Mediterranean. The Movement's roots are often incorrectly confused with the 1955 Bandung Conference of Asian and African states. It was conceived instead as a non-military alliance in the long aftermath of the 1956 Suez and Hungarian Crises, when superpower interests threatened both Yugoslav and Egyptian security. The centre of Yugoslav foreign policy throughout the 1950s was more focused in Europe than has previously been credited. In the 1960s Yugoslav diplomacy made a significant contribution to the Mediterranean region with keen interest in building an international movement and foreign policy of non-alignment. Finnish and Yugoslav foreign policies of neutralism and non-alignment were drafted as responses to the Soviet Union. They are an integral part of the narrative of modern European history as well.

1

INTRODUCTION

After the Second World War the European continent stood divided between two clearly defined and competing systems of government, economic and social progress. Historians have repeatedly analyzed the formation of the Soviet bloc in the east, the subsequent superpower confrontation, and the resulting rise of Euro-Atlantic interconnection in the west. The Cold War historiography of Europe between 1945 and 1989 has focused almost exclusively on this two-sided confrontation. This largely Western scholarship has served to track the formation of the Soviet bloc in Eastern Europe: its function as defensive buffer zone for Soviet security, its advantages for initial economic recovery, and its exclusionary role in filtering out influence from the West. This initial approach to the Cold War placed responsibility squarely on Josef Stalin's wartime and post-war policies, his expansionist desire for a Communist takeover in Eastern Europe.[1] By the 1960s, revisionists began to present the United States also as an expansionist power that was seeking economic hegemony in Europe.[2] Post-revisionists' writing before and after the Communist collapse of 1989 sees the Cold War more as a natural outcome of the Second World War that created a power vacuum from which two superpowers emerged.[3]

This study provides a new view of how two borderlands steered clear of absorption into the Soviet bloc during the early Cold War. It addresses the foreign relations of Yugoslavia and Finland with the Soviet Union and with each other between 1948 and 1958. Much can be learned from their separate yet comparable and, to some extent, coordinated contests with the Soviet Union. Consider first the often-discussed expulsion of Yugoslavia from the Soviet Cominform in 1948 and its long-term consequences for the conduct of the Cold War in Europe.[4] Ending the presumed partnership with the Soviet Union, the Tito-Stalin split launched Yugoslavia on its well analyzed search for the separate Communist regime that came to be known as workers' self-management.[5]

This focus coincides with that long-term interest in Soviet studies to examine the Soviet Party structure and the workings of the Kremlin first and everyday life and social history later by the revisionist. In the study of the Soviet Union after the Second World War these well developed and vital fields left the examination of foreign policy itself with less focus. Similarly, much less attention has been paid to Yugoslavia's search for an alternative foreign policy, one that previously unconsulted evidence suggests began before the split and helped to provoke it. After the split that search turned to avoiding violent conflict with the Soviet Union but while creating alternative international partnerships to help the still Communist state to survive in difficult post-war conditions. It will be argued here that the Finnish formulation of a foreign policy of neutralism towards the Soviet Union quickly became an important example for Yugoslavia.[6] Finnish-Soviet relations between 1944 and 1948 showed the Yugoslav Foreign Ministry that in order to avoid invasion, they would have to demonstrate a commitment to minimizing security risks to the Soviet Union along its European political border and to not interfering in the Soviet domination of domestic politics elsewhere in Eastern Europe. Moreover, it was this initial example of a policy of neutralism together with the wider Yugoslav international ties created globally since 1948 that inspired the state to lead the way towards the formation of the Non-Aligned Movement at the Belgrade founding conference of 1961.

Presidents Juho Kusti Paasikivi and Urho Kekkonen developed Helsinki's policy in the immediate aftermath of the Second World War.[7] Finnish neutralism came to be known as the 'Paasikivi-Kekkonen Line', after the two so-called 'line men', who drafted the policy in order to hold the line of the 800-mile long territorial Finnish-Soviet border, literally, against Soviet political or military invasion. Paasikivi and Kekkonen had concluded that this new strategy would be necessary for Finland to maintain its independence as the Cold War emerged. For Finland, neutralism meant limiting relations with Euro-Atlantic institutions to economic agreements, refraining from security alliances, limiting cooperation with Western intelligence agencies, and allowing a domestic Communist party to exist and be active. During the 1950s, along the same lines as this Finnish model, the Yugoslav leadership proceeded to expand Western economic relations, while demonstrating to the Soviets that Yugoslavia would never actively advocate that other East European states break from the bloc.

How first Finland decided to pursue 'neutralism' as a common strategy for foreign policy in the aftermath of the Second World War, and then Yugoslavia after the split with Soviet Union in 1948 are interesting questions. A more interesting one is how they both continued to do so through the 1950s, led by an autonomous Yugoslav Foreign Ministry and a Finnish President who were acting more independently than their respective political frameworks, Communist and multi-party parliament, would lead us to expect. In the process, we shall see a surprising coordination emerge between the Yugoslav and the Finnish Foreign Ministries on policies towards the Soviet Union. Their common focus on the European balance of power casts serious doubt on the long-standing Western, Russian and Yugoslav assumption of an early Tito-led turn to the Third World and the Non-Aligned Movement, as the centrepiece of Yugoslavia's foreign policy already by the mid-1950s. Instead, it will be argued here that the Non-Aligned Movement, the roots or which are often incorrectly confused with the 1955 Bandung Conference of Asian and African states, was formed primarily in the Mediterranean between 1958 and 1961. It was conceived of as a non-military alliance in the long aftermath of the 1956 Suez and Hungarian Crises, when superpower interests threatened both Yugoslav and Egyptian security in the Mediterranean. Yugoslav foreign policy throughout the 1950s was more focused in Europe than has previously been credited.

Finnish-Soviet and Yugoslav-Soviet exchanges also shared between Belgrade and Helsinki throughout the 1950s represent a unique feature of Cold War Europe as seen through the lens of neutralism. At the core of Yugoslav policy and of the Belgrade-Helsinki dialogue was an ongoing negotiation over the Cold War in Europe. At the conclusion of the Second World War, Stalin viewed Soviet foreign policy in Europe as crucial to Soviet recovery from the war and its political and economic ascendancy in the future.[8] Stalin's approach (as well as that of Nikita Khrushchev who was to follow) was not to confine Soviet defence and foreign policy in Europe to East Central Europe. Most Cold War literature on Europe focuses exclusively on states that later joined the North Atlantic Treaty Organization (NATO) or signed the Warsaw Pact.[9] However, Stalin's postwar foreign policy targeted the entire Soviet territorial and political border, extending in the north to Finland and in the south to Yugoslavia, which shared a border with Soviet bloc states Hungary and Bulgaria. Soviet efforts to subjugate Finnish and Yugoslav domestic and foreign policies after 1945 were frustrated on several levels. Lack of ability to control political developments in Finland and Yugoslavia became a concern after 1948 when Yugoslavia succeeded in surviving outside the Soviet bloc and the Soviet Union failed to force Finland to sign a treaty similar to those accepted by its emerging bloc regimes. Instead of an all-encompassing Finnish-Soviet Agreement on Friendship, Cooperation and Mutual Assistance, the Soviets received only 'a treaty without effective alliance' in 1948. Moscow feared that both Helsinki and Belgrade might escape its grasp and actively join the West European bloc. Soviet attempts to dominate both the Helsinki and Belgrade governments resurfaced in 1956 and 1958.

Stalin's death in 1953 generated a great deal of uncertainty for both Yugoslav and Finnish foreign policy. What was by then their common policy of neutralism had been based upon Stalin's foreign policy priorities. In 1953, it was unclear who would lead the Soviet Union, and whether Finnish and Yugoslav policies would still be tolerated. Again in 1956, the Hungarian Revolution tested Yugoslav and Finnish relations with the Soviet Union. Any significant support for Hungarian independence would have jeopardized the baselines of both Finnish and Yugoslav neutralisms. In 1958, the Yugoslav Communist Party leadership, essentially Josip Broz 'Tito' and Edvard Kardelj, again challenged neutral relations with the Soviet Union against the wishes of the Yugoslav Foreign Ministry with theoretical criticism of Soviet Communism. That same year, the Finnish Social Democratic Party, through a newly formed coalition government with the Conservative Party, challenged the Paasikivi-Kekkonen Line by expanding ties with the United States. After turning aside these challenges, Finland and Yugoslavia arrived at two different solutions in 1961: Finland decided to seek economic security increasingly from Euro-Atlantic economic integration by joining the European Free Trade Agreement (EFTA).[10] The Paasikivi-Kekkonen Line survived, but only within this context of deepening Euro-Atlantic trade relations, until the end of the Soviet control over Eastern Europe in 1989. In 1961, the Yugoslav Foreign Ministry, frustrated by recurring rhetorical eruptions between the Yugoslav and the Soviet party leaderships, directed Yugoslav foreign policy away from Europe and towards neutralism through the Non-Aligned Movement. Tito was eager to lead the movement that began as a non-partisan foreign policy initiative that sought to moderate east-west conflict and to represent small states through the formation of a multi-state coalition outside the east-west blocs. The movement promoted as a foreign policy strategy solidarity among nations less powerful in international relations. The inaugural conference of the Non-Aligned Movement was held in Belgrade in 1961.

Before directing these introductory remarks to the myths of the early Yugoslav non-alignment and Finland's early domestic subordination, we need to review the historiography of the split itself, Western and Yugoslav (or successor), Soviet and Russian. This study addresses issues raised by all of these historiographies, drawing on archival sources to make its case.

Yugoslav and Western Historiography of the Split

According to the initial Yugoslav, British and American scholarship the split with the Soviet Union in the spring of 1948 was not 'intended' by the Tito-led regime. Its leadership, fresh from their Partisan triumph in the Second World War, had set out to follow the example set by the Soviet Union directly, virtually copying the Stalin constitution of 1936.[11] Even the very latest English language account argues that relations between Moscow and Belgrade were basically harmonious until the end of 1947.[12] Yet by the fall of 1944 Tito's expansive and unwavering goal of leading a future Balkan Federation was also emerging without due Soviet coordination. By 1946 the Yugoslav leadership had dismissed the few personnel trained in Moscow from its ranks, semi-privately discussed their dislike of Soviet influence in Yugoslavia, provocatively continued to support Greek Communist guerillas in Northern Greece, bickered over Trieste with the Allies, and continued to propagate anti-Western rhetoric. As post-1989 research in Soviet archives makes clear, these provocations directly interfered with Stalin's immediate post-war foreign policy goals—to speed Soviet recovery by prolonging a working relationship with the West and to expedite peace negotiations in order to secure war reparations.[13] Independent foreign policy initiatives within the regional East European and Balkan context by Yugoslav Communists questioned the Soviet Union's primacy among Communist states. The strained relations between the Yugoslav and Soviet Communist leaderships spiralled into a dangerous open conflict in 1948. These Yugoslav initiatives and provocations led to the Soviet-Yugoslav split and to the Yugoslav security and economic dilemma posed by its geographic position between Soviet bloc states and NATO-member Italy. The Yugoslav revolt did not stem from ambition and opportunity alone. It was also inspired by basic disagreement over post-war Soviet foreign policy which Tito calibrated to be too conciliatory and cautious towards the Western Allies.

In the 60 years since the event, few detailed monographs have been written on the Tito-Stalin split, and only one focused directly on foreign relations following the split. Vladimir Dedijer's *The Battle Stalin Lost* published initially in Serbo-Croatian argued in 1970 that Yugoslavia was, through no desire or fault of its own, expelled unexpectedly from the Communist bloc by Stalin.[14] In 1975 Čedomir Štrbac's *Sukob KPJ i Informbiroa* (The Conflict between the CPY and the Cominform) concentrated on the anti-Yugoslav acts and tactics pursued by the Soviets through their satellites against Yugoslavia after the split and the eventual normalization of relations.[15] Ranko Petković's 1998 edited volume *1948: Jugoslavija i Kominform* (Yugoslavia and the Cominform) reviewed the split with support from documents published in Yugoslavia and in the *Foreign*

Relations of the United States volumes.[16] From Zagreb in 1988, Darko Bekić's *Jugoslavija u Hladnom Ratu* (Yugoslavia in the Cold War) placed the Tito-Stalin split within the context of US-Yugoslav relations and of Soviet-Yugoslav exchanges.[17] It became the standard text on Yugoslav foreign relations in the former Yugoslav states. From a similar point of analysis Tvrtko Jakovina's *Američki komunistički saveznik; Hrvati, Titova Jugoslavija i Sjedinjene Američke Države 1945–1955* (American Communist Ally: The Croats, Tito's Yugoslavia and the United States of America 1945–1955) (2003) gives an updated account of how the CIA and other US analysts understood the conflict as it unfolded.[18] This work also discusses the role and work of several American diplomats significant to Yugoslav-American relations in the early post-war years.

Prevalent since the dissolution of multinational Yugoslavia into ethnic nation-states have been histories of the constituent nations of Yugoslavia. They have left Tito-era foreign policy largely unexamined. When foreign policy is addressed, it is often times approached from the point of view of a former Yugoslav republic. The study of Yugoslav foreign policy has also been hindered by the location of the Yugoslav archives in Belgrade, which has experienced political instability since 1989. Access to the archives in Belgrade has been limited in practice. One notable exception is the Serbian language work of Dragan Bogetić whose *Nova Strategija Spoljne Politike Jugoslavije 1956–1961* (New Strategy of the Yugoslav Foreign Policy 1956–1961) (2008) both addresses Yugoslav foreign policy and uses archival sources exhaustively.[19]

Western scholarship on the split has also been limited. Only Adam Ulam's *Titoism and the Cominform* (1952), Milovan Djilas's *Conversations with Stalin* (1962), and Ivo Banac's *With Stalin against Tito* (1988) focus on the split itself.[20] Jeronim Perović's recent journal article 'The Tito-Stalin Split: A Reassessment in Light of New Evidence' (2007) gives a detailed account of the series of events.[21] Only Alvin Rubinstein's *Yugoslavia and the Non-Aligned World* (1970) concentrated on foreign relations in the 1950s and beyond.[22] Subsequent memoirs by Edvard Kardelj, a major Yugoslav diplomat whose work was also translated into English reinforced Rubinstein's argument for an early Yugoslav turn to the Non-Aligned Movement and Tito's leading role therein.[23]

These previous accounts, with the exception of Rubinstein's, focused on the question of whether the Tito-Stalin split was intentional or accidental from the Yugoslav perspective, on the state of Soviet-Yugoslav relations leading up to the split, and on what role the Yugoslav defection played in the tightening up of the East European regimes.[24] In 1952, Adam Ulam introduced the argument that despite Tito's ongoing plans for primacy in the Balkans, his party leadership were completely surprised by their expulsion from the Cominform in June 1948.²⁵ Accepting Belgrade's official account, Ulam argued that because of the wartime sacrifices and Communist commitment shared with the Soviet Union, the Yugoslavs could not have dreamed of purposefully criticizing or defying their great ally, even in 1948. Echoing Ulam's view are testimonies of great surprise at the split from important party figures, such as Milovan Djilas, Edvard Kardelj and as described by Vladimir Dedijer in his diary.²⁶

Ulam's work presented the now difficult to sustain view that the Yugoslavs did very little to provoke the split. His account acknowledged, yet dismissed, both private and semi-public expressions of negative feelings towards the Soviets within Tito's leadership. He emphasized instead Stalin's failed attempt to purge Tito's followers in the party and army, joining Djilas in noting the resemblance of these methods to those of the late 1930s purges in the Soviet Union.²⁷

Ulam's lasting contribution to the study of Yugoslavia is his identification of the Yugoslav Partisans and their Communist leadership's elevated role amongst the 'People's Democracies' of Eastern Europe. Wartime casualties and eventual successes made Yugoslavia a natural leader among the Communist parties in post-war Eastern Europe, despite the greater economic importance of Czechoslovakia and Poland.²⁸ Unlike these countries, Yugoslavia had fought and won the war with a home-grown Communist movement and a native leader, with only late Soviet assistance. Tito's wartime performance and his potential popularity within Eastern Europe appeared to threaten Stalin's primacy throughout Eastern Europe after the war. Ulam's account emphasizes the pragmatism and lack of ideological consistency in Stalin's policies during the Second World War and immediately after as a post-war dilemma. During the war, for example, Stalin had endorsed British attempts to persuade the Partisans to recognize the royal Yugoslav government in exile in London.²⁹ Stalin's efforts to diminish domestic Communist predominance were never admitted in the post-war environment in which Tito and the Partisans claimed their due recognition. Indeed, Ulam suggests that Stalin may have feared that the Yugoslavs would make this information public. Without reference to Stalin's fears or Yugoslav provocation, Denison Rusinow's 1977 study *The Yugoslav Experiment, 1948–1974* does point to the impossibility of any Soviet accommodation to separate Yugoslav initiatives after the 1947 Sklaraska Poreba meeting that established the Communist bloc and the Cominform; an unplanned response to the escalating Cold War.³⁰

Ivo Banac's later 1988 volume agrees that the Yugoslavs were surprised by the Soviet attack in 1948, but says they should not have been. As one of the only authors to that day he goes on to argue that serious conflict between the Communist Party of Yugoslavia (CPY) and the Soviet leadership had already been acknowledged during the war. In 1941, the Soviets contemplated recognizing the German partition of Yugoslavia that had resulted from the Axis occupation.[31] Drawing on early disagreements between Tito's leadership and Stalin, Banac astutely highlights the Partisans' over-zealous, hard left attitude during the war. While Stalin embraced a broad form of Russian nationalism as a rallying call during the war (reversing the Marxist-Leninist rejection of ethnic nationalism), the Partisans adhered strictly to the iconography of international Communism. Banac, like Ulam, draws on wartime experiences to make post-war conclusions. According to Banac, the Yugoslav Partisan takeover embraced none of the tolerance of a multi-party coalition that Stalin initially advocated as the war ended. Banac is the only historian of the Tito-Stalin conflict to refer to Finland, although in cursory fashion. He notes that at the first meeting of the Cominform in Szklarska Poreba in September 1947 Andrei Zhdanov grouped Finland within the cluster of anti-Fascist 'new democracies.'[32] Banac therefore infers a Soviet desire in 1947 to include Finland, like Yugoslavia, within the Soviet bloc. While it is problematic to recognize any sincerity in the call for the 'restoration of democratic liberties' in Stalinist foreign policy after 1946, Banac's work does spell out the separate and provocative way Yugoslav foreign policy was itself going even before 1947. He also calls attention to the early employment of Yugoslav Administration for State Security (UDBa) as a tool of foreign policy. Already in 1946, it was the UDBa that provided arms to the Communist Party of Greece (KKE) in the second round of the Greek Civil War.[33] Between 1945 and 1948, the post-war Communist leadership continued to act according to its wartime Partisan ethos, where the primacy of ultimate political goals for independence from outside political pressure and determination to build a one-party Communist state at any cost trumped all else. The split with the Soviets, he concludes, may not have been intended but was an inevitable consequence of both the Partisan leadership's overextended, unrealistic political goals and its political behavior.

None of this limited set of monographs on the split discusses the regional or international consequences of Yugoslavia's expulsion from the Soviet bloc. Prior to the split, the confident Communist leadership considered its territorial claims in Trieste and support of the KKE as domestic matters and initiatives that the Soviets would have to readily stand behind. Then, expulsion from the Soviet bloc quickly forced the Yugoslav regime to seek security in relations with non-Communist countries.[34] Absent from both Western and domestic historiography of Yugoslavia is any discussion of how the Finnish formulation of neutralism (between 1944 and 1948) as its policy towards the Soviet Union and Western Europe set an important example for Yugoslavia from 1948 forward.

Recent Soviet and Russian Historiography of the Split
The earlier work on the Tito-Stalin split discussed above was done largely in the absence of official Soviet documents. While Kardelj and Djilas provided first-hand accounts of the events from within Tito's immediate circle, both works function as biographies intended to deliver unambiguous political messages. In contrast, since the end of the Soviet Union work by Russian historians has tended to focus narrowly on foreign policy documents from the Soviet archives. The so-called 'let the documents speak' approach, described by Norman Naimark in his two essays on post-Soviet Russian historiography, has been applied to the Tito-Stalin split and presents facts emerging from archival party documents alone.[35] Attempts to analyze Soviet goals and policy towards Yugoslavia beyond what is directly stated in these documents (some of which are now compiled into large Russian volumes on Eastern Europe and others appear as collected articles in journals) are less frequent. By limiting themselves to the details in the documents, Russian scholars attempt to minimize the ideological agendas that distorted scholarly work in the Soviet period. Some very broad positions relevant to Soviet engagement in Eastern Europe immediately after the war are developed in current Russian scholarship on the Tito-Stalin conflict. The collections of documents assembled by T. V. Volokitina et. al. join Vladislav Zubok and Constantine Pleshakov's significant volume *Inside the Kremlin's Cold War* to argue that the forceful subjugation of East European governments was not Stalin's goal in the immediate post-war period.[36]

The Tito-Stalin conflict is viewed as the result of failed Soviet attempts to contain Tito's aggressive regional territorial advances in the Balkans.[37] According to the Volokitina volumes, Stalin feared that Eastern Europe might defy the Soviet Union if inspired by Western collusion with Yugoslavia. Documents published from the Soviet archives reveal an awareness that in many East European countries the public had not reacted well to the news of the expulsion of the CPY from the Cominform in June 1948.[38] The Volokitina studies on the split clearly describe Soviet strategy toward Yugoslavia as part of a broader plan for Eastern Europe illustrating the Soviet interpretation of the region's interconnectedness. By this view, Moscow's foreign policy vis-à-vis the West was pragmatic but the Communist political elites in Eastern Europe at this time pushed ahead to adopt the political systems under Soviet sponsorship that eventually became a burden to the Soviet Union. They were therefore also partially responsible for their adoption.[39]

In contrast to Volokitina, the veteran Russian historian Vladimir Gibianskii repeatedly engaged with the Tito-Stalin split and argues that Soviet hegemony over the East European Communist parties had already been defined as a primary goal during the war.[40] Gibianskii also underlines that, for the Yugoslav leadership, the Soviet Union was a 'natural center' and its primary source of necessary political support during the post-war period.[41] The crux of Gibianskii's argument is that the Yugoslavs and the Soviets were close allies and partners right down to the beginning of 1948.[42] He has often written about the importance of Yugoslav provocative steps in Albania in 1948. While he concludes that the Soviet Union gave other East European countries even less favorable evaluations at this time, his sources nevertheless also testify to a conflictual relationship between the Yugoslav and Soviet leaderships.

Gibianskii argues in one part of his extensive body of work that the notion of an increasingly negative Soviet view of Yugoslav leaders as early as the fall of 1947 was generated primarily by reports originating from the Soviet Ambassador in Belgrade Anatolii Lavrentev. His reports identified an increase in nationalist Yugoslav propaganda and overestimation of military and Communist credentials from the Second World War.[43] Even then, the head of the Balkan division of the Ministry of Foreign Affairs in Moscow, Aleksandr Lavrishchev, repudiated Lavrentev's claims in a telegram to Vyacheslav Molotov as late as October 1947.[44] Gibianskii's conclusion can thus be contested, but his many publications of and those citing Soviet documents include persuasive details left out of most monographs on Yugoslavia.

In addition to uncertainties about the background to the split, the opening of the Soviet archives has provided a broader perspective on Soviet foreign policy and Stalin's political circle.[45] Drawing on these documents and memoirs, Anatolii Anikeev's 2002 study *Kak Tito ot Stalin Ushel* (How Tito Walked Away from Stalin) has concentrated on the triangular relations between Yugoslavia, the Soviet Union and the United States in the early Cold War in a comprehensive way.[46] According to Anikeev, the Partisan leadership already made plans during the war for a future policy that would allow for Yugoslavia to play a leading role in the region. Anikeev strongly denies any surprise at the Tito-Stalin split or early pretense for Yugoslav obedience to Soviet leadership. He describes Tito's active role in interfering with the traditional hierarchical relations between Communist parties that were subjects to the Soviet party. Before the split, Anikeev argues that the Kremlin and Stalin had unwittingly acknowledged the Yugoslav claim for primacy by 'entrusting' it with control over political leadership in Albania and allowed Tito to support the Greek Communist insurgency. It has not been claimed elsewhere that Stalin willingly supported Yugoslav aid to the Greek Communists. Anikeev makes this valuable claim and has worked further on the effects of the Yugoslav-Soviet dispute on the Greek Civil War and the Balkan federation. Anikeev further argues that these privileges were not to be misinterpreted, as perhaps Tito did, to mean that Moscow was granting Yugoslavia a free hand in the Balkans. Anikeev maintains that the Yugoslav-American rapprochement followed the split largely as a consequence of necessity for Yugoslavia to overcome the economic blockade. Anikeev, like Volokitina and other Russian contemporaries, sharply criticizes Stalin's program of expansion into Eastern Europe after the war. Anikeev's work is valuable as it connects Stalin's foreign policy also to the enduring Russian and Soviet foreign policy—Bolshevik 'messianism' and old Russian imperial plans of expanding influence in the Balkans and the eastern Mediterranean. Many Russian historians today see an unfortunate causal relationship between post-war Soviet expansion into Eastern Europe and the collapse of the Soviet Union in 1991.[47] Anikeev's focus on Soviet goals in the Balkans instead of East Central Europe makes his work important for the examination of the Tito-Stalin split.

The Non-Alignment Myth in the Historiography of Yugoslavia

Despite the above noted differences, Western, Yugoslav and Russian scholarship on Yugoslavia has largely agreed that Yugoslav foreign policy was from the Tito-Stalin split forward built around a concept of non-alignment linked to non-European states and already formulated by 1955. The former British Ambassador Duncan Wilson traces Asian and African connections back to 1948 and to Tito. Wilson argues that:

> It was at this time [1958–61] that Tito began to develop more systematically than before the policy of 'non-alignment' in order to strengthen Yugoslavia's international position. From 1949 onwards the Yugoslavs had been constrained by circumstances to work towards some such policy. They were anathema to the Soviet bloc, and did not wish to ally themselves too closely with the West. Their best hope of diplomatic support lay in developing connections with the Asian and later African countries which were also trying to assert their independence…[48]

Wilson argues that Haile Selassie's visit to Belgrade in 1954 and Tito's visit to Ethiopia in 1955 paved the way to non-alignment: 'From this point on, Tito's own propensity for foreign travel and talent for diplomacy contributed much to the form of Yugoslavia's policy of non-alignment.'[49]

In existing scholarship, Yugoslav foreign policy during the 1950s is considered synonymous with the emergence of the Non-Aligned Movement although its geographic impetus is placed in Asia. The major Western work supporting such mythic importance for non-alignment is Alvin Rubinstein's aforementioned 1970 volume. Despite its title, *Yugoslavia and the Non-Aligned World*, Rubinstein traces the beginning of Yugoslav non-alignment to the Asian Socialist Conference of 1952, Nehru's subsequent drafting of Indian non-alignment, and the Bandung Conference of 1955.[50] Yugoslavia was not a participant in any of these initiatives, only sending an observer delegation to the Asian Socialist Conference and no one to the Bandung Conference.

Rubinstein argues that the Yugoslav leadership did not immediately seek partnership with the formerly colonized countries in 1948 because they counted the economic dependence of these countries upon former colonizers as decisive. He maintains that the independent positions of Burma, India and Egypt with regard to the Korean War changed this perception.

> More than any single event, the Korean War wrought a major change in Yugoslav views of the newly independent nations. Hitherto accepted assumptions came under searching review. Thus, the belief that economic dependence meant political subservience was contravened by the independent positions which nations such as India, Burma, and Egypt adopted towards the Korean War, despite their continued close and dependent economic links to the former metropole.[51]

Rubinstein (unlike many other authors) astutely admits Yugoslavia's absence from the Bandung Conference but argues that its failure left Yugoslavia to become 'a major beneficiary of the Conference's inability to establish a workable basis for cooperation.'[52] Tito was supposedly able to turn his early absence from a failed attempt at non-alignment to Yugoslavia's advantage: 'more than any other country, Yugoslavia helped to make of Bandung a prologue to political action rather than a footnote to futility.'[53] Tito did invite Gamal Abdel Nasser and Jawaharalal Nehru to Brioni in 1956. Rubinstein equates Yugoslav foreign policy with Tito's personal initiatives, and ignores the fact that, as noted below, Nasser came with his political authority yet to be established and Nehru with a narrower Asian agenda. Except for limited attention to Yugoslavia's relations with Italy, Rubinstein focuses solely on the non-European members of the Non-Aligned Movement. There is no discussion of Finnish or Austrian parallels in relations with the Soviet Union.

Against Rubinstein's Yugoslav-centered account Peter Willetts presents one of the most in-depth and analytical studies of the movement in *The Non-Aligned Movement: The Origins of a Third World Alliance* (1978).[54] The book makes a strong distinction between non-alignment as a principle of foreign policy in individual countries and the Non-Aligned as a unified movement in world politics. Willetts clearly shows by cluster analysis and with primary sources that only in the later 1960s did the movement begin to subsume some of the African-Asian protest. He instead links the birth of the movement most closely to Yugoslav and Egyptian foreign policy goals which united in avoidance of Soviet or British-French hegemony respectively since 1956 and the Hungarian and Suez crises.

In one of the early standard texts on Yugoslavia Fred Singleton, a leading British historian of Yugoslavia, argues that non-alignment was born of the Tito-Stalin split in 1948, and was fully in place through the 1950s. He concludes, 'The non-aligned policy was the cornerstone of Yugoslavia's foreign relations during the decade between the early 1950s and the early 1960s, and its high watermark was the Belgrade conference of 1961.'[55] Much of the most recent English language scholarship does not challenge this view. Sabrina Ramet boils Yugoslav foreign policy during this period down to a single paragraph, commenting that:

> The third leg in the triad—nonalignment—emerged in the mid-1950s, as Tito collaborated with Third World leaders, such as Egypt's Gamal Abdal al-Nasir and India's Jawaharlal Nehru, to develop a nonaligned movement in which member states would abjure both the passive role of unaligned or neutral states and any affiliation with either the Soviet bloc or the American-sponsored Atlantic Alliance.[56]

John Lampe similarly concludes, 'The emergence of a coordinated policy between these founding members [of the Non-Aligned Movement] dated from Tito's 1956 meeting with Nehru and the man who became his closest associate among these leaders, President Gamal Abdel Nasser of Egypt.'[57]

Tito did travel a great deal and his ambiguous statements, for example in 1955 that 'the uncommitted countries were Yugoslavia's true allies and greatest friends,' have been cited as proof of an already formed policy of non-alignment.[58] Yet they have not been enough to determine the Yugoslav direction as more than 'some such policy.'[59] Overlooking the crucial advantage taken from the 1954 establishment of trade relations with Italy, Duncan Wilson for instance argues that by 1955 Tito was leaning towards non-European non-alignment for economic reasons. He does admit that only two per cent of Yugoslav trade in 1954 was with 'developing countries.' This number shows no clear advantage.[60]

On the Russian side, Anikeev calls the Yugoslav leadership's increased fear of Soviet invasion a consequence of the Korean War. In a convincing argument Anikeev emphasizes that despite the normalization of Yugoslav-Soviet relations in the mid 1950s, Yugoslavia was firmly committed to a position outside the Warsaw Pact. Anikeev joins Western scholars in arguing that by 1955 Tito had begun to actively pursue foreign connections with Third World leaders.[61] Concluding his major study in 1957, a year after the Hungarian Revolution, Anikeev claims that by this time Tito had fully developed his commitment to the Third World. However, his work involves little discussion of Yugoslavia's Foreign Ministry, or the Ministry's possibly separate role.

There are few domestic works on Yugoslavia's non-alignment. First Radovan Radonjić's *Izgubljena Orientacija* (Lost Orientation) in 1985, and now Dragan Bogetić's *Nova Strategija Spoljne Politike Jugoslavije 1956–1961* (The New Strategy of Yugoslav Foreign Policy 1956–1961) in 2006, argue that the Yugoslav foreign policy was seeking African and Asian partners as early as the mid-1950s.[62] Both of their arguments rely heavily on the retrospective account of non-alignment's importance for the emergence of the less wealthy former colonial states. Bogetić's account relates perceptively and succinctly the content and importance of Yugoslavia's relations with Indonesia, Syria, Burma (Myanmar), Ethiopia, Ceylon (Sri Lanka), Sudan and many other states. Yet, although the Non-Aligned Movement stood against inequality between states, it developed a commitment to global reform in north-south relations only later in the 1970s. Radonjić's account relies more heavily on the work 'Historic Steps' from Edvard Kardelj, the party's chief ideologue.[63]

Indeed, the historiography of Yugoslav non-alignment has been heavily influenced by the personal accounts of Kardelj and Tito's biographer Vladimir Dedijer. Wilson speaks of Yugoslav foreign policy much as it is framed in their two person accounts: determined by Tito alone and having a great effect on world politics:

> [Tito's] pursuit of 'non-alignment' and efforts to co-ordinate the policies of non-aligned (mainly Asian and African) states have also had their importance on world scale. They have to some extent determined the shape of the confrontation or co-operation between 'North' and 'South'—the more and less developed countries of the world—on questions of investment and trade.[64]

In the much cited accounts of Kardelj and Dedijer, the world needs Tito. Fortified by his cult of personality and his reputation as a great East European leader in the Second World War, Tito alone could have influenced international affairs. Neither Kardelj nor Dedijer mention the Yugoslav Foreign Ministry in their major works. Nor do they even identify Koča Popović, the long-term Foreign Minister (1953–66). In the case of Kardelj this is understandable, as he viewed Popović as his primary competitor in shaping Yugoslav foreign policy.

In Kardelj's ideological frame of reference, Yugoslavia played an influential part in determining how far non-alignment should be equated with anti-imperialism and anti-colonialism, which in turn determined how far the movement was accepted by Soviet leaders.[65] This approach to non-alignment fails to explain how and why there came to be so many Yugoslav embassies and consulates world-wide, that their purpose was to create bilateral ties outside the Soviet Union and to counter the effects of Soviet influence and propaganda on Yugoslavia. Kardelj only briefly remarks that, 'The circumstances [from 1948] demanded that we maintain a particularly strong diplomatic service…in that way we were able to extend our activities in various countries as well as institutions and organizations.'[66] But countering the notion that Yugoslav diplomacy was concentrating on contacts with Asian and African states in the nascent Non-Aligned Movement, the Foreign Ministry sent delegations to tour Latin American states in 1946, 1949, 1954 and 1958. The goal of these visits to Argentina, Bolivia, Brazil, Colombia, Costa Rica, Cuba, Haiti, Honduras, Mexico, Peru, Uruguay and Venezuela was the extension of trade and political ties beyond Asia and Africa exclusively.

The conflict of interest between the Yugoslav Communist Party and its Foreign Ministry simply does not appear in the existing scholarship. The Ministry receives no separate attention. Summing up the Yugoslav non-alignment myth, Fred Singleton writes:

> The policy of non-alignment was the obvious one for Yugoslavia to take when she was cast out of the Cominform. It has been particularly associated with President Tito, who was clearly the inspirer of the series of non-aligned summit conferences. His tireless personal diplomacy, which included long journeys to Africa, Asia and Latin America during the 1960s, indicates the great importance he attaches to Yugoslavia's role in the Third World.[67]

This study argues that the case for an established Yugoslav role in the emerging Non-Aligned Movement by 1957 is hard to sustain. Jawaharlal Nehru, the Prime Minister of India since its partition in 1947 visited Yugoslavia briefly in 1956 in the context of the Suez Crisis and later concurrently with his visit to the Soviet Union in 1958. His 1958 visit was not to Belgrade alone, and its purpose was not solely connected to the future Non-Aligned Movement. In 1954, Nehru had begun to address the development of a foreign policy of non-alignment for India but within the context of Sino-Indian relations. The principles defining this policy included 'mutual respect for territorial integrity and sovereignty' and 'mutual non-aggression.' Nehru thereupon used the term 'non-alignment' to describe bilateral relations between India and China. In 1955, 29 Asian and African states convened at the Bandung Conference in Indonesia to discuss their position in relation to the developing two-bloc Cold War. The conference was organized by Burma (Myanmar), Ceylon (Sri Lanka), Indonesia, India and Pakistan. Yugoslavia was not invited to this meeting of Asian and African states. The Non-Aligned Movement's roots are often incorrectly confused with the Bandung Conference. This earlier meeting brought together communist states such as China and North Vietnam and Western allies such as Turkey and the Philippines. No European states such as Yugoslavia were represented and the Bandung final document included an endorsement for military pacts. Non-alignment on the other hand begun as and is a non-military alliance and did not endorse communism.

Gamal Abdel Nasser also participated in the meeting. He had become Prime Minister of Egypt only in 1954, and President in 1956. His founding of the United Arab Republic in 1958 with Syria preoccupied him until it collapsed in 1961. Nasser's partnership was not fully available to Tito until 1961. The three founding leaders of the Non-Aligned Movement, Nasser, Nehru and Tito, did meet briefly on Brioni in July 1956 and at the United Nations in New York in October 1960. The Brioni meeting is often cited as the one that led to the Non-Aligned Movement but the reason for the meeting was the building Egyptian conflict with Britain over Suez.[68] The Brioni communiqué issued at the meeting identifies three areas of concern, 'the Far East, the Middle East and Western Europe.'[69] It is telling that European issues are included, in particular vague references to the unification of Germany. The insertion of this topic relevant only to Yugoslavia suggests that no singular focus towards Asia and Africa is present yet in 1956. The first inaugural conference of the Non-Aligned Movement was held only in September 1961 in Belgrade.

Against the non-alignment myth, this study argues that following Yugoslavia's expulsion from the Soviet bloc, the Yugoslav party leadership increasingly granted its Foreign Ministry resources needed to establish a wider and more important range of diplomatic relations than those of any East European state. Extensive allocation of personnel, funding and the placement of Tito's closest associate Kardelj as Foreign Minister from August 1948 to January 1953 carried the process forward. It created a Yugoslav Foreign Ministry that produced political analysis independent from that of Tito's own committee on foreign relations—the League of

Communists of Yugoslavia Commission for International Relations. By 1953, the ministry explicitly regarded the Finnish model of neutralism as a possible solution to the Yugoslav security dilemma. It came to abandon that in favor of the Non-Aligned Movement only after 1958, when it became clear that relations between Yugoslav and Soviet parties would not be harmonious even after rapprochement.

'Finlandization' versus the Finnish Myth of Neutralism
Scholarship on post-war Finland, like Soviet and now Russian historiography, is highly politicized. 'Finlandization' as a pejorative notion from 1966, developed when the term was coined by German political scientist Richard Lowenthal to signify a partial membership in the Soviet bloc.[70] For critics such as Walter Laqueur, Finlandization came by the 1970s to mean that the new East-West détente might tempt other states to follow the Finnish pattern of avoiding NATO membership and accepting Soviet monitoring of foreign policy as including interference in domestic politics.[71] Laqueur defined Finlandization as 'that process or state of affairs in which, under the cloak of friendly relations with the Soviet Union, the sovereignty of a country becomes reduced.'[72] According to him, Finland was not a unique case but a dangerous precedent. He argued against those who in the 1970s believed that Western Europe, at all events, so far had little to fear from Finlandization, certainly less than Russia's East European satellites.' Laqueur pointed out that while after the Second World War Finland did not become a Soviet republic, a price was paid. Finland became a neutral country, but not vis-à-vis the Soviet Union, to which it had special obligations. The Kremlin required that Finland 'must not oppose any major Soviet foreign policy initiative, or enter into any commitments without Soviet approval.'[73] The size of Finland's army was limited by Soviet standards. Only political parties approved by the Soviet Union could participate in government. Alternative post-war accounts praise the maintenance of domestic independence against the military power of its neighbor, also highlighting Finland's 'heroic' war efforts against the Soviet Union during the Second World War. As with the historiography of Yugoslavia, critical examination of the 1950s is largely absent from the historiography of Finland. Finland's European Union (EU) membership in 1995 has focused attention on political developments since 1961, tracking the Finnish road towards the EU. The period of neutralism in the 1950s is neglected in favor of Finland's role in the détente of the late 1970s between the Soviet Union and the United States, and in the drafting of the Helsinki Agreement that created the Organization on Security and Cooperation in Europe (OSCE) in 1975.

Finnish scholarship tends to exaggerate the historical basis for neutralism. Jukka Nevakivi's journal article 'Finland and the Cold War' even dates Finnish political inclinations toward neutralism back to balancing between Prussian and Russian influences in the 1780s, before Finland's absorption into the Russian empire in 1809.[74] More realistically, neutralism emerged as an outcome of the 'Kekkonen-Paasikivi Line'—a strategy in Finnish foreign policy drafted at the end of the Second World War that sought to recognize that Finland's existence had always depended on relations with Sweden and Russia. Nevakivi also argued that neutralism's foundational role lay 'in the present philosophy of the nation,' i.e. Finland's commitment to democracy.[75] Nevakivi asserts that parliamentary democracy and a super-presidential system were also the foundations of neutralism. However, President Kekkonen established the Finnish super-presidential system firmly only in 1958, after the Kremlin suspended relations with Finland and following the formation of a Social Democratic-Conservative government. Kekkonen could thereby oversee and maintain the Paasikivi-Kekkonen Line beyond the influence of the Finnish parliament. Yet Nevakivi argues that parliamentary democracy was not compromised by neutralism, even if foreign policy priorities were. The limited scholarship on the period discusses how and why the events of 1948, namely the signing of the Agreement on Friendship, Collaboration and Mutual Assistance with the Soviets did not lead to a Soviet takeover. There has been no discussion of the subsequent Yugoslav-Finnish exchange and mutual interest in each others' relations with the Soviet Union.

Two significant further accounts were written in the 1980s, but without full access to Finnish or Soviet archival sources. Max Jakobson in *Finland: Myth and Reality* (1987) analyzes how and why Finland utilized the policy of neutralism to become a stabilized, democratic polity.[76] Jakobson does not construct a historical narrative of Finnish-Soviet relations as Nevakivi does, but stresses contingency, the influence of international events on Soviet foreign policy and their beneficial influence on Finnish-Soviet relations. Roy Allison describes post-war Finnish-Soviet relations as a matter of pragmatic coexistence since 1948.[77] While Jakobson, a journalist and later a Finnish career diplomat, had been privy to policy documents within the Finnish Foreign Ministry while serving it from 1953 to 1974, he had not had complete access to the Presidential Archives of Urho Kekkonen. They had been retained by his family and were closed until the 1990s to all other researchers except to Juhani Suomi who had access from the mid-1980s.[78] Neither account examines neutralism with reference to bilateral relations beyond the Soviet-Finnish case; with regard to Yugoslavia this is a critical omission.

The secondary literature on the very long presidency of Urho Kekkonen from 1956 to 1981 is clearly divided into accounts sympathetic to him and those challenging both his 'super-Presidency' and the Paasikivi-Kekkonen Line from the point of view of the Finnish Social Democratic Party. The historian recognized as most sympathetic to Kekkonen's persona and, therefore, also to the Finnish policy of neutralism is Juhani Suomi. With *Urho Kekkonen 1972–1976* he examines the Paasikivi-Kekkonen Line emphasizing its constructive role in the politics of détente between the US and the USSR.[79] Timo Vihavainen's *Kansakunta Rähmällään: Suomettumisen lyhyt historia* (A Nation on its Forehead: A Short History of Finlandization) on the other hand describes the 1970s as the culmination of Finlandization under the Paasikivi-Kekkonen Line.[80] However, Vihavainen argues that the Kremlin sought to influence Finnish domestic politics and that the causes of Finlandization as a whole were internal. Kekkonen in return sought to use Finnish-Soviet relations to strengthen his own domestic position.

What is the myth of post-war Finnish neutralism and why was it constructed? According to this myth Finland since 1945 was a republic with a parliamentary democracy that functioned without Soviet control. According to this representation, the Kremlin was not able to effectively influence the outcome of Finnish parliamentary or presidential elections, and Soviet-Finnish relations did not dominate Finnish foreign relations. This myth was created to maintain an untarnished reputation for President Kekkonen and support a positive view of Finnish democracy. These goals also sought mutually to support Finnish independence against further Soviet threat. According to this narrative, although Kekkonen remained as President from 1956 to 1981, this unbroken tenure and unchecked authority in foreign relations is supposed to have worked strictly to the advantage of Finnish parliamentary democracy.

This study argues that while President Paasikivi had in 1948 involved the Finnish Parliament directly in deciding the course of Finnish-Soviet relations, Kekkonen withdrew this oversight from the Parliament in 1958. By breaking up the Social Democratic-Conservative government that challenged the Paasikivi-Kekkonen Line, and erecting in its place a minority government from of his own party, Kekkonen maintained the Finnish foreign policy of neutralism, but allowed the Kremlin to influence Finnish domestic—not foreign—politics. The Finlandization theory is therefore supported in arguing that the Kremlin influenced Finnish politics during the course of the Cold War. As we shall see, however, this influence did not appear fully effective until after 1958. Without the powerful threat of Soviet invasion, Kekkonen would not have survived as President for 25 years. He would not have been able to break the government in 1958.

The myth of benign Finnish neutralism, like the Yugoslav myth of early non-alignment, is centered around the head of state. Both Kekkonen in Finland and Tito in Yugoslavia came to be venerated as grand political leaders that defeated the Soviet threat without shots being fired. These images resonate in the age of nuclear weapons and in the far longer period in which we are tempted to explain a country's foreign relations as the policies of a single striking persona. The desire to protect the legacies of these two personae has remained. It is partly for this reason that many capable contemporary researchers have faced difficulties gaining entry to the presidential archives of Tito and Kekkonen.

Soviet-Finnish and Soviet-Yugoslav Relations: Yugoslavia's Northern Connection

This study engages two broad themes: the formation of the policy of neutralism in Finland and in Yugoslavia during the early Cold War (1948–58), and the history of their diplomatic relations with the Soviet Union, led by Yugoslavia's surprisingly autonomous Foreign Ministry and left by Finland's Foreign Ministry to the control of a surprisingly independent President. Little has been written about either country's Foreign Ministry. Some former members of the Yugoslav ministry have offered insight. In his *Subjektivna Istorija Jugoslovenske Diplomatije 1943–1991* (A Subjective History of Yugoslav Diplomacy 1943–1991), Ranko Petković provides portraits of the most influential Yugoslav Foreign Ministers including Edvard Kardelj, Koča Popović and Marko Nikežić.[81] Mita Miljković and Arso Milatović draw on their personal diaries describing their daily work as Yugoslav ambassadors in the 1950s in Sofia, Bucharest and Warsaw respectively.[82] Similarly, a Finnish language *Ulkoasiainhallinnon historia. 1: 1918–1956* (History of the Foreign Ministry, Volume 1, 1918–1956) offers short biographies of Finnish diplomats and their work.[83]

The general aim of this study is to revise our understanding of the long-term consequences of the Tito-Stalin split. The Tito-Stalin split stands out as an unexpected development in the immediate aftermath of the Second World War. It is generally accepted that the split had far-reaching consequences for the internal development of Yugoslavia. Largely neglected in scholarly literature are the ways in which the split not only broadened, but also changed the practice of Yugoslavia's foreign policy. Elsewhere in Eastern Europe, as is well known, the split served as a warning to Communist regimes under direct Soviet control. Along its long northern border with Finland, Soviet foreign policy faced another independent government whose separate interests in neutralism and independent relations with Yugoslavia created a complex and less manageable dynamic. That historically neglected dynamic predates Yugoslavia's turn to the Non-Aligned Movement in 1961.

My inquiry draws on the archives of the former Yugoslavia, the former Soviet Union and Finland. I have also benefited from consultation of the United States National Archives in College Park, Maryland and the National Archives of Great Britain in London during my graduate studies. My sources range from the Archive of the Office of the President Josip Broz 'Tito,' the Archive of Serbia and Montenegro and the Archive of the Foreign Ministry of Yugoslavia in Belgrade, to the Archive of the Finnish Foreign Ministry and the Archive of the Finnish Protection Police in Helsinki. The Archive of the Yugoslav Foreign Ministry and the Finnish Protection Police archive gives permission to a limited amount of scholars at a given time. At the Finnish Foreign Ministry archive I made use of special files that contain the transcripts of President Paasikivi's exchanges with his cabinet during the 1948 negotiations for the Finnish-Soviet Agreement on Friendship, Cooperation and Mutual Assistance. I also consulted the Archive of President Urho Kaleva Kekkonen in Orimattila, Finland. I made reference to documents from the Foreign Ministry Archive of the Russian Federation (Arkhiv vneshnei politiki Rossiiskoi Federatsii AVP RF), some of which I was able to find through references in collections of documents published by T. V. Volokitina and others. I have also consulted documents from the Russian State Archive of Socio-Political History (Rossiiskii gosudarstvennyi arkhiv sotsial'no-politicheskoi istorii RGASPI). The RGASPI now houses the documents of the former Russian Centre for Preservation and Study of Records of Modern History, here referenced by its original acronym, RTsKhIDNI.

This work is comprised of five thematic chapters. Chapter 1 examines the Yugoslav and Soviet leaderships' appraisals of each other before and after the Tito-Stalin split in June 1948. It argues that the Yugoslav leadership did not actively avoid conflict with the Soviet Union, but instead pursued its foreign political objectives despite Soviet objections. Examined here are Tito's and Kardelj's letters to Stalin and Molotov. This extensive correspondence from March to May 1948 underlines the spontaneity of the Yugoslav outbursts at the Soviets that aggravated the brewing conflict. Chapter 2 turns to the Finnish analysis of the Yugoslav-Soviet conflict and the conclusion of the Finnish-Soviet Agreement on Friendship, Cooperation and Mutual Assistance in 1948. It argues that the Kremlin placed similar political tests to the Yugoslav and Finnish leaderships in 1948. While Tito and Kardelj failed their test, Finland was able to pass its by signing the 1948 treaty, and by offering trade relations to the Soviet Union. This chapter argues that the Finnish President Paasikivi's decision to include the Parliament in the process of ratifying the treaty was crucial. It placed the responsibility for Finnish policy of neutralism on all political actors represented in the Parliament. Attention is also paid to the early formation of Yugoslav-Finnish ties in Belgrade immediately after Yugoslavia's expulsion from the Cominform.

The next three chapters narrate the rise and fall of similar Finnish and Yugoslav policies of neutralism from 1953 to 1958. Chapter 3 presents Finnish-Yugoslav collaborative analysis of the effects of Josef Stalin's death upon Soviet policy in Europe in 1953. Yugoslav interest in Finnish analysis of the future of Soviet foreign relations is shown here. The Yugoslav Foreign Ministry's interest in Finland emerged as a consequence of the changing role of the Yugoslav ministry. In 1953 new Foreign Minister Koča Popović worked to transform the ministry and separate it from its previous connection with the Yugoslav Secret Police. I argue that the ministry's autonomous role was solidified during the early years of Popović's tenure, while Tito and his inner circle concentrated on domestic challenges. Yugoslav-Finnish ties are seen to grow in the aftermath of Stalin's death as a result of frequent and broad cultural exchanges. This chapter argues that while Yugoslav interest in Finland was born after the Tito-Stalin split in 1948, the Yugoslav foreign policy of neutralism was born after Stalin's death in 1953. While the Finnish Paasikivi-Kekkonen Line had served as an example since 1948, under Popović's influence the Ministry gained enough autonomy to institute this policy.

Chapter 4 compares Finnish and Yugoslav responses to the Soviet invasion of Hungary in 1956. The events in Hungary threatened both Finnish and Yugoslav policies of neutralism, and the Yugoslav and Finnish Foreign Ministries carefully weighed the other's responses to Soviet military action in Budapest. While Khrushchev's new regional foreign policy in Scandinavia benefited Finland, Yugoslav-Soviet rapprochement in 1955 was frustrated by renewal of the ideological conflict between the Yugoslav and Soviet parties in 1956. Tito's personal role in Yugoslav-Soviet relations resurfaced in a series of antagonistic statements against the Soviet leadership, echoed by Edvard Kardelj and followed by Soviet reprisals. However, by 1956, a professional Yugoslav Foreign Ministry, independently conducting foreign policy analysis through a wide network of Yugoslav embassies, found the Tito-Khrushchev war of words detrimental to Yugoslavia's main foreign policy goals: world-wide bilateral trade and political relations.

Chapter 5 analyzes the renewed conflict between the Soviet and Yugoslav Communist parties in 1958 and the Kremlin's clash with the Finnish Social Democratic-Conservative government. I argue that, as in 1948, so in 1958 the Kremlin took similar approaches to Soviet-Finnish and Soviet-Yugoslav relations. Frustrated with the Yugoslav party leadership in

Belgrade, and the Social Democratic-Conservative coalition in Helsinki, Moscow froze relations with both capitals. A new direction of the Yugoslav foreign policy away from Europe towards Asia and Africa addressed the Yugoslav-Soviet clash. In 1958, the Yugoslav ministry decided to prioritize bilateral relations outside of Europe in order to avoid both the Soviet bloc and rhetorical Yugoslav-Soviet party conflicts. President Kekkonen, in personal, private contact with Soviet intelligence as his diary reveals, repaired Finnish-Soviet relations by an unprecedented intervention in domestic politics, forcing out an elected coalition government and ignoring the Foreign Ministry entirely. My conclusion points to the post-1958 period, when Yugoslav and Finnish foreign policies did indeed go their separate ways, ending a decade of close connection and common reliance on a policy of neutral independence.

2

1948: THE SOVIET TEST FOR YUGOSLAVIA AND THE TITO-STALIN SPLIT

On 28 June 1948, the Cominform announced the expulsion of Yugoslavia from the organization, and called for the leadership of the Communist Party of Yugoslavia to be replaced. The *Cominform Journal* of 1 July 1948 publicly cited the CPY's 'incorrect line on the main questions of home and foreign policy, a line which is a departure from Marxism-Leninism' as the reason for the expulsion.[1] This document, which appeared within weeks in the languages of all of the Soviet bloc states, actually directly addresses the primary reason behind the Tito-Stalin split, Yugoslav disapproval of Soviet foreign policy couched in the rhetoric of Communist ideology.

The CPY was condemned for 'beg[inning] to identify the foreign policy of the Soviet Union with the foreign policy of imperialist powers,' and in particular for 'defaming Soviet military experts.'[2] This the Yugoslavs did. While Tito and Stalin bickered over numerous issues between 1945 and 1948 (including a future Balkan federation), the underlying, but often misunderstood, reason for the split was the Tito leadership's objection to Stalin's post-war foreign policy. The Yugoslav leadership felt that Stalin was overly accommodating to the wartime Western allies, ready to grant them their sphere of influence in Western Europe, and that the Soviet Union was not ready to recognize the Yugoslav right to a 'leading role among the East European Communist parties.' Moreover, Tito's leadership was not willing to compromise its independence from the Soviet party, acquired during the war but now rejected by Soviet foreign policy in 1948. The Comintern document publicly declared that the Soviet Union sought the replacement of the Central Committee of the CPY, starting with the removal of Tito, Milovan Djilas, Edvard Kardelj and Aleksandar Ranković. The document even lists the names of nominees to replace the 'purely Turkish terrorist regime.'[3] Sreten Žujović and Andrea Hebrang were therein characterized as 'advocates of friendship between Yugoslavia and the Soviet Union.' Both men had in fact already been purged by Tito's regime for their alleged 'pro-Soviet views.'[4]

The Soviet leadership resorted to these extreme measures towards a fellow Communist state in the spring of 1948 as a consequence of the long-standing refusal of Tito and his inner circle to accept Stalin's foreign policy as it emerged in the second half of the Second World War. This chapter moves from analysis of the origins of this rift to the Soviet response, culminating in the formal expulsion of Yugoslavia from the Cominform by June 1948.

Already in January 1948, we see the Soviet response taking shape. Although neglected in Yugoslav accounts, a Soviet offer of a trade agreement was made during that same month and then withdrawn by February 1948. On the Yugoslav side, internal party discussions indicate that its leadership played a more active role in the split than has previously been maintained. Contrary to both the original Yugoslav argument of Vladimir Dedijer and the more recent revisionist view of Ivo Banac, discussions over the Soviet offer of a trade agreement within Tito's inner circle indicate that it also saw the break coming.[5]

The Soviets offered a trade agreement to Yugoslavia in January 1948 as a political test of loyalty for the Tito leadership. By then, the Kremlin had grown frustrated with the Yugoslav leadership because of their assistance to the Greek Communists in the renewed civil war, their contention with the Western Allies, and their uncoordinated manoeuvres to promote a Yugoslav-Bulgarian Balkan Federation.[6] This political test of Tito parallels the Soviet attempt to consolidate political power over Finland through a similar Finnish-Soviet Agreement of Friendship, Cooperation and Mutual Assistance. The Finnish agreement, negotiated that same spring of 1948, is the subject of Chapter 2. In both cases, post-war Stalinist foreign policy prioritized the closely linked goals of territorial security and economic gain. As the Tito leadership failed to agree to a trade policy with the Soviet Union, by March of 1948 it had also failed the political test. The Kremlin moved swiftly to consolidate political power over Yugoslavia alternatively through the replacement of the Yugoslav leadership.

Soviet Wartime Collaboration with Western Allies and Post-war Yugoslav Objections

Since the proclamation of the Federal People's Republic of Yugoslavia (FPRY) on 29 November 1945, its Communist leadership had pursued its own domestic and foreign policy goals independent of the Soviet Union. More importantly, starting already in 1941, Tito and Stalin had continuously disagreed about the fundamental role and goals of the Partisan force's war efforts. Although issuing a directive via the Comintern on 22 June 1941 urging the CPY to organize resistance to the Nazi German dismemberment of Yugoslavia, the Soviet government proceeded to accredit royal Yugoslavia's King Peter II, in exile in London, as the state's highest representative. The Soviet Union and the Yugoslav government in exile raised their respective legations to the status of embassies. In contrast, the Soviet leadership had not yet accorded Tito's representation in Moscow the status of an embassy as late as January 1948. While wartime Soviet contacts with the royal Yugoslav government cast doubt on the political legitimacy of the Partisan resistance movement, Soviet military assistance to Tito was also not forthcoming. The Partisan command first informed Moscow that they had prepared an airfield in Bosnia in order to receive Soviet supplies, of mortars, arms and ammunition as early as December 1941.[7] Requests of troops, medical supplies, and military materials from the Comintern followed, in February and in March 1942. No such request was ever honored, even when a small Red Army mission finally arrived in 1944 and a realistic Soviet capacity to provide aid now existed.[8]

In official Comintern replies to Tito's requests for assistance in March 1942 and March 1943, the Soviets repeatedly advised Tito to cooperate with the non-Communist Yugoslav government in exile in London.[9] In March 1942 for example, the Soviets characteristically congratulated the Partisans for their military successes while urging Tito to:

> take into account that the Soviet Union has treaty relations with the Yugoslav King and Government and that taking an open stand against these would create new difficulties in the joint war efforts and the relations between the Soviet Union on the one hand and Great Britain and America on the other. Do not view the issues of your fight from your own, national standpoint, but also from the international standpoint of the British-American-Soviet coalition.[10]

Moreover, the Soviet leadership repeatedly encouraged the Partisans not to emphasize that they were fighting a civil war against the rival royalist Chetnik movement, which, like the exiled Yugoslav government, expected the return of monarchy to Yugoslavia.

Despite Tito's repeated telegrams claiming that the Chetniks were collaborating with the Nazi enemy, the Comintern continued to remind Tito in March 1942, that 'for reasons of [Soviet] policy...it is not opportune to emphasize that the struggle is mainly against the Chetniks. World public opinion must first and foremost be mobilized against the invaders; mentioning or unmasking the Chetniks is secondary.'[11] Tito protested on numerous telegrams to Stalin by openly arguing that the Soviet government's policy was not helpful to the goals of international socialism. For example, on 25 November 1941 Tito complained of Russian propaganda in favor of Chetnik leader Draža Mihailović being reported on Radio Moscow.[12] The Partisan correspondence with the Soviet leadership over complaints of Soviet support of the Chetnik enemies continued into 1944. Tito formed his provisional government in November 1943. After this the Soviets informed the British Foreign Office on 21 December 1943 that the Soviet government wished to promote a partnership between the Yugoslav government in exile and the Anti-Fascist National Committee for the Liberation of Yugoslavia (AVNOJ). Stalin seemed to be effectively asking Tito not only to resolve his differences with the London government but to accept a subsidiary position for himself and the Partisan movement.[13] It was only in November 1944 after the joint Soviet-Partisan liberation of Belgrade that Stalin and Molotov expressed their full support for Partisan predominance over the London government, asking the London government's representative, Ivan Šubašić to reconcile with Tito and cooperate in forming a Communist-led government.[14]

Launching an Independent Yugoslav Foreign Policy 1945–1948

Following the end of the Second World War, Yugoslav foreign policy continued to contradict Stalin's immediate post-war goals in Eastern Europe. With no sympathy for the Soviet inability to assist the Partisans during the war, for whatever reason, the Yugoslav leadership around Tito adopted, semi-privately, adversarial attitudes towards the Soviets.[15] In October 1944, Stalin had agreed with Winston Churchill in the Kremlin (in their now famous 'percentages agreement') that while Russia was to hold 90 per cent predominance in Romania, Britain would have 90 per cent in Greece in the post-war period. Hungary and Yugoslavia would be divided 50–50, and the Soviet Union would have 75 per cent control in Bulgaria.[16] Between October 1944 and January 1948, Stalin held up his end of the percentages agreement; but in the eyes of Tito and his leadership, the situation in Greece resembled the situation that the Partisans had experienced during the war. The Greek Communist Party faced an adversary, the royal forces, that like the Yugoslav government in exile during the Second World War, enjoyed Allied support for its return to power.[17] British troops had established that authority in December 1944 by putting down the Communist-led effort to seize control of Athens in what has been called the Second Round of the Greek Civil War.[18] A temporary agreement in 1945 with the KKE leadership to disarm their wartime resistance movement (EAM/ELAS) broke down by the 1946 elections. Reconstructing EAM/ELAS as the Democratic Army of Greece (DAG) they launched the Third Round of the civil war, this time from the northern region bordering Yugoslavia.[19] Without consulting the Soviet leadership and against their wishes, Tito supplied arms to the new force in the winter of 1946–47.[20] This Yugoslav aid also included the use of Yugoslav territory as sanctuary for DAG forces, as well as radio broadcasts of 'Radio Free Greece' emanating from Belgrade.[21]

Yugoslav actions caused immediate difficulties for Stalin. The Truman administration was not convinced that the Yugoslavs had independently provided support without Moscow's approval. This perception of Moscow's intention to align Greece with the Soviet Union through the KKE triggered an American agreement to pick up the support for the royal government that the British could no longer continue. On 12 March 1947, President Truman requested Congress's approval for military aid to Greece and Turkey, on the grounds that it would prevent Soviet takeover and not just Communist victory.[22] To complicate matters further, the KKE leadership itself had been directly asking the Soviets for military assistance. Between 1944 and 1946, the Soviet Union had been relatively inactive in guiding national Communist movements, preferring what the Yugoslavs then called 'imperialistic agreements' with the US and UK. The Yugoslav provision of many more arms to the Greek Communists than even those promised by Moscow contributed to the Yugoslav argument that the Soviets had forsaken the international Communist cause. This embarrassment even forced Stalin to provide the DAG with some limited assistance in June 1947, following sizeable Yugoslav support.[23]

Two key features in Yugoslav foreign policy between 1945 and 1948 underlined the growing conflict between the Soviet Union and Yugoslavia's ambitions to establish itself as the new regional power: plans for a Communist Balkan Federation and the Yugoslav leadership's vocal anti-Western/anti-capitalist rhetoric. Whether honoring the percentages agreement or not, the Western powers by the summer of 1947 had effectively withdrawn their support for internal opposition to the Communists' Bulgarian Workers' Party (BRP). Yet it was not clear what the Soviet zone of influence over Bulgaria meant in practice. Party leaders for example, interpreted alignment with the Soviet Union in major international questions as still offering them some autonomy in their relations with other Communist parties within the Soviet zone of influence.[24]

At the Szklarska Poreba meeting in August 1947, held to coordinate the activities of these parties under Soviet leadership in Eastern Europe, a new Communist Information Bureau (Cominform) with its headquarters in Belgrade was set up to direct this consolidation. European Social Democratic parties previously considered desirable allies were now condemned as 'the most dangerous agents of imperialism.'[25] Yet it remained unclear to what extent inter-party contacts were to be regulated by Moscow. The mere choice of the Yugoslav capital as the location of the Cominform headquarters served as a public Soviet endorsement of Tito's leadership. At the conference the Yugoslavs were praised for their 'revolutionary activism.' The Bulgarian Communist leader Georgi Dimitrov interpreted Stalin's endorsement of the Yugoslavs' independent activism as primarily an endorsement of future autonomous initiatives of other East European party leaderships.[26]

In response, Dimitrov began to cultivate closer contacts with Tito in 1947. In August 1947, Tito and Dimitrov signed the Bled Agreement—a treaty of alliance that focused on economic and cultural cooperation. Tito and Dimitrov discussed a possible future Balkan Federation, an idea first introduced by Stalin in 1944.[27] However, no specific agreement on the federation was reached. Previous Soviet-sponsored discussions of a possible Balkan Federation originated from the controversy over the conflicting ambitions of Yugoslavia and Bulgaria in Macedonia after the Second World War. At the end of the war, Stalin had mentioned the federation to Tito as a possible solution to the Macedonian question but abandoned the idea a year later.

The ambitious Yugoslav leadership, especially Edvard Kardelj, considered the federation a realistic possibility.[28] But from the outset in 1944, the Yugoslav and Bulgarian representatives disagreed on its structure. An equal association of two states was deemed inappropriate by the Yugoslavs, as this would reduce the status of leading federal republics Croatia, Slovenia and Serbia. The Yugoslav proposal that Bulgaria would become a seventh constituent republic of Yugoslavia was not surprisingly unacceptable to the Bulgarian leadership. Moreover, such a configuration would have bolstered the Yugoslav position too much to have been accepted by Moscow and would have been resisted by Britain for fear that it would threaten Greek interests and the Mediterranean lifeline to the Suez Canal.

In 1946 Stalin again flirted with the idea of a Yugoslav-Bulgarian federation but only if the Soviet Union were to be fully in charge of setting the terms and conducting the negotiations. The idea was abandoned for the second time in June 1946 due to lack of interest both in Belgrade and in Sofia. A shift in Bulgarian policy over the Macedonian question in July 1946 that allowed more concessions to Yugoslavia swiftly sparked a third attempt at the federation between Bulgaria and Yugoslavia, discussions to which the Soviets were not party. The Bled Agreement of August 1947 called for the strengthening of economic ties, simplification of border controls, and the foregoing of significant war reparations from Bulgaria to Yugoslavia. In Bled, it was agreed that Macedonia would not be ceded to Yugoslavia until the formation of a possible future federation.[29] Stalin felt that the Yugoslavs and Bulgarians had taken undue advantage of the independence he had extended to their parties. He was outraged that the agreement had been signed without Soviet consultation. Both the Yugoslav and the Bulgarian leadership were reprimanded by Moscow. Stalin immediately wrote to Tito and Dimitrov:

> The opinion of the Soviet government is that both governments have made a mistake, having made a treaty, moreover, of unlimited duration…despite the warnings of the Soviet government. The Soviet government believes that the impatience of these two governments has facilitated the actions of reactionary Anglo-American elements, giving them an additional excuse to intensify the military intervention in Greek and Turkish affairs against Yugoslavia and Bulgaria…The Soviet government must be given advance notice, as it cannot take responsibility for agreements of great importance in the area of foreign policy that are signed without consultation with the Soviet government.[30]

Only after the conclusion of the Bulgarian peace treaty on 15 September 1947 did the Soviets agree to the signing of a modified Bled Agreement in November 1947.

More than the often cited independent actions of the Yugoslav and Bulgarian leadership in negotiations over a future federation was also outrage over the Tito leadership's unwavering expansionism. Recent documentary evidence shows that Tito at various times included not only Bulgaria in proposals for a federation but different versions of it would have possibly included even Italy and Czechoslovakia.

From the fall of 1947 and early 1948, an increasingly negative view of the Yugoslav leadership appeared in the reports originating from the Soviet embassy in Yugoslavia. Ambassador Anatolii Lavrentev identified an increase in Yugoslav 'nationalist propaganda' and cited an overestimation of Partisan military credentials gained during the Second World War.[31] The reports criticized Tito's self-aggrandizing speeches and considered him as challenging Stalin's leading position. Through an agent in the Yugoslav Politburo, the Soviet leadership learned that in January 1948 the Yugoslavs within the Central Committee continued to discuss their grievances toward the Soviets in private, as they had done in 1945.[32] In the winter-spring 1948 the TsK VKP (b) Apparat (the Central Committee of the All-Union Communist Party (Bolsheviks)) under Mikhail Suslov wrote secret analytical reports and critiques of four Communist party groups—Yugoslavia, Hungary, Poland and Czechoslovakia—where charges of nationalism and underestimation of the role of the USSR play a central role.[33] These culminated in Suslov's report, entitled 'About the anti-Marxist positions of the leadership of the Communist Party of Yugoslavia on questions of foreign and domestic politics,' filed on 18 March 1948.[34] The Soviet documents discussed the preparation of replacements for those within the Yugoslav leadership who had not expressed views favorable closer to cooperation with the Soviet Union with those who had. Plans to replace key figures were already under way in the winter of 1947–48.[35] Denouncing the Yugoslavs served as an opportunity to reject all 'national roads to socialism.' Stalin worried that the East European regimes might defy the Soviet Union if inspired by possible Western collusion with Yugoslavia in the future.[36]

Stalin was already concerned about independent Yugoslav actions in the Balkans, as noted above. Ironically, the foundation of the Cominform in August 1947 only intensified contacts between Yugoslavia and Bulgaria. It coincided with the signing of the Bled Agreement and allowed their leaders to keep talking about a future Balkan Federation. On 17 January 1948, Dimitrov was interviewed by foreign journalists on his train returning from Romania following the signing of the Bulgarian-Romanian Treaty of Friendship, Collaboration and Mutual Assistance. He commented that a larger federation, stretching from Poland to Greece, was possible in the future.[37] Dimitrov listed as projected members of this future federation, 'our peoples of the popular democracies will decide whether it shall be a federation or confederation of states…"Bulgaria, Albania, Romania, Yugoslavia, Hungary, Poland, Czechoslovakia and even Greece".'[38] Dimitrov told the foreign journalists:

> When in yesterday's speech I called these treaties alliances, I was not throwing out a chance word; I mean alliances, and we are allies. That is the sense applied to the treaties Bulgaria has signed with Albania, Yugoslavia and Romania, and it is the meaning of the treaties she will sign with Czechoslovakia, Hungary and Poland. We are allies as we are allies de facto with the Soviet Union… [39]

Dimitrov went on to emphasize Moscow's role in these projected proceedings. 'The federation plans to cooperate with Russia on a large scale, and if possible would seek trade relations with the United States, Britain and France.' Again, the US interpreted these independent Yugoslav and Bulgarian moves as being directed from Moscow. Even the *New York Times* speculated on 11 January 1948 that 'one of the basic European aspects of Soviet foreign policy seems to be the encouragement of a federation of Balkan and Danubian states.'[40] The article reported Dimitrov's listing of potential members as 'at least Albania, Yugoslavia, Bulgaria and Romania—truly Balkans states—and Hungary, their Danubian neighbor [that] have Communist dictatorial governments in common.'[41] As evidence, the article cited the Soviet Union's bilateral treaty of military assistance that existed with Yugoslavia, and noted that similar pacts were being drawn up with the four other countries. The *Times* considered it 'logical to anticipate that the Soviet Union would like a federation system extending from Poland on the Baltic Sea to Greece in the Aegean, and including all intervening countries.'[42] The Western press also cited bilateral pacts between Poland, Czechoslovakia and Yugoslavia, as well as between Yugoslavia, Bulgaria, Albania and Romania. From the perspective of the *Times*, these steps were natural, since 'the lands affected already have common foreign policies, and all of them are coordinated by Moscow.'[43] Moscow's disclaimer was not aided by the placement of two Yugoslav divisions of troops in Albania 'to ward off the insurgency taking place in Greece' one week after Dimitrov's statements.

Again, neither Dimitrov nor Tito had consulted Stalin before making their moves.[44] On 24 January 1948, Stalin sent a harshly worded letter to Dimitrov:

> The part of your statement at the press conference in Romania concerning the federation or confederation of people's democracies, including Greece, Poland, Czechoslovakia, etc., is viewed by Moscow friends as harmful, detrimental to the countries of the new democracy, and as facilitating the struggle of the Anglo-Americans against these countries...We consider your statement about a customs union between countries having treaties of mutual assistance equally careless and harmful...It is hard to figure out what could have made you make such rash and injudicious statements at the press conference.[45]

On 28 January, *Pravda* flatly denied any movement towards an East European federation as widely reported in the Western press.[46] Stalin quickly summoned both Dimitrov and Tito to the Kremlin.[47] However, only Dimitrov made an appearance. The still defiant Tito sent Kardelj, accompanied by Djilas (who was already in Moscow), in his place. At the meeting on 10 February, Stalin insisted that Bulgaria and Yugoslavia were not to engage in provocations of the West at this time. In Stalin's view, it was unlikely that the Greek insurgency would succeed in bringing about a Communist regime to power, and it was equally unlikely that the US and Britain would allow a Communist government in the Eastern Mediterranean.[48] Therefore Yugoslavia's and Bulgaria's persistent efforts to undermine the percentages agreement were futile and destructive. Stalin in no way accepted Dimitrov's suggestion of a larger confederation, asking of Dimitrov, 'What historic ties are there between Bulgaria and Romania? None! And we need not speak of Bulgaria nor Hungary nor Poland.'[49] Stalin accepted only the idea of a Soviet sponsored Balkan Federation between Bulgaria and Yugoslavia, into which Albania could later enter, with the possibility of separate federations between Hungary and Romania and Bulgaria and Poland respectively. Neither Bulgaria, nor Yugoslavia were to have any part in these. In the meeting Molotov exalted, 'Yugoslavia did not warn us and didn't even inform us about this decision [to send troops to Albania] until after the fact. We believe that this speaks of serious differences existing between us.'[50] The Yugoslavs withdrew their forces at once from Albania but were angered by the Soviet disapproval which quickly extended into wrangling over trade relations.

On 12 February, Stalin asked both the Bulgarian and the Yugoslav regimes to sign declarations that they would consult the Soviet Union before undertaking foreign policy initiatives.[51] By January 1948 there were several areas of disagreement between the Yugoslav and the Soviet leaderships, including enduring disappointment at the Soviets' lack of wartime support and resentment of the hard Soviet terms, as noted below, in several 'joint companies.' However, the real conflict between Stalin and Tito underlying the dramatic turns of events between 1945 and 1948, was that the Yugoslav leader and his closest associates were not willing to let the Kremlin preside over their foreign relations. Not only did the Tito regime have difficulty in giving up their independent ties with Bulgaria; they were eager to forge close independent ties with other Communist parties outside the Balkan border set by Moscow, extending for example to the Czechoslovak Communist Party. To show that Tito, unlike Stalin, remained loyal to the international Communist movement the Yugoslavs refused to abandon their anti-Western rhetoric and territorial claims in order to aid Soviet goals of non-conflictual relations with the West. Specifically, this meant that the Yugoslav regime was unwilling to give up its claim to Trieste in favor of Italy. For Stalin, Tito's giving up this Yugoslav claim would have aided Soviet bargaining with the West on German reparations and other issues. The Yugoslav claim to Trieste that continued into the post-war period received initial Soviet support but soon became a position that challenged the early Cold War propaganda of accommodation in Stalin's foreign policy, just as identified in the Cominform expulsion letter. On 24 April 1945, Nazi Germany had surrendered Trieste to the Allies. Tito's Partisan units arrived at the port of Trieste ahead of Anzac units from New Zealand.[52] The US and Britain demanded that the Partisans withdraw from Trieste. On 9 June 1945 a compromise was reached and thereafter the border region of the Free Territory of Trieste (FTT) was administered in two zones, Zone A and Zone B. Trieste and its route to Austria was placed in the Zone A administered by the Allies.[53] Included in Zone A was also Pula at the tip of the Istrian Peninsula. Zone B would be administered by Yugoslavia. In the summer 1946 a US proposal for a permanent solution would have placed Trieste in Italy and moved the common border even further east into Yugoslavia than previous Allied proposals.[54] This sent Tito reeling, and Yugoslav army units were moved forward to the border of Zone B. The Yugoslav air force begun to monitor American flights over Yugoslav territory with increasing hostility. They presented a list of a total of 172 unauthorized American flights over Yugoslav territory between 16 July and 8 August 1946. The Yugoslav air command forced an unauthorized American C-47 transport plane down in early August and shot down another one killing the entire crew on 19 August.[55] Despite these incidents the Yugoslav government did not curtail its anti-Western rhetoric but rather reinforced it. On 20 March 1948, amidst the growing Soviet-Yugoslav contention, the American, British and French governments in the so-called 'Tripartite Proposal' suggested that the whole Free Territory of Trieste would be placed under Italian sovereignty.[56] When Tito's leadership would not budge, the US government moved to release only $30 million dollars from Yugoslav pre-war gold reserves for 1948.[57]

By 1948 these independent actions, together with Tito's wartime record and his widespread popularity in the Communist-controlled Poland and Czechoslovakia, constituted a significant problem for Stalin and the Kremlin.[58] The Soviets wished to maintain their pre-eminent leadership within the emerging Soviet bloc and sought actively from January 1948 to consolidate it.

Edvard Kardelj's Prominent Role as Foreign Minister

The Yugoslav approach was based on the strong convictions of a small group around Tito. Between 1945 and 1952 all Yugoslav policy decisions came collectively from a core group of three men: Tito himself, Djilas and

Kardelj. Kardelj as Yugoslav Foreign Minister from 31 August 1948 to 14 January 1953 grew accustomed to consulting Djilas and then guiding foreign policy as Tito's closest confidant. In telegrams to Tito across the period 1948–52, Kardelj repeatedly used the sentence 'Djidje [meaning Djilas] and I think you should' carry out the initiative put forward.[59] Throughout 1948 and 1949, Kardelj hardly ever advised Tito on a state policy decision or drafted a foreign policy document without consulting Djilas, or at least referring to his legitimating concurrence. In his recent survey of Yugoslavia's foreign relations, Ranko Petković points out that, 'these dates of Kardelj's tenure, in spite of the fact that they are exact, should be treated conditionally in light of the fact that Edvard Kardelj was a special super-Minister of Foreign Affairs of Yugoslavia before and after [1948]. Not only because he wanted to be one, but because he was able to act as one.'[60] Kardelj's special role is rightly said to stem from the 'authority of power' within the value system of Communist Yugoslavia. His Partisan credentials were of the highest order, as he had been involved in building the movement with Tito all along the way. He was a member of a regional committee of the CPY in Slovenia from 1932, on the staff of the CPY Politburo in Paris in 1937, and member of the Central Committee of the CPY from 1938 onwards. Kardelj became a member of the Politburo in 1940. He participated in the Partisan uprising in Slovenia in July 1941 and edited the CPY publication *Borba* during the war in the Serbian liberated area Užice in 1941. He became Vice-President of the AVNOJ Executive Committee in 1942, Vice-President of the People's Committee for the Liberation of Yugoslavia (NKOJ) in 1943, and Vice-President of Yugoslavia in 1945. In all these roles Kardelj had remained loyal and close to Tito. He is the only Foreign Minister of Yugoslavia (or any Soviet bloc regime for that matter) to have attained, and maintained, this most prestigious party position while acting as Minister.

Following the Tito-Stalin split, Kardelj followed a list of predecessors to the post whose Communist credentials remained unimpressive. In fact, Josip Smodlaka, Ivan Šubašić and Stanoje Simić all lacked any credentials as party members or participants in the Partisan movement during the war, let alone any access to Tito's circle afterwards. In fact, the position of Foreign Minister had remained generally insignificant until Kardelj's ascendancy, as demonstrated by the fact that all three former ministers had been appointed for the purpose of appeasing outside actors. Smodlaka (1943–44) and Šubašić (1944–45), were both pre-war Croatian political figures who had been representatives of the royal Yugoslav government in exile. They were given their positions only in response to Allied calls for cooperation between the Partisans and the Chetniks.

Simić (1945–48) was placed in the post to appease the Soviet leadership. He had spent three years of the Second World War as envoy of the exiled Yugoslav government in London to the USSR in Moscow.[61] He resigned in 1944 and made himself available to Tito's government. In the aftermath of the Tito-Stalin split, his background was no longer viewed as a political asset. Not only was Simić accused of being 'the Russians' guy,' due to his prolonged stay in Moscow, his views on foreign policy were not far from Stalin's, which were now considered too 'pro-Western.'[62] These official reasons for Simić's dismissal do not tell the entire story. After all, if anyone was guilty of collaboration with the Soviets, it was Tito and Kardelj. Both of them had publicly proclaimed their loyalty to the Soviet Union many times since 1945. However, Tito justly or unjustly feared that Simić was one of the figures like Hebrang and Žujović with whom the Kremlin sought to replace his circle. The Kremlin had previously endorsed Simić. In March 1945, Stalin, through a letter from Molotov, reprimanded Tito and Kardelj for not including Simić in their government. The telegram read:

> In the interest of avoiding misunderstandings, we consider it necessary to inform you that the Russian friends of Yugoslavia in Moscow were stunned to learn that the new Yugoslav government was to include such figures as [Milan] Grol…This incomprehension is compounded by the fact that Simić has been excluded from the government, although his sympathy for the national-liberation movement is beyond question. Since we had no opportunity earlier to know of these changes in the Yugoslav government, we find it necessary to inform you, if only at this late date, that we consider these changes to be an effort fraught with potential political complications.[63]

Kardelj was already Tito's most trusted foreign representative, the one Tito had regularly sent in his place when he would not personally meet with Stalin. Kardelj's replacement of 'Moscow's man' Simić was also a symbolic insult to Stalin.

Kardelj was placed in the position of Foreign Minister almost immediately following Yugoslavia's formal expulsion from the Cominform. In the aftermath of the split, the Foreign Ministry immediately acquired the extended and significant role of analyzing and countering the Soviet anti-Yugoslav propaganda which would soon be circulated though all East European states loyal to Moscow. This was not the function of a propaganda section of the Ministry of the Interior which could in other circumstances be expected. For example, on 13 February 1949, the daily *Tribuna Ludu* in Warsaw commented 'Anglo-American occupiers are supporting Tito's clique in Trieste.'[64] The article grouped the Yugoslavs with the Western Allies claiming that Tito was acting in unison with the colonizing powers to 'occupy Trieste mutually.'[65] On 19 February, *Radio Bucharest* commented that:

> When the Yugoslav government no longer adopts the unfriendly politics which is depriving it from help of socialist countries of the National Democracies, and the Soviet Union in the first place, only then on its own Yugoslavia will understand that in economic respects it can reach the same success as the countries of the National Democracies are enjoying with only with the enormous help of the socialist countries.[66]

On 21 February, *Radio Prague* announced:

> All students are demonstrating and signaling loyalty towards the democratic front in the world and love towards the Soviet Union. They are insisting with the university, even while holding back horrible torment, that 'we, Yugoslav students in the USSR, completely sympathize with the position in which our fellow students in Yugoslavia find themselves in, because after we became aware of the Cominform resolution, we were approached by force by strange men from the Yugoslav embassy telling us to interrupt our schooling and to abandon the brotherly USSR.'

On 22 February, *Radio Budapest* stated that 'the nation of Yugoslavia (with the exception of the kulak and the reactionaries) were it not subject to the [secret police] UDBa terror, would throw out Tito and his clique tomorrow, so far that none of them would ever be heard from again. The position of Yugoslavia is as it were facing the mouth of a pistol and only the order to fire needs to be given.'[67]

Although Kardelj's selection as Foreign Minister was inspired by political loyalty and rhetorical goals, it produced impressive results for Yugoslav diplomacy in the next years not only in terms of countering anti-Yugoslav Soviet propaganda. Under Kardelj, Yugoslavia quickly became a member of the United Nations (UN), and Yugoslavia achieved a term as a non-permanent member of the Security Council as early as January 1950. These achievements were perhaps more the result of Western support aimed at embarrassing the Soviet Union. The Yugoslavs for their part did not betray expectations. Already in 1950, at the UN General Assembly (GA), Yugoslavia notoriously accused the Soviet Union of having started the Korean conflict. Kardelj desired an internationally visible role for

Yugoslavia in order to air Yugoslav grievances against the Soviet Union in a public forum. Kardelj's and the Tito-leadership's domestic popularity rose accordingly—the foreign policy addressed both domestic and international audiences. After his participation at the opening of the 6th regular session of the GA, Kardelj 'returned to Belgrade to be greeted like "Caesar", because small and independent Yugoslavia was chosen as Vice-President of the large General Assembly of the UN.'[68] In addition, from the domestic Yugoslav perspective, with Kardelj's political authority also came financial leverage for the ministry. Budgetary resources allocated to the ministry made it a more autonomous body than other Yugoslav ministries. The choice of Tito's closest confidant as its head increased its autonomous internal workings as oversight was largely entrusted to someone Tito relied upon. Kardelj sought immediately to expand the Foreign Ministry's network of embassies world-wide. Although his actions were directed against the Soviet Union from within Tito's inner circle, it was through these actions, with Western support that the Yugoslav Foreign Ministry quickly gained international stature. Yugoslavia's role in the UN body benefited the Ministry, which would continue to gain autonomy from the Yugoslav Politburo and from UDBa after Kardelj's tenure ended in 1953, seven weeks before the death of Stalin.

Escalating Yugoslav-Soviet Differences, January–March 1948
Past scholarship on the Tito-Stalin split maintains, as noted above, that although the original Partisan leadership wanted to remain independent from the Soviets, it did not seek a split with the USSR. It was supposedly Stalin who acted precipitously in expelling Yugoslavia from the Cominform.[69] Djilas's memoirs also argue for the unintentional nature of the break with the Soviet Union by describing the efforts of Kardelj, Ranković and himself to convince Tito of the senselessness of a clash with the Soviets.[70] Archival evidence, however, suggests that the Partisan leadership was not surprised by the split in March or in June. In fact, an escalating confrontation of problems with the Soviets had been predicted, if not sought, by the Yugoslav leadership since late January 1948.

By January 1948, the Tito-Kardelj-Djilas troika in the Office of the President of the Republic was not willing to compromise on any of their accumulating differences with the Soviet Union. This defiance culminated in Tito's confident, confrontational letter to Stalin with a concise statement of independence in April:

> We are of the opinion that there are many specific aspects in the social transformation of Yugoslavia which can be of benefit to the revolutionary development in other countries…This does not mean

that we place the role of the CPSU and the social system of the USSR in the background. On the contrary we study and take the Soviet system as an example, but we are developing socialism in our country in somewhat different form. [71]

Before then, the personal correspondence of both Tito and Kardelj indicates that for both of them their position was based on a belief in their 'earned' right to an independent but still Communist policy—a right earned by the party's pre-war consolidation under Tito and their struggle in the Second World War against the various Fascist forces without Soviet assistance. There were altogether six significant letters exchanged between Tito and Stalin or Molotov between March and June 1948.[72] Kardelj drafted Tito's replies. These often studied letters already show the thus far frequently neglected Yugoslav disposition not to compromise with the Soviets.[73] With virtually no changes, the drafts were dispatched from the President's Office to Moscow. For example, their crucial reply of 13 April 1948 to Stalin's complaint over an anti-Soviet atmosphere in Yugoslavia on 27 March 1948 was initially handwritten by Kardelj simply on the back of 33 sheets of stationary from Tito's President's Office.[74] Then transcribed verbatim, the letter was signed by Tito, and sent to Stalin. Here provocative statements such as 'no matter how much each of us loves the land of socialism, the USSR, he can, in no case love his country less, which is also developing socialism—in this concrete case FRNJ, for which so many thousands of its most progressive people fell' made the Yugoslav argument.[75]

In fact, these letters reflect the decision by Tito's inner circle to cease ready cooperation with Moscow in January 1948 which is clear from the course of Yugoslav-Soviet trade negotiations.[76] The Soviet leadership had suggested to the Yugoslavs that these negotiations begin in Moscow in January 1948. Tito sent Djilas and Bogdan Crnobrnja, only the Assistant Minister of Foreign Trade, to Moscow for the talks. Indifferent to the outcome of these trade negotiations, Tito simultaneously provoked Moscow by dispatching the two divisions of Yugoslav troops to Albania. There are no documents on this Albanian decision in the Archives of Yugoslavia because neither the preparations or the decision to send troops across the border were discussed in the Politburo. Dijlas was already in Moscow, and not even Kardelj was privy to the details. Tito made the decision alone, outside of the party, the Foreign Ministry and his inner circle. He only consulted the key military people needed to execute the act: Ranković, the head of UDBa, Koča Popović who would succeed Kardelj as Foreign Minister, Ivan Gošnjak, a general in the Yugoslav People's Army (JNA) and Lieutenant-General of the JNA Svetozar Vukmanović-Tempo, who had been in charge of Partisan operations in Albania during the war.[77] Tito argued that Albania was endangered by "'Greek reaction," and, "imperialists hiding in Greece" and needed Yugoslav support to "save and defend Albania".[78] Djilas has suggested that by sending in these divisions, Tito was trying to ensure that a potential Yugoslav-Albanian unification would still be possible in the future. [79] However, it seems more likely within the context of the events in Moscow, that Tito was asserting his superiority in the Balkans as he had done since 1945 with symbolic acts while also testing Moscow for its reaction. Dimitrov's coincidental comments over the possible future of the Balkan Federation on 11 January added to the tension. In response to clear Soviet displeasure, Tito sent Kardelj to Moscow where he listened to Stalin's rebuke on 10 February. The Soviet leadership announced a delay in the trade agreement on the same day. Djilas and Kardelj quickly departed from Moscow without an agreement. In order to maintain the appearance still desiring a trade agreement, Crnobrnja remained in Moscow until 3 March at the behest of the Yugoslav Ministry of Foreign Trade. Crnobrnja took back with him the first draft of the Soviet Trade Agreement now being offered to the Yugoslavs again after the January-February delay. But despite a promise from Crnobrnja to the Yugoslav representative in Moscow, Vladimir Popović, that he would send back an official Yugoslav reply, such a reply was never even drafted. Popović, like the rest of the Yugoslav government outside Tito's inner circle continued to work under the assumption that Yugoslav-Soviet trade relations would continue.

Popović had become concerned over the lack of Yugoslav action to achieve a trade agreement even before Crnobrnja's arrival. Already in January, Popović had pleaded in an unusual, direct letter to Tito: 'Pardon me, that I am engaging you on these questions, but all our previous urging towards the Ministry of Foreign Trade until today did not produce results. It is urgent, namely it is needed, that our Ministry informs us when we will complete the Soviet Trade Project Agreement.'[80] It seems that Tito's leadership had no longer seriously pursued a trade agreement with the Soviet Union since January and expected a serious break with the Soviets from the first days of March. Therefore, it was the policy of the Yugoslav Foreign Ministry to continue its work as previously and not to inform people outside of Tito's immediate circle, including Popović in Moscow, of the heated exchanges.

On 12 February 1948 Popović repeated his complaint, this time to his regional section supervisor in the Yugoslav Foreign Ministry that, 'we here have received the impression that in Yugoslavia not one institution works seriously and systematically to achieve [the trade and technical assistance] agreement' with the Soviet Union.[81] By mid-February, still unaware of

Tito's personal decision not to complete the trade agreement with the Soviet Union, Popović had become thoroughly frustrated with being unable to determine the shape of trade relations with the Soviet Union, relations which were important for propaganda purposes as well as for the economy. Popović explained in his letter to the Ministry that this task was especially difficult because no such comprehensive agreement between Yugoslavia and the Soviet Union had been concluded in the three years since the end of the Second World War.[82] In the absence of instructions from Belgrade, Popović had established 'a local position on things, because exactly no one [from Belgrade] informed us [in Moscow] what should be done despite the fact that there exists a hardworking group and experts who are located in Yugoslavia and who are competent on these questions.'[83]

The frustrated tone of Popović's communication reappears in several of his February and March 1948 letters.[84] He had understood that his role as the Yugoslav representative was to seek a trade agreement with the Soviet Union. A trade agreement could guarantee commercial exchange with the East European states already establishing formal trade relations with the Soviet Union. Popović also hoped that it would include some Soviet aid to benefit a Yugoslav economy still recovering from war damage.[85] The Soviet Union was the largest regional Communist ally of Yugoslavia, and since the Second World War it had continued expanding its influence and presence in neighbouring Eastern Europe. To reinforce his efforts, Popović wrote several memorandums on the promising content of Soviet trade agreements with Romania, Bulgaria and Poland.

Well beyond Popović's efforts, Crnobrnja was in fact withdrawn from Moscow specifically because of Tito's decision not to conclude a trade agreement with the Soviet Union. In addition, Crnobrnja's analysis of the Soviet proposal that he filed immediately upon his return did not favor the conclusion of the agreement on its economic terms. The Soviet side had proposed a shipment protocol according to which Yugoslav exports would amount to $57.5 million in value and Soviet imports to $58.6 million.[86] Crnobrnja found crucial commodities to be pork, cement, caustic soda and dry plums. However, the Yugoslavs could not foresee favourable terms of trade with the Soviet Union on any of these goods:

> Pork we cannot conclude because the Soviets cannot give us this product; cement we cannot conclude because cement we can sell on the world market for 17–18 dollars per ton, and the Soviets will give us only something close to 11 dollars. In 1946 we could agree to this because the difference was smaller between 15 and 16 dollars.[87]

Moreover, Crnobrnja did not appreciate Soviet tactics: 'We did not conclude an agreement on caustic soda because the Soviets offered too low of a price. In the world market Yugoslavia can get $300, but the Soviets will only pay $75, which is how much they pay for soda from Romania. This would be against the interests of our country. In long negotiations, the Soviets went up to $150, and we lowered our asking price to $200 although at the time we were able to receive between $260 and $270 on the world market. On the next day the Soviets went down to only $75.'[88]

Much more than being denied a one-year trade agreement was at stake from the beginning of Stalin's policy decision to offer the Yugoslavs these unfavorable terms. From January to March 1948 the Soviet leadership were drafting more comprehensive trade agreements with East European states. One was also proposed for Finland. These were to serve as the first steps towards a formulation of a comprehensive Soviet economic and security bloc in Eastern Europe. The Soviet offer to the Yugoslavs worked within the framework of these treaties but also served as a political test to oblige the unruly Yugoslavs to accept unfavorable terms.

Despite arguments of economic necessity and the impending danger of a conflict with the Soviet Union, Tito's all-powerful Office of the President of the Republic was no longer seriously pursuing a trade agreement with the Soviet Union. Having sent troops to Albania in January and having been reprimanded over the action in February, the Yugoslav leadership was already reconsidering its close cooperation with Moscow. As discussed above it had already been in conflict with the Soviet Union over its foreign policy. Moreover, for that matter, the Yugoslav leadership in Belgrade had already regarded close relations with the Soviet Union with caution because Soviet technical experts attached to the several Yugoslav-Soviet joint companies formed in 1945 reported to Soviet military intelligence. In addition, there was the exploitative reputation quickly established by the several Joint Companies, obliging the Soviets to disband them by 1947.[89] In his memoirs Kardelj explains that in early 1946 the Soviets (wishing to establish joint Soviet-Yugoslav companies) sent a delegation to Belgrade to establish cooperative companies for the navigation of the Danube and for civil air transport. Kardelj, studying similar Romanian and Hungarian agreements with the Soviet Union, was astonished to find that 'no attempt had been made to conceal the obvious inequality, the brutal hegemony of the Russians. I did not know what to think. The agreements seemed politically stupid and legally absurd.'[90] The Soviet terms offered to Yugoslavia for the joint companies were similar to those for Hungary and Romania. For example, the Soviet-Yugoslav Civil Air Transport Company (JUSTA) had pressed unsuccessfully to maintain all air service between Yugoslavia and foreign countries, leaving the domestic Jugoslovenski

Aerotransport (JAT) without a single foreign route.[91] From January 1948, it was therefore not only the Kremlin that stalled the signing of a Trade and Technical Assistance Agreement with Yugoslavia, but Tito as well. He made it seem as if bureaucratic problems in the Yugoslav Foreign Ministry were delaying the deal.

Instead of informing Popović in Moscow of the change in Yugoslav foreign policy, the President's Office simply avoided questions about the trade agreement. As Yugoslavia was officially a Soviet ally, the Foreign Ministry was in no position to make a decision to abandon serious trade relations and close 'technical' contacts with the Soviet Union. Moreover, after discovering Soviet penetration of meetings of the Central Committee in Belgrade, the leadership feared that any official communiqué could find its way to Moscow.[92] Therefore, only a close circle of officials in Belgrade were made aware of this policy.

In the spring of 1948, Tito's Office continued to analyze the content of Soviet trade agreements with other East European states through the Yugoslav Foreign Ministry. On 19 February 1948 Romania signed an agreement for 1948 amounting to net trade of $30 million marking a $5 million increase from 1947.[93] According to the agreement, Romania was to receive cotton, metals, machine tools and unrefined fuel from the Soviet Union.[94] Oil and petroleum derivatives together with lumber were designated as Romania's exports.[95] The Romanian Embassy in Moscow gave the information about the content of the agreement to the Yugoslavs in mid-February 1948.

As Yugoslavia adopted a diplomatic strategy to delay the signing of its trade agreement with the USSR, the Soviets sought to limit Yugoslavia's ability to establish international protocols and privileges of independent statehood. The Kremlin, for example, agreed to Yugoslavia's request for the right to engage in flights over occupied Berlin only in principle. By insisting in March 1948 that the Yugoslavs sign an official agreement with Aeroflot before the privileges could take effect, the Soviets effectively denied the Yugoslav request.[96] The Yugoslav Military Mission in Berlin had made repeated requests to the Foreign Ministry to establish a Belgrade-Prague-Amsterdam aviation route that needed to pass over Berlin. Overall, the Soviets intentionally prolonged the signing of the discussed Agreement on Air Transport and Aviation Affairs that would have authorized flights over Berlin.[97]

On 18 March 1948 Nikolai Bulganin, Moscow's Minister of Defence informed General Barskov, the Head of the Soviet Military Mission in Yugoslavia, that the Soviet government would abruptly and immediately withdraw all its military advisors and instructors from Yugoslavia because 'they [we]re surrounded by hostility…they [we]re not treated in a friendly fashion in Yugoslavia.'⁹⁸ The following day the Soviet government called for the withdrawal of all civilian experts as well. Tito's leadership cried foul and claimed that they were 'amazed and [could] not understand' why the Soviets would withdraw their military personnel without any discussion or prior complaint.⁹⁹

In fact, a new Soviet complaint was at hand, and it also concerned the economy. The Soviet commercial representative Lebedev had made inquiries to Yugoslav Assistant Minister Boris Kidrič about Yugoslav economic data. The Yugoslavs had simply refused to surrender any economic and industrial statistics to the Soviets. Instead, they referred the Soviet representatives to the highest level of the Central Committee. These referrals were diversionary tactics both to prevent further Soviet espionage and to hold off trade and economic cooperation with the Soviet Union. In March the Yugoslav politburo also passed a resolution calling for a more independent course in economic and military industrial areas.¹⁰⁰

The original western analysis of the Tito-Stalin split suggested that the strains on the Soviet-Yugoslav relationship grew heavier in early 1948 because of dissension over a future Balkan Federation.¹⁰¹ However, as documents from the Office of the President of the Republic demonstrate, the exponential growth of Soviet frustration with Belgrade was rather a result of Yugoslavia's tacit refusal to sign a Trade and Technical Assistance Agreement and their attempts to frustrate Soviet influence through other measures.¹⁰² The trade agreement was a political test for the Yugoslavs, as noted above, but Stalin also sought secure and integrated Soviet influence in Eastern Europe, still needing resources to recover from the war and to compete with the West in the future. This agreement would have begun to link the Yugoslav economy to that of the Soviet Union to the latter's benefit. Through a trade agreement the Yugoslavs could begin making up for some of their previous political independence by contributing to the Soviet economy.

The Tito-Stalin Exchanges of March–June, 1948

Tito raised the issue of a Trade and Technical Assistance Agreement in the often quoted letter to Molotov on 20 March 1948, following the Soviet withdrawal of its technical and civilian experts. This would be the first of the aforementioned six letters over the next three months. Their exchanges became an airing of old grievances that culminated in Yugoslavia's expulsion from the Cominform on 28 June. Tito's letter of 20 March, rejected Soviet reasons for withdrawing their military personnel, claiming that Yugoslav relations with the Soviets in Belgrade were 'not only good, but actually brotherly and hospitable, which [was] the custom towards all Soviet people in the new Yugoslavia.'¹⁰³ With a certain amount of sarcasm,

Tito's letter concluded that he was 'forced to reject the reasons about some sort of "lack of hospitality and lack of confidence" towards Soviet experts and Soviet representatives' and asked to be 'informed of the true reason for this decision by the Government of the USSR.' Moreover, Tito reminded Molotov that 'none of the [Soviet representatives] ha[d] complained to [him] of anything like this, although they ha[d] all had the opportunity to do so personally with [him], because [he] ha[d] never refused to see any of the Soviet people.' Tito also referred at the end of his letter to information 'the Government of the USSR [was] obtaining from various other people…because such information [was] not always objective, accurate or given with good intentions.'[104] By 'various other people' Tito most likely meant representatives of other East European governments he believed to be reporting to Soviet intelligence through their delegations in Belgrade.

Popović personally delivered Tito's letter to Molotov in Moscow. Upon receiving it, Molotov 'became visibly angry and said little and emphasized that the Soviets had sufficient evidence' for their claims.[105] As far as Popović, outside Tito's inner circle as we have seen, knew in March 1948, Belgrade was still looking for a possible reconciliation with Moscow. He even suggested investigating the 'main culprit in the affair further.'[106] By this Popović meant lower level personnel who could be blamed for the emerging rift, perhaps allowing the budding dispute to be framed as a misunderstanding from which both sides could then emerge as 'not guilty.' In his own description of events, Popović emphasized to Tito personally the extreme and unprecedented nature of Molotov's anger upon reading Tito's letter. The Yugoslav representative also fastened on Tito's sarcastic offer to meet personally with any Soviet representative as a tactical success in keeping the door open for reconciliation.

Yet, Molotov left Popović with no indication that the conflict could be resolved. Yugoslav representation in Moscow faced increasing difficulties itself from late March 1948. It did not receive even delayed replies to the simplest requests, including the licensing and transport of Yugoslav cars from Eastern Europe to Moscow for the delegation's use. The Soviets also refused to send the previously promised construction experts from the Soviet Union for the urgent task of starting construction on the huge housing project in the Yugoslav capital called New Belgrade. Popović concluded (and informed Belgrade) incredulously that not only the Soviet Foreign Ministry but also the entire Soviet governmental bureaucracy had clearly been instructed to complicate relations with Yugoslavia.[107]

The correspondence between Tito's and Stalin's offices was handled in secrecy. Tito's letters as drafted by Kardelj were hand delivered to Moscow, as were Vlado Popović's full reports of his meetings with Molotov to Belgrade. Only the most general information was included in telegrams.

The correspondence now took on an increasingly argumentative tone. In his letter of 27 March Stalin reminded Tito that Yugoslavia had already asked the Soviet Union to reduce the number of its military advisers by 60 per cent and that some high ranking Yugoslavs had allegedly said that this was because 'the rules of the Soviet army were hidebound, stereotyped and without value to the Yugoslav army, and that there was no point in paying the Soviet advisers since there was no benefit to be derived from them.'[108] Stalin named names from the ranks of Tito's closest collaborators in making these charges. These included Koča Popović, the Yugoslav Army Chief of Staff, who had requested this large-scale reduction of Soviet military advisers in 1946. The salaries of the Soviet military experts were set by Moscow at 30,000–40,000 dinars, while commanders of the Yugoslav National Army at the same time were paid only 9,000–11,000 dinars. The Soviets refused to lower their salaries, so the Yugoslavs asked the Soviet Union to reduce their numbers. Stalin also claimed that the Soviets had evidence that a group of 'questionable Marxists—Djilas, Svetozar Vukmanović-Tempo, Kidrič, Ranković' had circulated rumours, for instance that 'the CPSU is degenerate,' [that] 'great power chauvinism is rampant in the USSR,' [that] 'the USSR is trying to dominate Yugoslavia economically' and [that] 'the Cominform is a means of controlling the other parties by the CPSU.'[109] Stalin identified Velemir Velebit, as an 'English spy' who had nevertheless been given the position of First Assistant Foreign Minister.

Stalin's listing of Tito's closest collaborators served to create a record of the people that the Kremlin wanted to expel from the Yugoslav leadership. Later Stalin would seek to discredit the leaders closest to Tito by connecting them to the earlier enemies of the Soviet state as identified in the purge trials of the 1930s. Hence their association by Stalin with the heresy of Trotsky, the mistaken anti-collectivization economic theories of Bukharin and the criminal pre-1917 revisionism of the Mensheviks.[110]

Stalin sought to present 'facts' de-legitimizing the current Yugoslav Party in this correspondence, referring to the CPY as not 'completely legalized and still having only a semi-legal status.' Worse yet, Stalin complained that the 'decisions of the Party organs [we]re never published in the press, neither [we]re the reports of Party assemblies.' Moreover, the Central Committee was criticised because the 'Personnel Secretary of the party [wa]s also the Minister of State Security [Service] UDBa,' placing party cadres under the supervision of the Minister of State Security. The Soviet complaint was that instead of the party controlling state organs in Yugoslavia, a state agency, namely the Ministry of Security, controlled the party.[111]

Stalin also complained that the Yugoslav security apparatus watched over the activities of the Soviet representatives in Yugoslavia, including the representative of the CPSU to the Cominform Pavel Yudin, which indeed they had. Soviet representatives had not been subjected to such scrutiny in other East European states since 1945.

In response on 13 April, Tito openly accused Stalin of employing and recruiting Soviet spies within Yugoslavia. Another Kardelj-drafted third letter told Stalin:

> There are many reasons why we are dissatisfied…it is impossible to mention all the reasons in this letter but we will mention a few. First, we regard it as improper for the agents of the Soviet intelligence service to recruit people in our country, which is moving towards socialism…This is done in spite of the fact that our leaders and [State Security Administration] UDBa have protested against this and made it known that it cannot be tolerated…For example, Colonel Stepanov did not hesitate in 1945 to recruit one of our comrades who was working in the central division of coding and decoding in UDBa…who reported this to the present Marshal Tito as he should. Such recruiting is not done for the purpose of a struggle against some capitalist country, and we must come to the conclusion that this recruiting is destroying our internal unity…This work by the agents of the Soviet Intelligence Service cannot be called loyal and friendly towards our country.[112]

The Soviet accusations against the Tito-led Central Committee of the CPY that were developed over the correspondence of the spring 1948, were simply restated for the document expelling Yugoslavia from the Cominform. Despite Tito and Kardelj's continued claims of 'surprise at the tone and content' of Stalin's letter and the Cominform document, they could hardly have been surprised.[113] Kardelj was after all the author of Tito's confrontational letters to Stalin between March and May.

Summarizing the Split

The Soviet justifications for the break with the Tito leadership had been well established within this correspondence from mid-March onwards. Moreover, Tito, Djilas and Kardelj had collectively drafted the decision, upon Djilas's and Kardelj's return from Moscow in early February, to refuse to sign a trade agreement. Surprise and disbelief as a response to the expulsion was nonetheless the official policy and rhetoric of the Tito-led regime. Yet the expulsion of Yugoslavia from the Cominform was neither sudden and unforeseen by the Yugoslavs, nor unintended by the Soviets.

The expulsion of Yugoslavia from the Cominform was a Soviet attempt to replace the Yugoslav leadership with a more subservient one in order to consolidate the Soviet bloc in 1948. It was not, as has been suggested by some interpretations, an accidental consequence of, for example, a rogue individual in the Balkan Section of the Soviet Foreign Ministry.[114] It was not, as per the official Yugoslav argumentation transmitted to Molotov by Yugoslav representative Popović in Moscow in April 1948, a formulaic mistake of lower level officials but a conflict between the Soviet-Yugoslav parties.

Relations between Tito and Stalin had been strained since 1941, as we have seen. Relations between the Yugoslav and Soviet Foreign Ministries in trying to establish protocol for diplomatic relations had been strained since 1945. Relations between economic representatives in Moscow and Belgrade had been frozen since early 1948. Although the Tito-Stalin correspondence in the spring of 1948 assumed the form of personal attacks, their collision course was not due to a simple conflict between powerful leaders. Although Tito became unsympathetic to Stalin personally, the Tito-Stalin split resulted from broader and more fundamental disagreements. The Yugoslavs simply refused to assume a subsidiary role in relation to the Soviet Union, one requiring Soviet surveillance of the Yugoslav military, and oversight of foreign policy. Yugoslav resistance to Soviet control interfered with Soviet goals of forming a unified security and military defence bloc, or buffer zone, in Eastern Europe.[115] Their resistance also irritatingly, if less significantly, interfered with Soviet economic goals.

In response to Stalin's wild accusations against members of his inner circle, Tito's 13 April letter named Hebrang, and Žujović, together with Simić, as anti-party elements responsible for 'providing inaccurate and slanderous information to the Soviet representative in Yugoslavia.'[116] Tito's April letter explained that Hebrang and Žujović had given this misinformation about Tito to the Soviet leadership in an attempt to 'hide their anti-Party work and their tendencies and attempts, exposed earlier, to break up the unity of the leadership and the Party in general.'[117] In very stark terms, Tito explained to Stalin how his, Tito's, domestic future did not depend on Soviet good-will. Tito wrote that Yugoslav popular support for the Soviet Union, in a country of many Orthodox Christians, did not come naturally:

> Among many Soviet people there exists the mistaken idea that the sympathy of the broad masses in Yugoslavia towards the USSR came of itself, on the basis of some traditions which go back to the time of Tsarist Russia. This is not so.[118]

Tito had already warned Stalin in March that the support for the Soviet Union had to be earned. Now, his April letter elaborated. 'Love for the USSR did not come of itself. It was stubbornly inculcated into the masses of the Party and the people in general by the present leaders of the new Yugoslavia, including the first rank, the very ones so falsely accused in the letter.'[119] Tito threatened Stalin in no uncertain terms by referring to the possibility of withdrawing Yugoslav support for the Soviet Union.

Tito also emphasized the uniqueness and importance of Yugoslavia amongst East European states by noting unkindly that in Yugoslavia the CPY 'formed the nucleus of the People's Front' and therefore 'there [was] no danger of its dissolving into a People's Front' as had been necessary in Bulgaria and Poland.[120] Such comments reminded the Soviets that, in contrast to other East European countries, in Yugoslavia there was essentially no political opposition to the CPY. Some of Eastern Europe, Tito's comments implied, could still be lost to Soviet control. Tito also bragged about Yugoslavia's stature: 'the great reputation of our Party, won not only in our country but in the whole world, on the basis of the results it has obtained, speaks for itself.'[121] Moreover, Tito threatened Soviet authority by speaking about a larger Yugoslav role within the future Communist bloc: 'we are also of the opinion that there are many specific aspects in the social transformation of Yugoslavia which can be of benefit to the revolutionary development in other countries, and are already being used...We are attempting to apply the best forms of work in the realization of socialism.'[122] It is clear from these statements that Tito had, since early 1945, very little intention of subordinating the Yugoslav regime that they were forging to Soviet management. Collectively, Tito's leadership were a hardened group of Party cadres from various ethnic and class backgrounds who survived the war by making high-risk military and political decisions. Having taken those heavy risks and won, they were ready to follow Tito and Kardelj in defying Stalin and Molotov in the spring of 1948. What then were the consequences of Soviet failure to consolidate political hegemony by replacing Tito's leadership in Yugoslavia? As this chapter illustrates, this led to the appointment of Kardelj as Foreign Minister (on 3 August 1948), and from there the mandate for the creation of a powerful Foreign Ministry and a new Yugoslav foreign policy of neutralism, even before the death of Stalin in 1953.

Simultaneously the Soviet leadership were unable since 1945 to attach Yugoslavia to its economic network in a way which would have benefited Soviet economy and technology. They were still unable to achieve this in the spring of 1948. Trade plus technical cooperation would have constituted a first step towards a formal 'Friendship, Assistance and Cooperation Agreement.' It was this kind of agreement that the Soviets attempted first to sign with Yugoslavia that foresaw the fate of the Finnish-Soviet financial deal in 1948 that was part of the broadly designed (also political) Agreement on Friendship, Assistance and Mutual Cooperation. From the Yugoslavs the Soviet leadership expected a show of willingness to become part of a broader East European economic network under Soviet control and with that a show of commitment to Soviet foreign political goals and leadership among Communist states. From Finland the Soviet leadership expected a commitment to not joining Western defence or intelligence organizations, the presence of an active Communist party and a commitment to trade with the Soviet Union that benefited its economy. This treaty and its consequences for the Finnish policy of neutralism is the topic of the next chapter.[123]

3

1948: THE SOVIET TEST FOR FINLAND AND THE COMPROMISE ON NEUTRALISM

On 22 February 1948, Stalin, as the Chairman of the Council of Ministers of the Soviet Union, wrote to Finnish President Juho Kusti Paasikivi, requesting 'that Finland and the Soviet Union make a Friendship, Cooperation and Assistance Agreement similar to those signed between Hungary and the Soviet Union, and Romania and the Soviet Union.'[1] Stalin reminded Paasikivi that 'two of the three states bordering the Soviet Union which fought on the German side, Hungary and Romania, have already signed treaties of bilateral assistance in case of a possible attack by Germany.'[2] Finland was the third. On 22 February, just as Stalin's test for Finland begun, the Kremlin broke off a comparable test for Yugoslavia. It may well be only a coincidence that the high-level Yugoslav trade delegation, led by Edvard Kardelj and Foreign Minister Stanoje Simić, were forced to abandon talks on a similar agreement on the very day that the Kremlin requested negotiations with a Finnish delegation. Yet, from the divergent Yugoslav and Finnish experiences with these trade treaties in 1948 would come a common approach to relations with the Soviet Union across the 1950s that the remaining chapters will explore. The best name for that approach is neutralism.

Finland and Yugoslavia hardly faced common circumstances in these early post-war years. Finland shared an 800-mile territorial border with the Soviet Union, while Yugoslavia shared a political border with the emerging Soviet bloc in Eastern Europe. In the inter-war period, both states had emerged as newly independent but then faced overwhelming challenges as the Second World War began. Finland lost close to 10 per cent of its territory to the Soviet Union in the Winter War of 1939–40, and Yugoslavia was broken apart entirely after the German Nazi invasion of 1941. Finland had subsequently cooperated with Nazi Germany during the war and futilely fought the Soviet Union in 1944. The Finnish-Soviet Armistice of 1944 required Finland to pay the Soviet Union $300 million worth of commodities over six years.[3] The Paris Peace Treaty of 1947 reconfirmed this heavy obligation. Finland was forced to accept a 50-year lease of the territory and waters of Porkkala Island to a Soviet naval base in the Gulf of Finland.[4] The treaty required Finland to grant the Soviet Union the use of railways, waterways, roads, and air routes for the transportation of personnel and freight to and from Porkkala.[5] In total, Finland handed over to the Soviet Union 17,760 square miles, nearly 10 per cent of its territory, mainly in Karelia.[6] Finland was also required to return Petsamo—on the shore of the Barents Sea—to the Soviet Union. This area contained a strategically valuable ice-free port as well as nickel and copper mines. The territorial losses also cut in half the 30-mile canal that connects the Gulf of Finland to the Saimaa Lake. The Finnish armed forces were to consist of no more than 34,400 army troops, 4,500 naval personnel with total tonnage of 10,000 tons of equipment, an air force of 60 aircraft and 3,000 men.[7] No such limitations or loss of territory were applied to Tito's Yugoslavia.

The initial Finnish approach to post-war relations with the Soviet Union was obviously going to be one seeking some relaxation in the post-war settlement. It was driven by the decisions of two key leaders, though it was supported by a broader parliamentary process. Their strategy was to regain the domestic sovereignty which they believed had been compromised under the Moscow Armistice of 1944. The Soviet leadership's initiation of negotiations in February 1948 did not come as a surprise to President Paasikivi. On 18 January 1945, Andrei Zhdanov, the Soviet head of the Allied Commission in Finland, had proposed to the then Finnish President Carl Gustaf Emil Mannerheim a future assistance treaty between 'two sovereign states,' similar to those the Soviet Union had signed with France and with Czechoslovakia.[8] Zhdanov asked Mannerheim 'not to mention the issue to anyone else because the airing of the issue would cause a backlash within the Kremlin.'[9] Mannerheim, however, informed his Prime Minister, then Paasikivi. In fact, Soviet documents show that Foreign Minister Vyacheslav Molotov had reprimanded Zhdanov for overreaching in an attempt to redefine Soviet-Finnish relations. On 18 January, Molotov wrote to Zhdanov in Helsinki, 'You have gone too far. A pact with Mannerheim of the sort we have with Czechoslovakia is [the] music for the future. We have to reestablish diplomatic relations first. Do not frighten Mannerheim with radical proposals.'[10] He was asked just to clarify his position. Without reference to the corresponding Finnish documents, Russian scholar Dmitri

Volkogonov has interpreted these events from the perspective of Stalin's relationship with Zhdanov, whose obedience Stalin was testing in January.[11] From a reading of the Soviet documents, Zhdanov's suggestion for redefining Finnish-Soviet relations apparently concludes with Molotov's rebuff of 18 January. The more recent study of Vladislav Zubok and Constantine Pleshakov argues that:

> The Finnish attempt to obtain an early, better deal in comparison with the general terms of armistice ran contrary to the Stalin-Molotov grand diplomacy in Europe. It would certainly have been a violation of the principle to settle a post-war world in the concert of three great powers, something that Stalin still highly valued. Zhdanov, who was on the margins of this grand diplomacy, failed to see this obvious fact.[12]

Be that as it may, Finnish Foreign Ministry documents show that Zhdanov did not drop the inquiry. On 24 January, Mannerheim met with Zhdanov again, 'informing him that both he as the President and Paasikivi as Prime Minister were interested in the matter,' but without soliciting a further response from Zhdanov.[13] On 12 May 1945, Zhdanov repeatedly 'asked Prime Minister Paasikivi whether Finland would support a radical program for the betterment of Finnish-Soviet relations.'[14] Zhdanov went on to emphasize revealingly that 'the Russians do not wish to touch Finnish business or conditions, but that they want Finland to remain independent and economically successful, further asking whether Paasikivi had a chance to get acquainted with Soviet treaties with France and Czechoslovakia.' Paasikivi replied that he considered 'the treaty with Czechoslovakia not to be bad, but that this was his personal opinion, and that signing of a treaty with the Soviet Union depended on the Parliament.' The matter proceeded no further at the time. On 31 May 1945, Zhdanov informed Paasikivi that 'the Soviet government in principle supported a treaty, that a treaty is being prepared in Moscow and the Soviets would inform the Finns further.' However, this did not take place until a Finnish trade relations delegation visiting Moscow in November 1947 brought up the possibility of a Soviet-Finnish treaty.[15]

The 1945 Mannerheim-Paasikivi-Zhdanov exchange suggests that from the early post-war period both the Soviet and Finnish sides wished to achieve a political solution through an economic agreement on bilateral trade. This was a clearly different starting point than that of Yugoslavia, where Josip Broz Tito and Edvard Kardelj enjoyed Partisan credentials that encouraged overconfident foreign relations with an emotional and tumultuous relationship critical of the Kremlin as argued in Chapter 1. The

Finns, first under the leadership of Mannerheim and later Paasikivi, pursued a cautious working relationship with Moscow from 1945 to 1948. Zhdanov, had participated in the Finnish-Soviet armistice negotiations and spent several years in Helsinki. He himself proceeded with caution in revealing to Mannerheim Moscow's desire for economic benefit from Finland and the possibility of a permanent solution to Finnish-Soviet relations. The exchange represents more than 'Zhdanov swallow[ing] Molotov's remonstration' and Stalin's simple conclusion that 'the 'Sovietization' of Finland would be a bloody and protracted struggle,' an 'open wound' which the Soviets should not add to the existing struggles in the 'Western Ukraine and the Baltic.'[16] Stalin wished to rebuild the post-war Soviet economy and saw Finland as a source of assistance. Paasikivi, and later Prime Minister and President Urho Kekkonen, felt that economic concessions were preferable to political and territorial ones. They believed that Finland's unequivocal acceptance of harsh Allied peace terms was necessary for any chance of future political independence. Nevertheless, the only other person to whom Paasikivi had relayed the information of the sensitive discussions with Zhdanov concerning a possible future treaty was Foreign Minister Carl Enckell, making Stalin's letter of March 1948 a surprise for most of the Finnish political establishment, if not Paasikivi.[17]

Finnish members of parliament, like international observers, were unaware of the 1945 Soviet proposals. Instead, they associated the Soviet initiative with the recent coup in Czechoslovakia, where the Soviet-backed Communist Party took control of the government in February 1948. Yet the coup signaled to Paasikivi that Finland's position was growing increasingly difficult. Prior to the Communist seizure of power, Western observers had been guardedly optimistic that Eduard Beneš's coalition government could remain at least in some measure internally independent in exchange for its adherence to Soviet foreign policy.[18] Czechoslovakia had already established favorable relations with Moscow, on the basis of the Soviet-Czechoslovak Treaty of Friendship in 1943.[19] Beneš himself had cultivated such ties during the war. The Soviet Union had wanted to show all states in the path of the Red Army (and Western states with large Communist parties, such as France and Italy) an example of amicable Soviet relations with a non-Communist leadership. The Czech coup carried out in February 1948, in the wake of Georgi Dimitrov's announcement of a future Balkan Federation, helped to convince Western governments that Stalin's intentions in Europe were expansionist. It made the Finnish policy of incipient neutralism more difficult to pursue, given its goal of political independence from Moscow.

President Paasikivi and Speaker of the Parliament Kekkonen therefore considered Stalin's 1948 invitation a political test for Finland based on the

1945 proposals, a test both leaders were determined that Finland should not fail. In sharp contrast to the cocksure attitude of the Yugoslav leadership towards Soviet criticism of Yugoslav foreign and domestic policy in 1948, the Finnish leadership considered it important to engage deferentially with the Kremlin. The Soviet side requested that a Finnish ministerial delegation arrive in Moscow for negotiations, but offered simultaneously to send a delegation to Helsinki.[20] The Finns considered it important to appear as agreeable as possible in all non-essential diplomatic matters and dutifully arranged to travel to Moscow by Soviet aircraft.[21] And so the Finnish leadership accepted the Soviet invitation, and the Finnish-Soviet negotiations for the Agreement on Friendship, Cooperation and Assistance began in Moscow on 25 March 1948. The Finnish delegation consisted of Prime Minister Mauno Pekkala, Speaker of the Parliament Kekkonen, Foreign Minister Enckell, Deputy Foreign Minister Reinhold Svento, Interior Minister Yrjö Leino, Members of Parliament Karl Gustaf Söderholm and Onni Peltonen, and Finnish Ambassador to Moscow Carl-Johan Sundström. By this time the Soviet-Yugoslav dispute was already underway: the Soviets had proceeded to withdraw their military and economic advisers from Belgrade on 18 March, and Tito had sent his first letter of protest to Molotov on 20 March.

Paasikivi considered Soviet goals for Finland to be more geopolitical and economic than ideological. Upon receiving the invitation, the Finnish Foreign Ministry had deemed these negotiations primarily a test to determine whether Finland could be trusted politically not to join a Western security alliance. In Paasikivi's opinion, 'the Russians [were] trying to get to the Mediterranean, while other big powers can make attempts to get to the Soviet Union through Finland.'[22] Ambassador Sundström, already concluded in Moscow in 1947 that:

> The Russians based on their experiences of Finnish politics in the independence period see a close connection between [Finnish] domestic and foreign policy. Not to mention that in the previous course of hostile political relations [the Finnish leadership] was not even willing to create good commercial and cultural relations with the Soviet Union.[23]

This Sundström considered a foolish misstep not to be repeated. The Finnish Foreign Ministry, unlike Tito and Kardelj, generally welcomed an opportunity to better relations with the Soviet Union by any means other than armed conflict. Sundström's analysis emphasized that for the post-war Soviet Union, economic and cultural relations with territorially or politically bordering countries constituted political tests to secure their foreign policies.

In fact, based on their analysis of Soviet goals, the Finnish Foreign Ministry expected drawn-out negotiations without the signing of an actual concluding document. The Finnish delegation considered 'the Soviet leadership to fear the international climate' if they forced a military treaty on democratic Finland.[24] Paasikivi also considered the negotiations an opportunity. All Finns were hoping to gain concessions modifying the Finnish-Soviet Peace Treaty, especially the harsh stipulations of free passage for Soviet troops and personnel to and from Porkkala Military Base and cutting Finland off from use of the Saimaa Canal. The Finnish Foreign Ministry had requested negotiations over the canal in the beginning of February 1948.[25] The discussions within the Finnish delegation to the negotiations for the Agreement on Friendship, Cooperation and Assistance in Moscow reveal their ambitious judgement that if the Soviets could gain assurance through a treaty that Finland would not allow a land-attack on the Soviet Union, perhaps Finland could regain sovereignty over both Saimaa and Porkkala. In other words, the ultimate goal of the post-war Finnish foreign policy in the spring of 1948 was to better define and establish territorial independence. Paasikivi first in 1944, and Kekkonen later in 1946, had proceeded to draft a foreign policy strategy for Finland after it became clear that Finland would lose the war to the Soviet Union. Both concluded that a new strategy would be necessary for Finland to regain and then maintain its sovereignty next to the Soviet Union as a non-Communist state. For Finland, neutralism meant limiting relations with Euro-Atlantic institutions to economic agreements, refraining from security alliances, limiting cooperation with Western intelligence agencies, and allowing for the existence of an active Communist Party. This strategy came later to be known as the Paasikivi-Kekkonen Line in the sense of upholding a border line as noted in the introduction. It sought through diplomatic means to regain and retain territorial sovereignty and secure freedom from further Soviet demands.[26] However, before the 1948 Soviet political test for Finland, and the subsequent conclusion of the Finnish-Soviet treaty, the specific content and parameters of the Paasikivi-Kekkonen Line had not been defined.

Finnish-Soviet negotiations in the spring of 1948 demonstrate that, whereas Yugoslavia—a Communist state under Tito's leadership facing the Soviets only along a political border—was able to secure independence from Moscow's political influence by refusal to cooperate in a prolonged conflict, Finland—a democratic republic located on the Soviet geographic border—had to negotiate a carefully configured political, security and economic package agreement for its independence. In 1948, wartime experience still mattered for the survival of both states. Tito's Partisans had fought exclusively against the German or Italian forces, or their presumed local allies the Croat Ustaša and Serb Chetniks. Despite numerous disagreements between Tito's and Stalin's wartime leaderships, these credentials still mattered in 1948. Finland had collaborated with Nazi Germany and consequently suffered heavy territorial losses, giving the new post-war Finnish leadership no leeway to refuse the Soviet request in 1948. The request for a friendship agreement was viewed as an opportunity to gain Soviet concessions but also as possibly threatening a lose of independence. As in the Yugoslav case, despite the involvement of Finnish parliamentary process (through Paasikivi's appointment of two Parliamentarians to the Negotiations Committee), top leaders on the Finnish side were dominant, namely President Paasikivi and the then Speaker of the House Kekkonen, in their defacto capacities as Soviet experts.

The Paasikivi-Kekkonen Line and the Origins of Finnish Neutralism

Paasikivi's turn of the century political career combined the experience of a Tsarist-era advocate for Finnish national independence and an early twentieth-century decision to apply his legal education to finance. Born in 1870 and a Doctor of Law by 1902 after study in Sweden as well as in Finland, Paasikivi soon turned to banking and international finance. He became the Head of the Treasury of the Russian Grand Duchy of Finland (maintaining that position until 1914) but also entered politics. He joined the Fennoman Conservative Party (from 1918 the National Coalition Party -NCP), which opposed Russian ties and proposed an independent Finnish republic in the form of a monarchy. The Party's slogan, 'Swedes we are no longer, Russians we can never be, so let us be Finns,' originally coined in 1809, summarises well the party's nineteenth-century romantic-nationalist political ethos.[27] Paasikivi was elected to the Finnish Parliament Eduskunta in 1907 but resigned in 1909 in protest of Tsar Nicholas II's attempts to change the laws that governed the autonomy of Finland. The Tsar had, for example, proposed the abolition of the Finnish senate.

The principle of independence for the Finnish state governed Paasikivi's political thinking throughout his career. He was not afraid to resign in political protest, and his 1909 resignation was only the first of many such acts. He served briefly as Prime Minister of the first government of independent Finland in 1918. Staying involved in Finnish-Soviet relations, Paasikivi headed the Finnish delegation in Tartu, Estonia that signed the Finnish-Russian peace treaty in 1920. In the inter-war period Paasikivi established himself as a prominent banker in the private sector, only to be appointed in 1936 as Finland's Ambassador to Sweden, a country of primary political importance to Finland now facing not only the Communist Soviet Union but also Nazi Germany.

Kekkonen was born in 1900, 30 years later than Paasikivi and thus further removed from Finland's past as part of the Russian Empire. Kekkonen, like Paasikivi, sided with the White government during the Finnish Civil War (1918) between the Reds and the Whites. Kekkonen fought as a troop commander taking part altogether in nine battles in six months. Like Tito, Kardelj and Paasikivi's, Kekkonen's career prior to 1948 had revolved around intimate knowledge of and relations with the Soviet Union.[28] He resigned his commission from the White Army in June 1918 and in July he became an investigator for the Military Police. Young Kekkonen was fiercely anti-Communist and his primary political ambition was to support independence of the Finnish state. In 1921 while enrolling as a student at the University of Helsinki's Faculty of Law, Kekkonen simultaneously begun his professional career with the *Etsivä Keskuspoliisi* (EK) (Investigatory Central Police). The EK was founded in 1919 as the Finnish state's secret police. It became the *Valtiollinen Poliisi* (State's Police) in 1939 and the *Suojelupoliisi* (Protection Police) in 1949. Throughout the 1920s and the 1930s Kekkonen was therefore involved in the creation and subsequent organization of the Finnish Protection Police. This was none other than the Finnish counter-intelligence service that evolved from in the immediate aftermath of Finnish independence and civil war. The EK had its roots in the pre-1917 Finnish Independence Movement and intelligence gathering during the Civil War. According to its 1919 mandate the EK's purpose was to act 'as a police department whose jurisdiction encompasses the entire state to monitor and prevent, when possible, all attempts and actions that are guided against the independence of the state, or which can hinder general security of the state or its legal system.'[29] Kekkonen felt a sense of duty to work for this organization whose principal task in the 1930s became counter-intelligence against the Soviet Union. His career within the police went ahead quickly, and the EK even sponsored his legal studies.[30] Already in 1923 he became an Investigatory Detective and a Senior Investigator in 1925. Kekkonen worked for the Secret Police until 1927. For almost ten years following the Finnish Civil War Kekkonen's 'primary opponent was the Soviet intelligence service, that practiced multilateral intelligence gathering in Finland, as well as on all Finnish Communists.'[31] In 1927 Kekkonen having become a Doctor of Law entered politics by becoming an attorney for the Agrarians' Party (AP). He served as Justice Minister from 1936–37 and as Minister of the Interior from 1937–39.

During the Second World War, Paasikivi worked at the centre of Finnish-Soviet diplomacy. From October 1939, Paasikivi served as the

Special Finnish Representative in Moscow and led Soviet-Finnish negotiations prior to the outbreak of the Winter War in November. In March 1940, Paasikivi headed the Peace Commission to negotiate the Finnish-Soviet peace treaty. In this capacity, Paasikivi was required to sign the treaty by which Finland ceded approximately one-tenth of its territory. Paasikivi's long-established credentials as a supporter of independence allowed his political career to survive the signing of this increasingly unpopular agreement. During the Second World War, he was hardly sympathetic to Nazi Germany. He had served as Finland's Minister to Moscow from March 1940 but resigned from the post in May 1941 when it became clear that the Finnish government would side with Nazi Germany against the impending Soviet summer offensive. From March 1944 Paasikivi served as negotiator of the Finnish-Soviet Peace Treaty in Moscow and as Prime Minister. Paasikivi then became President from March 1946 to February 1956, as elected in 1946 by the Parliament and in 1950 by the Electoral College.[32]

During the Second World War Kekkonen did not serve in government, which allowed him a more prominent post-war political role afterwards. His patriotic image was strengthened through his work with Karelian refugees from 1940 to 1943. By the end of the war, he had become a harsh critic of the Moscow Peace Treaty that Paasikivi had signed. Kekkonen served as the Minister of Justice during the Finnish war-crimes trials of 1944–46. Here Kekkonen's duties included prosecuting those political leaders responsible for involving Finland in the war on the German side. Kekkonen had also accumulated an extensive amount of information on the Soviet and Finnish Communist leadership by 1948. In him, Paasikivi recognised a junior partner who was not a socialist and whose political philosophy mirrored his own recognition that the future of the state depended primarily on Finland's relations with the Soviet Union.

Beyond his unwavering commitment to an independent Finnish nation-state, Paasikivi was against public ownership of property. His political rivals most often came from the ranks of the Social Democrats and the Communists. From the minutes of his meetings as President with his cabinet it is clear that Paasikivi was prone to speak frankly, not hesitating to criticize his colleagues. Perhaps because he had not supported the Finnish wartime alliance with Nazi Germany in 1941, Paasikivi was able to commit Finland to pay heavy war reparations to the Soviet Union in full; this Paasikivi perceived as necessary for the development of an untainted, post-war foreign policy within a parliamentary democracy. Despite his conservative ties to the private sector, Paasikivi was less concerned with the NCP than with the integrity of the Finnish state. His career was more like that of a state representative than a party member. Ready to work across party lines, Paasikivi therefore sought out a leading role in Finnish negotiations with the Soviet Union. The origins of Finnish neutralism came not only from this readiness but also from a disposition to work around parliamentary pressures when needed.

Fateful Negotiations in Moscow, 25 March–6 April 1948

Paasikivi sent the delegation to Moscow in March 1948 despite the fact that nearly 80 per cent of the Finnish Parliament were against any negotiations because they feared that these might lead to a treaty of military alliance. Kekkonen, attached to the Moscow negotiations, made certain that all decisions were finalized in Helsinki by Paasikivi. The earlier discussions between Zhdanov and Paasikivi had indicated that the Kremlin unsurprisingly preferred to deal only with a few key figures.

While Tito had not travelled to Moscow at Stalin's summons in February 1948, Paasikivi was also absent from these negotiations. This was most likely due to security concerns. The Finnish leadership feared a possible Soviet-led coup against the sitting government (as had occurred the previous month in Czechoslovakia) if its most prominent figure, Paasikivi, were to leave the capital. Tito may have had similar concerns, but his decision to send his closest advisors, Kardelj and Djilas, in his place was primarily an act of defiance. Paasikivi intended no such defiance. He cleverly instructed both Prime Minister Pekkala and Minister of the Interior Leino, both from the left-wing Finnish People's Democratic League (SKDL), to join the Negotiations Committee, simultaneously appeasing the Soviets and removing the two most prominent left-wing figures from the Finnish capital. If Stalin intended to orchestrate a coup in Finland on the Czechoslovak model, the absence of the two most visible left-wing leaders would stand in his way.

The content of the actual negotiations was carefully guarded. The Finnish President's Office received only one copy of the record of the meetings and scrambled telegrams which deliberately contained only a rudimentary description of the proceedings. Shortly after treaty negotiations began, Paasikivi admitted to his cabinet, which remained in Helsinki, that 'the handling of this kind of matter in this type of democracy is very difficult. Finnish plans [discussed in this meeting] cannot be made known to the Soviets, and cannot be leaked to newspapers—here [within the cabinet] we must maintain strict silence and secrecy...We are now facing a situation' in which secrecy was necessary.[33] The Foreign Ministry rearranged its operations to keep the Secretariat open 24 hours a day, manned only by the Secretary of the Foreign Minister or his deputy in order to maintain confidentiality.[34] In the first two days of meetings, when one telegram (number 6) was accidentally sent without coding the Foreign

Ministry responded, in the strongest possible terms: 'Open telegrams on these issues cannot be permitted to be sent.'[35]

Despite Paasikivi's absence from the bargaining table in Moscow, the negotiations were ultimately conducted from Helsinki. Kekkonen served as Paasikivi's unofficial voice within the Finnish delegation. Kekkonen and Paasikivi belonged to opposing political parties, the AP and the NCP respectively, and Finland was about to face contentious parliamentary elections in the spring of 1948 immediately following the talks with the Soviets. More strikingly, Kekkonen's own Agrarians' (renamed the Centre Party in 1956) vehemently opposed any military treaty with the Soviet Union, while Paasikivi supported one if it could lead to retaining territorial sovereignty.[36] The electoral atmosphere and the anti-Conservative but not pro-Soviet propaganda of the left-wing SKDL made Paasikivi's and the cabinet's efforts to proceed with diplomacy in Moscow more difficult. SKDL coalition included the Finnish Communist Party (SKP). Kekkonen regularly telephoned Paasikivi personally from Moscow with the news from the Delegation.[37]

Most often, Kekkonen would inform other members of the Negotiation Committee of these telephone conversations only after the fact. While the delegation 'dragged its feet and delayed informing the President and his cabinet for at least one and a half days' after the initial Soviet proposal, Kekkonen in Moscow often deferred to Paasikivi; he repeatedly emphasized to the Negotiations Committee the authority of the presidency over the Parliament.[38] Kekkonen defended Paasikivi or the presidency in the delegations' internal discussions by reminding them 'that the majority of the Parliament opposed Paasikivi's initial readiness to send a Delegation; the President is deliberating whether to support the Delegation, he is isolated; the position of the President is even more difficult than ours.'[39]

Kekkonen's loyalty to Paasikivi in 1948, despite their ties to opposing political parties and future electoral rivalries, was based on their shared vision for the future of Finnish foreign policy, centred upon security from the Soviet Union, their common intimate accumulated knowledge of the Soviet Union, and also their similar educational backgrounds discussed earlier in this chapter.

In the initial meeting in 1948 the Finns suggested a treaty according to 'unofficial previous talks providing, in case of an attack on Finland, or through the territory of Finland against the Soviet Union, the attack would be defended by mutual forces in the circumstance that Finnish forces were not sufficient.'[40] Earlier in February 1947, Paasikivi had stated that:

> the Finnish nation wishes to remain outside all possible kinds of conflicts. The Finnish nation wishes to maintain and develop friendly

relations between Finland and the Soviet Union and fulfil the Finnish-Soviet Peace Treaty diligently. The Finnish nation is ready as she is obliged by her independence to defend without hesitation her own territory against attacks and to resist each attack, which against Finnish territorial sovereignty, would be made against the Soviet Union.[41]

This Finnish formulation for neutralism appeared in their first draft of the agreement handed over to the Soviets for consideration. It underlined 'Finland's intention to stay out of international conflicts', to which the Soviet representatives predictably objected.[42]

The Kremlin sought instead a treaty comparable to their agreements signed with Hungary and Romania.[43] Both the Hungarian and Romanian treaties contained a clause according to which both states 'undertook the responsibility to negotiate [with the Soviet Union] in all important international matters,' which was absent from the Czechoslovak treaty.[44] In response, Finnish leaders again requested that the Czechoslovak treaty from 1943 be considered as a model. Paasikivi's cabinet agreed that the Romanian and Hungarian treaties contained ambiguous language that could be dangerous to Finland's future.[45] Paasikivi worried in particular that such wording could raise international concern over Finland's political position and might be interpreted as extending to Finnish trade relations with the West.[46] The long 20-year duration of the Romania and Hungarian treaties also troubled Paasikivi, given Finland's ambitions for Scandinavian integration and bilateral trade with Western states.[47] But he did give 'the Delegation permission to go up to 20 years, although adding that 10 years would be better.'[48] To avoid an analogous agreement, he asked that Finland be recognized as being in a different geopolitical position from Hungary and Romania.[49]

The Soviet side was however concerned with the treaty's expeditious signing as a show of some Soviet authority and was therefore willing—to the great surprise of the Finnish delegation—quickly to abandon the concept of an analogous agreement based upon previous models and to consider a Finnish draft as the basis for negotiation. The Soviet-Romanian Agreement on Friendship, Cooperation and Assistance had been signed on 4 February, only two days after the arrival of the Romanian delegation in Moscow on 2 February 1948, and just weeks after Dimitrov's announcement of the future Balkan Federation to the international media.[50] In mid-March, the Finnish side was not aware that Soviet difficulties with Yugoslavia were probably pushing them to come to terms with Helsinki. This pressure became clear only after Yugoslavia's expulsion from the Cominform in June. Yet already in March, the Soviet press had signalled the urgency of an agreement prior to the commencement of the negotiations. *Izvestia* published news of Stalin's proposal on 5 March, and *Pravda* on 14 March. *Izvestia* commented that 'the democratic circles in Finland have received Comrade Stalin's request with approval...as recent historic experience has demonstrated that aggression against the great Soviet Union stole from Finland its national neutrality and changed it into the weapon of foreign aggressors' (note that this language hardly defines the Finns as 'foreign' themselves).[51] The official voice of the Soviet government insisted in an increasingly forceful tone that 'only politics of friendship with the Soviet Union can guarantee to Finland its national neutrality and state sovereignty. As the reactionary international forces are currently attempting to resurrect the power of Germany, it is natural, that democratic nations begin procedures to prevent the revival of German aggression.'[52]

Soviet acceptance of a non-analogous agreement guaranteed that the treaty would address only Finnish territory and thus would not obligate Finland to respond to an attack outside its borders. The Finnish side considered this an accomplishment. However, the Finnish leadership had miscalculated the tactical and strategic Soviet goals for the negotiations. Paasikivi had assumed that the Soviets were not actively seeking a treaty with Finland, any more than they were with Yugoslavia. Based on its understanding of Stalin's foreign policy at the time, the Finnish Foreign Ministry had anticipated that the Soviet Union wished to avoid a reaction from the Western powers, and that they would hold some kind of negotiations to clarify Finnish-Soviet relations but stall on signing an actual treaty, as they were doing with Yugoslavia since February. But already on 29 March, four days after their arrival, the Finnish delegation was handed a Soviet revision of the Finnish proposal 'that went very far [into detail] very fast' leading Prime Minister Pekkala in Moscow to conclude that 'our assumptions were completely mistaken.'[53]

The Soviets did however push for military privileges in Finland. The Soviet proposal countered the Finnish argument that 'Finland should in the first place defend its own territory' by suggesting that the Soviet Union would defend the territory of Finland 'in agreement with Finland.'[54] Finnish territorial defence was crucial to its goal of maintaining Finnish political and territorial independence. The Finnish delegation, according to Paasikivi's instructions, countered that Finnish sovereignty itself 'obliges Finland to fight against an invasion against the Soviet Union through Finland...defence will take place because of independence.'[55] The Finns feared a return to mere political autonomy—a concept that was familiar from Finland's past as a Grand Duchy of Russia until 1917. Paasikivi and political theorist K. G. Idman, who had helped the President draft the ideological background of the Finnish position of political neutrality, had both served under the Tsarist political establishment in the beginning of their political careers. They had spent their youth advocating for Finnish independence instead of autonomy.

Paasikivi had briefed the delegation on several guidelines prior to departure. The first was that 'the agreement needs to be by its content and wording absolutely clear, so that it leaves no room for interpretation, which can violate the [Finnish] state's independence and the nation's sovereignty.'[56] Secondly, 'the purpose of the agreement can only be to deter an attack by Germany or its allies.'[57] Thirdly, 'if Finland's own strength is not enough to deter an attack, the Soviet Union should upon Finnish request give Finland the necessary help.'[58] According to Paasikivi's instructions, 'the treaty could only concern Finland's own land, sea, and aerial defence, and procedures could only become effective during wartime.'[59] The initial Finnish proposal drafted in the language familiar from Paasikivi stated that 'the Finnish nation sees it as its duty and its honour to defend its land and territory.'[60] Paasikivi's primary goal in these negotiations was to secure territorial independence and parliamentary democracy. These goals could be served by trade agreements and Finnish concessions in them if necessary.

Territorial self-defence was the tool by which, according to the emerging Paasikivi-Kekkonen Line, Finland would guarantee Soviet territorial security in order to maintain its own political independence. Paasikivi considered the Soviet revisions completely contrary to Finnish expectations and goals of independent territorial defence, as the Soviets sought to defend Finnish territory 'in agreement with Finland.'[61] The Finnish delegation in Moscow nervously argued amongst themselves about how to approach both the Soviet leadership and Paasikivi. Interior Minister Leino had feared a coup in Helsinki during the negotiations and had in fact approached the Finnish military prior to leaving for Moscow, asking it to guarantee Finland's independence if necessary. Kekkonen pressed the delegation to consult the opinions of military experts and their knowledge of historical agreements between states to enable Finland to define the terms of the agreement in such a way that would leave Finland in charge of its own defence.[62] The rather ineffectual Leino provided little reasoning to rescue the situation and argued self-servingly in an effort to move decision making to the delegation and himself that 'this is a political question,' and that the 'negotiations Delegation should itself have enough sense to state its own opinion before consulting any experts for theirs.'[63] This provoked Kekkonen, to comment, 'yes, I am ready to state my own opinion, which will not change on account of experts, but hearing the opinions of experts would be beneficial' for the analysis of texts and subsequent drafting of a legal counter-argument.[64]

Back in Helsinki, Paasikivi was greatly dissatisfied with the Delegation's counter-proposal, which would have changed the revised Soviet wording, from 'Finland would defend its territory together with the Soviet Union' to 'Finland will defend its territory with the help of the Soviet Union and together with it.'[65] Paasikivi emphasized that Soviet assistance could be accepted only in the event of official requests from the Finnish government. He feared that 'with the help of the Soviet Union' could be interpreted as granting the Soviets power to decide when they should 'help' Finland—which would undermine his own goal for Finnish-Soviet relations: the guarantee of territorial independence. For once, Paasikivi felt insufficiently informed of the events in Moscow, commenting angrily that 'the proposal of the Negotiations Delegation was not sufficient, and that he himself [Paasikivi] did not have anyone to negotiate with' for further recourse.[66] Disturbed by his own initial miscalculation of Soviet goals, dissatisfied with the proposed Soviet language and fearful of his isolation from events in Moscow, where he had been privy to key events since 1939, Paasikivi decided to stall the negotiations that had been proceeding swiftly up to this point. While the delegation considered changing Paasikivi's emphasis on the agency of 'the Finnish nation' in the treaty's wording to the 'Finnish state's leadership', Paasikivi did abandon this nationalist rhetoric before the delegation had time to do so. But he then turned to a series of stalling tactics. First, he stated that 'the signing and empowering of the treaty [would] have to take place strictly according to the [republican] constitution.'[67] Through the Presidential Office, Paasikivi could have authorised the delegation either to sign or refuse the agreement. Instead, he first called in his cabinet, followed by the Government's Foreign Affairs' delegation and the Parliamentary Groups' Chairmen, initiating an independent Parliamentary process of group meetings.[68] Involving the oppositional Parliament would likely hinder agreement on a treaty with the Soviet Union. To make certain that his tactics succeeded, Paasikivi started this process without consulting the delegation in Moscow or Leino who wished to retain decision making, informing only Kekkonen of his decision over the telephone.

In Moscow, Kekkonen steadfastly refused to support Pekkala's recommendation to overrule the President's initiative to involve the Parliament in the treaty process, announcing in the clearest of terms, 'I am not with you, if we hurry this decision in order to blackmail [Paasikivi], but I am with you in requesting [further instructions from the President].'[69] Moreover, Kekkonen refused to comply with the SKDL members, proposal to remove Paasikivi's wording concerning 'the Finnish nation's desire to remain outside international conflicts' from the Finnish proposal, remarking that this was a 'sentence pronounced by the authority vested in the [President's] own authority.'[70] Paasikivi specifically requested that 'Kekkonen and someone else be sent to inform him of the events in Moscow' after the first five days of negotiations.[71]

Paasikivi acted quickly in Helsinki to stall a decision on the unexpectedly prompt Soviet proposal. He told representatives in the parliament 'that the government through its cabinet, and I as President would like to receive some kind of information regarding the changes so that a treaty might pass through the parliament.'[72] This invitation made sure that lengthy discussions would follow. Paasikivi told his cabinet meeting that in addition to countering the fast Soviet response, he wished to place the 'Parliament in front of the real decision making process.'[73] Whatever support this would win for the Paasikivi presidency, this approach would force the Kremlin to publicly recognize Finland's elected, multi-party parliament as an equal partner in the negotiations. Paasikivi knew very well that 'the majority of the Finnish people would rather not have seen such an agreement made' and admitted that 'we do not make this [agreement] gladly, but now that wars are what they are, we cannot do anything [to prevent a treaty].'[74] Beyond stalling on the treaty, Paasikivi wanted Finland to acknowledge as broadly as possible that it could not defeat the Soviet Union or maintain independence through any possible war. The best way for the state to cope with the circumstances was to distribute the burden of this acknowledgement across political party lines. Then on that basis, a treaty with the USSR could be signed.[75]

Although Finnish foreign policy had in Paasikivi and Kekkonen a two-person spearhead for its goals and direction, the President's recourse to the Finnish parliamentary process stood in stark contrast to the unilateral decision making of Kardelj and Tito. They alone in the spring of 1948 determined Yugoslav policy towards the Soviet Union, in the form of hastily drafted letters to Stalin. During wartime in Finland, it had been accepted procedure for the Prime Minister and the President to make foreign policy decisions through their executive offices without consultation. Now, three years after the war had ended, Paasikivi placed the matter of the Soviet-Finnish treaty directly before the parliament, stating that 'this is the business of the entire nation.'[76] The delegation negotiating in Moscow was angered by Paasikivi's actions, as the parliamentary process he had initiated could not easily be curtailed. The Minister of the Interior Leino argued that irrespective of Paasikivi's procedure, 'the President can despite Parliamentary groups [involvement] agree to a particular solution.'[77] Nevertheless, the delegation worried that 'if the [delegation] should have to make an agreement, which the Delegation has the authority to do, it is possible that the Parliament despite this will not accept it.'[78] More than anything, the Socialist Unity Party leader Pekkala feared that Soviet goodwill would be forfeited by Paasikivi's turn to the slow parliamentary process.[79] Both Leino and Pekkala feared losing votes in the impending elections. Eventually, in July 1948 their fears turned out to be true when the SKDL to which both belonged, became the largest loser in the parliamentary elections dropping a total of 11 seats in the parliament. At Paasikivi's request, Kekkonen and the Finnish Ambassador in Moscow returned to Helsinki to brief Paasikivi and the parliament on the course of events.[80]

In the end, after having consulted with Kekkonen, Paasikivi and his cabinet decided to authorize the delegation to sign the Agreement on Friendship, Cooperation and Assistance on 6 April 1948. Ratification through Parliament took much longer than the Soviets would have liked, but Moscow seemed satisfied with the Finnish agreement. Paasikivi was also satisfied, noting that 'Molotov in particular had shown a certain amount of fairness by agreeing to the Finnish agreement's wording' in the end rather than insisting the text be based on the Romanian and Hungarian agreements.[81] This wording showed that Zhdanov in 1945 had been correct: the Soviet goal in regards to Finland was not to equate it with Romania and Hungary, but instead to benefit economically from the Finnish loss in the war and to seek Soviet territorial security. With the signing of the treaty, the parameters of the Paasikivi-Kekkonen Line had now been drawn in practice to the satisfaction of both Paasikivi and Kekkonen. The early Cold War was a time in which Soviet policies in Eastern Europe were still difficult to predict. Soviet intentions for the role of the other one-party states in Eastern Europe remained unclear as the international press polemic over the Balkan Federation discussed in Chapter 1 points out. Paasikivi was aware of the unsettled situation across the political Soviet border with Europe and cautiously commented in the final meeting with his cabinet over the treaty that 'matters of foreign policy are such that in them one cannot tell whether the decision is the right one or the wrong one until 10–15–20 years after…In my view I am for the signing of this agreement. But one cannot tell absolutely in matters of foreign policy. The chances favor the signing of this treaty.'[82]

The final terms of the signed agreement stated that if Finland or the Soviet Union through Finland would be attacked by Germany or an ally of Germany, Finland would as an independent state fight to resist the attack by all means necessary by land, sea or air and would do so if necessary 'with the help of the Soviet Union or together with it.' However, article two stated that Soviet assistance was not automatic but 'only determined by negotiations in the case that the threat of a military attack had transpired.' Finland also reconfirmed its commitment to article three of the 1947 Paris peace treaty preventing Finland from joining or forming any alliances that were directed against the Soviet Union.

The Trade-Off Policy: Independence, Expanded Economic Ties and Curtailed Civil Liberties

The day after the signing, the Finnish delegation quickly began pursuing the treaty's secondary goal: a trade agreement with the Soviet Union.[83] Privately, Paasikivi had instructed the delegation that 'first the treaty should be concluded, and afterwards economic matters could be discussed.'[84] Paasikivi sought first to verify the political content of the treaty—the guarantee of Finnish independence—before fortifying the agreement through economic exchange. On the basis of his conversation with Stalin on 6 April, Pekkala observed encouragingly that 'this idea of trade negotiations is not foreign to Soviet goals either', adding that 'in order for us to reduce the amount of war reparations there are several tactics at our disposal.'[85] The Finnish delegation presented the Soviets with the somewhat tenuous proposition that after the signing of the agreement 'the entire situation is completely different, the whole territory now serves as Leningrad's security buffer. The Saimaa Canal should for also be accounted as a difficult economic issue.'[86] The Saimaa Canal is the 43-kilometre-long sea-way that connects Lake Saimaa with the Gulf of Finland in close proximity to the Finnish-Soviet border and the city of Vyborg as it was renegotiated after the Second World War. Finland lost the authority to administer the canal as a condition of the Paris peace treaty. With its tenuous argument that the new friendship treaty guaranteed Soviet security, the delegation pointed out that the Kremlin could no longer claim a security threat from Finland. Therefore it asked that, the administration of the Saimaa Canal and other territory lost in the Paris peace treaty should now be returned to Finland. Without mentioning the deep-seated desire in Finland to regain at least some of the territories lost in the treaty, the Finns requested 'a correction' to the quantity of reparations Finland owned to the Soviet Union, as compensation earned from the signing of the Friendship and Cooperation Agreement.[87] Popular opinion in Finland urged the initiation of negotiations to regain the lost Karelian territories. Paasikivi and for that matter the delegation also privately understood, clearly that 'the Soviets would not negotiate over territory.'[88]

The Finnish Ministerial Delegation had been told in meetings as early as November 1947 that 'war reparations are an economic [and not political] matter.'[89] After the signing of the 1948 treaty, People's Commissar for Internal and Foreign Trade Anastas Mikoyan and the Finnish Ministry of

Economy were placed in charge of the negotiations. Yet for Kekkonen, the Finnish politician most skilled in Soviet matters in Moscow at the time, the question of reparations '[was] not an economic question, but a political one.'[90] The Yugoslavs, having pursued trade negotiations through the Ministry of Economy, failed to reach an agreement. They had failed the test of granting the Soviets favourable economic terms, or to negotiate over them to reaffirm political loyalty in the aftermath of Tito's dealings with Dimitrov. Kekkonen considered it crucial to pursue the economic counterpart for the political Agreement on Friendship, Cooperation and Assistance precisely as a device for political leverage. He stated that 'even if the Friendship and Cooperation Treaty passed within the Parliament, I am certain, that the Delegation will be heavily criticised if it leaves without proposing some amendment to war reparations.'[91] Kekkonen, using the ratification of the treaty as leverage and political capital, directly initiated the Finnish approach to Molotov the very next day.[92]

Kekkonen succeeded in his initiative to consolidate this Finnish policy of neutralism. The economic negotiations proceeded according to the Finnish plan. In June 1948 the Soviet Union announced that it would reduce its claims for the remainder of war reparations by 50 per cent, which amounted to approximately $75 million.[93] The reduction was mostly applied to timber and cable deliveries.[94] On 10 November a Finnish Ministerial trade delegation arrived in Moscow. The new trade agreement signed on 17 December 1948 was greeted by the Finnish government as a success.[95] Although the Soviet side had focused on acquiring metallurgy and machine tools, the largest Finnish exports to the Soviet Union were to become 500,000 square metres of wooden houses and cellulose products.[96] The most important Soviet imports to Finland were wheat, corn, sugar, iron, petrol and petro-chemical derivatives. The Soviet Union agreed simultaneously to reduce two-thirds of the penalties applied towards goods not delivered in the previous year (1947). This amounted to $600,000. The Finnish-Soviet trade in 1948 grew by 80 per cent from the previous year to $90 million.[97]

Transformation of the Finnish Foreign Ministry Following the Finnish-Soviet Treaty

The role of the Finnish Foreign Ministry, like that of its Yugoslav counterpart, was transformed as a consequence of the events of 1948. While the Yugoslav Ministry became a more extensive and professional organization throughout the 1950s, the Finnish-Soviet treaty established a new domestic role for the Finnish Ministry in curtailing the public expression of anti-Soviet views. Both ministries dealt with and managed Soviet propaganda originating from Moscow as a matter of state security.

That a dialogue between the Soviet leadership and those in Helsinki and Belgrade was carried over in the context of public propaganda in the Soviet and Soviet bloc press is in fact a curious feature of the politics of Cold War neutralism. As discussed in Chapter 1, in the Yugoslav case its ministry analyzed Soviet rebuffs and carried out threat assessments based on anti-Yugoslav announcements as indicators of Soviet threat level. The Finnish Foreign Ministry on the other hand struggled, especially in the early post-war years, with its new task of restraining various expressions of anti-Soviet, anti-Russian, and anti-Communist sentiment in Finland. Ministry officials tended not to discuss the reasons behind such feelings or to argue against their existence. But in their correspondence they recognized, especially following the Tito-Stalin split of 1948, the detrimental effect of the expression of anti-Soviet sentiments on the maintenance of the Paasikivi-Kekkonen Line. Their correspondence did discuss the unfortunate consequences of anti-Soviet expressions in Finland for Finnish foreign policy. The Soviets themselves carefully monitored Finnish popular sentiment and used evidence of anti-Communism to suggest a security risk to the Soviet Union given the border with Finland. The Paasikivi-Kekkonen Line was based upon the elimination of any security risk to the Soviet Union along this territorial border. The Foreign Ministry did not consider that pursuing this strategy would crucially jeopardize the functioning of Finnish civil society and thus have a detrimental effect on parliamentary process, but they nonetheless felt obliged to limit freedom of expression in Finland. From 1946, the Finnish Foreign Ministry considered the preservation of autonomous Finnish parliamentary procedure a goal best served by observing the Kekkonen-Paasikivi Line even if it meant curtailing the freedom of expression.

Pushing Ministry officials into this new role were Moscow's protests against anti-Soviet manifestations directly to them rather than to other ministries or to the judiciary. In December 1948, Soviet Ambassador Fedorov wrote an official complaint against the staging of the Aarne Sihvo play *Infantryman's Bride* and Jean-Paul Sartre's *Dirty Hands* in two theatres in Helsinki.[98] The Soviet Ambassador claimed that these plays were 'mean-spirited and served as provocations against the Soviet Union...[and that] these and other cases are not in harmony with Finland's obligations.'[99] In the difficult conditions following the Tito-Stalin split, Enckell and the Finnish Foreign Ministry staff had developed a formulaic response to Soviet attempts to control Finland's civil society. He requested an official response from the Ministry of Education to the Soviet complaint, which read:

The Ministry of Education has asked for an explanation [of the staging of *Dirty Hands*] from the Director of the Finnish National Theatre, Eino Kalima, and from the Secretary of the Finnish Theatre Organizations Union, Verner Veistäjä...our understanding is that it is impossible to think that Professor Kalima, who is known as a sincere friend of the Soviet Union, would have staged the play Dirty Hands with the intention of humiliating the Soviet Union. The musical 'Infantryman's Bride' is not being shown in its original format but as a musical comedy.[100]

Yet upon reading the Finnish translation of Fedorov's letter, Enckell simply crossed out Fedorov's typewritten word 'obligations' and wrote over it by hand, 'neutrality' in private protest.[101] Both plays were then removed from the stage within five days of the original Soviet complaint.[102] The Interior Ministry ordered the Ministry of Education to carefully consider whether the showing of the original film version of *Infantryman's Bride* should be banned.[103] In response to this incident (and a concurrent physical altercation between Soviet Embassy officials and Helsinki police officers in December 1948), the Finnish Interior Ministry filed a 'general note to the department of criminal investigations' on the day the plays were officially removed from the stage bill.[104] This note asked that:

for the purposes of the common good of the country and the nation it is indispensable that irresponsible persons do not commit acts or propose statements which can create a danger that the relations of Finland towards a foreign state are harmed. On this account, the Minister of the Interior encourages the police to carefully observe these, R.L. number 4, a section of the Law of 8 May 1948, declaring that punishable acts endangering the country will not take place in any shape or form and that expedient and effective procedures will be carried out immediately upon discovery of any such acts.[105]

The Finnish strategy in the aftermath of the Tito-Stalin split and the signing of the Friendship and Cooperation Treaty was thus entirely different from that of the Yugoslavs. While Tito's leadership answered complaints over anti-Soviet feelings in 1948 with contempt and sarcasm, the Finnish Foreign Ministry dutifully and efficiently appeased the Soviets in controlling civic and cultural conduct. Copies of the internal instruction to prevent anti-Soviet manifestations were included in Enckell's reply to Fedorov, along with a reassurance that 'the Finnish authorities have continuously paid careful attention to the expression of anti-Soviet opinions.'[106] As the extent of the Finnish Foreign Ministry's response to Moscow's demands was still being defined, Enckell had added in his first draft of the letter to Fedorov that on that very day, 'A construction worker at a shop in Nokia had been arrested on the order of the President of Finland to the Interior Ministry; this person had made insulting comments against leading persons of the Soviet Union in Tampere and has been placed under subpoena on account of his insulting statements.'[107] In the final version, Enckell scratched out this sentence, so as not even to inform the Soviets of the incident. The arrest itself nevertheless illustrates the determination of the Finnish authorities to prevent any occasion for Soviet complaint and the serious role the Ministry had to perform.

It was the Foreign Ministry that was initially responsible for spelling out the specifics of Finnish neutralism as its Soviet policy. Enckell, of secondary importance in Paasikivi's cabinet and correspondence until May 1948, now acquired a key role in shaping how the neutralism would be implemented as a domestic policy. As indicated above, Enckell himself would decide which information to forward to the Soviets regarding anti-Soviet demonstrations, and how to subsequently appease the Soviet Foreign Ministry. The success of the Paasikivi-Kekkonen Line, Finland's territorial security and economic future rested on his performance. In Yugoslavia, the initial response to Soviet attempts to confirm Yugoslavia's loyalty was set by Tito, Kardelj and Djilas. Yet, as we shall see in subsequent chapters, after Kardelj became the Foreign Minister in the second half of 1948, the content and execution of this new policy of independence begun to transfer with him as Tito's confidant to the Foreign Ministry of Yugoslavia. After Kardelj's departure in 1953 the autonomous role of the Yugoslav Ministry increased throughout the 1950s, culminating in the Ministry's role in the turn to non-alignment after 1961. The Yugoslav Ministry grew into this role the through the increase of resources and the placement of Tito's trusted confidant as Foreign Minister. The Finnish Ministry received no additional funding to execute its complicated task of enforcing neutralism across all state institutions, especially through the domestic police and judicial system. At the same time, the Finnish incentive to watch Soviet foreign policy as closely as possible encouraged a connection with its Yugoslav counterpart that would fall into place after Stalin's death in 1953.

Western and Yugoslav Responses to the Soviet-Finnish Agreement

Western observers were concerned that the Finnish trade agreement and its political trade-offs with the Soviet Union would undermine the neutralism promised by the Paasikivi-Kekkonen Line. On 1 March 1948, the *New York*

Times linked the Soviet proposal to Finland directly to the recent coup in Czechoslovakia. The article warned that:

> In the familiar style introduced by Hitler, Stalin his erstwhile partner and eager imitator in enslaving other countries, has quickly followed up the conquest of Czechoslovakia by reaching out to grab Finland. He has served a blunt demand on the Finnish government for an immediate 'pact of friendship, cooperation and mutual assistance' which, like similar Soviet pacts with the Baltic and the Balkan states, could only mean the end of that country's independence and a first step towards its ultimate sovietisation.[108]

The *Times* article further concluded that the Soviet-Finnish 'pact is also directed against the United States' because the Soviet proposal mentioned Soviet agreements with Romania and Hungary, 'treaties that are not merely against Germany but also against "any other state which would directly or in any other form unite with Germany in a policy of aggression." Since Germany is included in the European Recovery Program, and since that program is denounced by Russia as a measure of American "imperialist aggression," the pact is also directed against the United States.'[109]

The Finnish leadership was aware of international wariness about neutralism. The delegation's military adviser had reminded them in Moscow, that they should carefully consider that 'this agreement will be interpreted in the world, and especially in Sweden and Norway, under a magnifying glass. For this reason, its stipulations on territorial defence should be as clear as possible' to avoid unnecessary international fears over the Soviet military's role in Finland. In the aftermath of the Tito-Stalin split and the signing of the Finnish-Soviet Agreement, individual analysts and policy-makers were questioning neutralism's ability to succeed next door to a strong military power. Did not the Soviet ability to directly monitor Finnish public life represent a dangerous level of Soviet influence over Finland?

No government was more sceptical of the Paasikivi-Kekkonen Line's ability to succeed in securing Finnish political independence than that of Sweden. In November 1947, a rumour reached the Dutch Ambassador in Stockholm, according to which 'the government of the Soviet Union had proposed to the government of Finland that it join the Soviet Union.'[110] Such baseless reports were taken seriously, as Finnish neutralism after the Second World War depended on the careful configuration of security arrangements between Scandinavian countries. While Norway and Denmark would quickly join NATO in 1949, Swedish membership would have brought the Western alliance to the border with Finland. The Swedish leadership, from the early post-war period in 1947, felt that the Finnish commitment to neutralism was not stable enough to prevent overt Soviet predominance in any period of increased tension. The Swedes did not wish to exchange their Finnish neighbor for a Soviet one. While neutral status had helped Sweden to escape most burdens of the atrocities of the Second World War, the Swedes remained suspicious of the Paasikivi-Kekkonen Line from its inception and fearful of Soviet infiltration. Rumors of the permeability of Finnish domestic and foreign policy to Soviet influence, as reported by the Swedish government, were commonplace in the late 1940s and early 1950s.

Despite the critical attitude in the Swedish government and the American press, Finland found superpower support for its neutralism from the US State Department. It led the way in strong, but mostly unpublicized Western support for Finnish policy in 1948 and later in more public support for the Yugoslav version of the 1950s. The Finnish Foreign Ministry kept the United States informed through its Washington embassy on the status and progress of Finnish-Soviet relations. By 1946 the Finnish Foreign Ministry had established a pattern of consultation with the State Department on the course of Finnish-Soviet relations. In the spring of 1946, on the concluding day of the visit of a Finnish ministerial delegation to Moscow, Finnish representative Lauri Havinki in Washington visited the State Department to provide a briefing on Finnish-Soviet relations. For its part, the State Department 'expressed optimism toward the progress of Finnish-Soviet peace treaties negotiations in Paris', concluding that the early success of the Finnish-Soviet negotiations 'points towards the Soviet Union being increasingly more interested in cooperation.'[111]

These periodic debriefings became routine even as US expectations of 'Soviet cooperation' faded after 1946. During the Finnish-Soviet Friendship and Cooperation Treaty negotiations, Finnish representative M. Waltimo visited the State Department to brief officials on the events in Moscow. The Truman administration, unlike the American press, did not worry about the implications of the Soviet-Finnish negotiations but had expected them and understood the difficult Finnish position as a state physically bordering the Soviet Union. 'The State [Department] expects Finland to sign some kind of a treaty with the Soviet Union, [and the State Department] has been very pleased with the way Finland has handled the negotiations so far.'[112] The State Department's judgement of the Soviet approach at the time, as communicated to a Finnish diplomat, was that 'the attacks against Scandinavian countries in the Soviet press serve the purpose of frightening these states away from the Marshall Plan, but the State Department is convinced that the actual effect [of the Soviet policy] will be opposite, heralding a closer than before cooperation with Scandinavian western powers.'[113]

The Finnish leadership also kept the Yugoslav Foreign Ministry informed throughout the course of the Finnish-Soviet negotiations in the spring 1948. On 15 March 1948, during the reception for the 100-year anniversary of the Hungarian revolution in Belgrade, Finnish chargé d'affaires Ville Niskanen described to the Yugoslav Foreign Minister Simić the Finnish outlook on Moscow's proposal for treaty negotiations.[114] Niskanen explained the parliamentary opposition to the proposed pact. Simić expressed the somewhat surprising view that Finland should agree to a pact with the Soviet Union 'now especially after the war when [according to the Paris Peace Treaty] Finland is only allowed minimal army; [Finnish] domestic forces are not enough even to begin a defence' of the country.[115] But Simić and the Yugoslav leadership were also interested in finding out 'whether the Soviets had proposed any special protocols' for Finland. Niskanen underlined Moscow's growing pressure on Finland in recent months as exerted through the Soviet press. Simić remarked that 'if Finland refused to sign the pact sooner or later this will lead to an accident'. While Tito and Kardelj had abandoned any Yugoslav opportunity for a treaty, Yugoslav Foreign Minister Simić was not, as noted in Chapter 1, a member of this inner circle. Like his ambassador in Moscow he would not have known about the abandonment, helping us to understand why he was suggesting here that Finland should agree to a treaty. Simić asked Niskanen 'if Finland was afraid that a pact with the Soviets would mean that the old relations with the West would get cold, or whether Finland feared "all-consuming Communism"?' Niskanen cautiously replied that 'Finns fear both.'

Niskanen sent the report of this conversation as a special communiqué for the Negotiations Committee being prepared in Helsinki, with the curious remark that 'Simić is neither a member of the Communist Party of Yugoslavia, nor a "secret Communist," indicating that the diplomatic exchange between the Finnish representation and the Yugoslav Foreign Ministry should be marked not as one coordinated by the Communist leadership in Belgrade but as an autonomous and informative exchange. Niskanen even compared Simić's political background to Paasikivi's. Niskanen knew that Simić, a veteran of the Serbian army in the Balkan Wars and the First World War, had served in the Foreign Ministry of the Kingdom of Serbs, Croats and Slovenes from 1920 and as Counsellor in the Yugoslav legation in Paris from 1935 until retiring in 1938. Reactivated in 1939, Simić became the London government's Ambassador to Moscow from 1943 to late 1944. Only then did he resign from that government to join Tito's, first as its first ambassador to the US from April 1945 to

January 1946 and then as Foreign Minister from February 1946 to August 1948. Like Paasikivi and Kekkonen, Simić had special experience with the Soviet leadership, having spent part of the war in Moscow. While the two Finnish leaders' Soviet experience would be counted a valuable asset by the Finnish political establishment in 1948, Simić's background cost him the position of Foreign Minister in the same year. The need for some non-Communist presence in the post-war Communist governments of Eastern Europe, initially at Soviet insistence, had long since passed in Yugoslavia when the split with Stalin pushed the Tito regime to advertise its own Communist credentials.

In addition to such personal conversations, Niskanen in Belgrade noted in April 1948 that the conclusion of the Finnish-Soviet negotiations 'received much attention from the official circles in Yugoslavia...because it was recognized that [Finland and Yugoslavia] were approximately in the same geopolitical position.'[116] On 9 April 1948, the Yugoslav daily *Politika* republished an article on the Finnish-Soviet treaty from *Izvestia* complete with the Soviet announcement that 'from the negotiations between the Soviet Union and Finland it can clearly be seen that the Soviet Union treats Finnish national independence and state sovereignty with full respect'. State sovereignty was already an issue which the Yugoslav Communist Party wished to emphasize in April 1948. After the treaty was signed at the very end of May 1948, Niskanen marked a change in the way he was treated by Simić: 'I feel that the Foreign Minister has become more helpful; we have been looking for some space for the representation for three months without being able to gain the Foreign Ministry's permission. Now after the signing of the treaty, the Foreign Ministry instead helped us to find a property where we can move into.'

Finland after the Split

The eruption of the Tito-Stalin split seems to provide only a sharp contrast to the Finnish agreement with the Soviet leadership guaranteeing Soviet security along its territorial border, along with favourable trade relations in exchange for Finnish state sovereignty. There were however important similarities that paved the way for Finnish and Yugoslav policies towards the Soviet Union. Finland and Yugoslavia were both close to the expanding and solidifying Soviet influence in Eastern Europe. Both states were led by strong political partnerships in Tito and Kardelj, Paasikivi and Kekkonen, who guided their national political frameworks in determining the course of their foreign relations with the Soviet Union. Following Kekkonen's initiation of a collaborative relationship with Paasikivi during the 1948 Finnish-Soviet negotiations, Kekkonen ultimately emerged as Paasikivi's successor as President in 1956. Kardelj similarly emerged as Tito's closest collaborator in Yugoslavia after solidifying his relationship with Tito through his role as Foreign Minister in the difficult times of 1948. In the end, Helsinki was able to secure a treaty. Initially risking parliamentary opposition in order to gain time and build multi-party consensus, these key leaders' steadfast collaboration and cautious vision for the post-war Finnish-Soviet relations prevailed.

The events of 1948 admittedly spelled out different futures for the Finnish and the Yugoslav states, aside from providing independence from the Soviet Union. Finland continued to function as a multi-party parliamentary democracy, while Tito's party alone governed Yugoslavia. Tito, unlike Paasikivi, was not interested in a negotiated relationship with the Soviet Union in 1948, and the Soviet-Yugoslav relations did not find stability until the very late 1950s when the Yugoslav Foreign Ministry gained primacy in Yugoslav-Soviet relations.

In Finland, Paasikivi would retain the office of President until 1956. Although losing his presidential bid to Paasikivi in 1950, Kekkonen remained Prime Minister in separate governments, 1950–53 and 1954–56. He served as Foreign Minister in 1953 and 1954 as well. It is no coincidence that Kekkonen, with his professional police background, became Paasikivi's formidable successor, purposefully taking control of Finnish neutralism policy back for the executive office of the President from 1956 to 1981, as we shall see in Chapter 5. Paasikivi had involved the Parliament in the 1948 treaty negotiations to prevent a treaty similar to Soviet treaties with Romania and Bulgaria, and in order to successfully establish the Paasikivi-Kekkonen Line. Only by underlining the difference between the Soviet political process with one-party Communist states and Finland with its freely elected parliament did Paasikivi feel that he could establish neutralism as a policy in 1948. However, the cooperation between Paasikivi and Kekkonen during the 1948 negotiations shows that both clearly wanted to manage Soviet relations themselves despite referring to the parliament for the ratification of the treaty. This was tactical. As Soviet-Finnish relations in 1948 after the ratification of the treaty that the Foreign Ministry would be in charge of handling Soviet demands for curtailment of Finnish anti-Soviet public expressions and anti-Soviet politics.

Yugoslavia and Finland found themselves in similar positions vis-à-vis the Soviet Union at the end of that year. Both states, outside the Soviet bloc but under continuous Soviet political pressure, placed high value on correct analysis of their relations with the Soviet Union. Contacts between Finland and Yugoslavia begun to be built in Belgrade in 1948 after Yugoslavia's expulsion from the Cominform. But they could only solidify, as we shall see in Chapter 4, once the death of Stalin had opened the way for Yugoslavia to come to terms with the Soviet Union on a path that was now comparable to the Finnish one. That path was neutralism.

4

THE DEATH OF STALIN AND THE BEGINNING OF A BEAUTIFUL YUGOSLAV-FINNISH FRIENDSHIP

> At the conclusion of the Finnish-Soviet Agreement of Friendship, Cooperation, and Mutual Assistance in 1948, we had a 'moderate' opinion about the significance of the agreement, while now we must say that the results of the agreement exceeded our most daring hope.[1]
>
> *6 April 1953 V.M. Molotov*

Josef Stalin's death was announced on 5 March 1953. Finnish and Yugoslav representatives were both reporting that members of Moscow's international diplomatic corps feared an immediate hardening of the foreign policy of the Soviet Union.[2] These accounts predicted that this hardening would manifest itself in the Soviet-controlled territories of Eastern Europe, and especially in East Germany. Many in Moscow did not perceive Soviet foreign policy as directed toward East Asia, despite the Korean conflict. At least for the diplomatic observers quoted in Finnish and Yugoslav reports in March 1953, Europe was more important for Soviet military strategy. Although the growing east-west competition would probably become global, the prospect of further consolidation in Eastern Europe was unsurprisingly more worrying to regimes bordering the Soviet bloc.

On the eve of Stalin's death, Yugoslavia's representation in Bonn reported an American expectation 'of the onset of a period of internal accounting [in the Soviet Union] which could lead to unforeseen consequences…demonstrating a concern that Moscow could at any moment easily enter into threatening war adventures. Stalin had been against such threats and now the onset of the strengthening of the danger of war is widely expected in all local diplomatic and political circles.'³ The Yugoslav diplomats in Bonn were confused. After his death, Stalin's leadership was suddenly being regarded as having maintained pragmatic restraint in post-war Europe. Diplomatic observers from Sweden and Norway as well as West Germany feared the onset of a military-led reactionary leadership in Moscow.

The Yugoslav Ministry for Foreign Affairs, highly sensitive to any such turn in Soviet leadership, directed its immediate attention to Helsinki in March 1953.[4] The ministry, keen to gauge the perhaps dangerous but also possibly opportune future for Soviet-Yugoslav relations after Stalin's death ordered the Helsinki Embassy separately and specifically to note 'all, and the least, details which would demonstrate the changing of Soviet internal and external politics; these need to be recorded diligently, analysed and inform Belgrade about [them].'[5] The Yugoslav Ministry did not look for advice in the NATO capitals of Western Europe that expressed fears of a hardening in interpreting the consequences of Stalin's death because their position was different. Instead, the Ministry sought out the position and sources of information of Finland, termed in a 11 March report 'a Nordic state...on the Soviet-European border,' and considered to be of best use to them immediately upon Stalin's death.[6] On the basis of his sources in the Finnish Foreign Ministry, Yugoslav Ambassador in Helsinki Slavko Zore completed a five-part, 21-page analysis titled 'Stalin's Death' by early April.[7] According to Zore, the Finnish Foreign Ministry disagreed with the fearful expectations originating in Bonn. His main argument was that the Finns perceived Stalin's death as a political opportunity and were not fearful of the future of Finnish-Soviet relations. Zore concluded that the Soviet Union was instead actively seeking engagement in Europe. Yugoslav interest in the Finnish reading of Soviet affairs would grow from this point forward. This Finnish position, and the Yugoslav Foreign Ministry's interest in bettering relations with Moscow, formed the basis for Yugoslav-Finnish dialogue in 1953 and is the main topic of this chapter.

Stalin's death would irrevocably alter the power structure of Soviet domestic politics, although these changes were not immediately apparent. At the top, these changes culminated in Nikita Khrushchev becoming Soviet party leader in 1953 and Soviet Prime Minister in 1958.[8] His accession combined with the focus of Soviet foreign policy on Europe worked to the strategic advantage of Finland and Yugoslavia. As the Soviet leadership sought internal order in the aftermath of Stalin's death, both states were able to extract political and economic concessions from the Soviet Union between 1953 and 1955. Helsinki and Belgrade found themselves in the common process of renegotiating their respective bilateral relations with Moscow. Cultural, political and economic contact between Finland and Yugoslavia grew exponentially from 1953 forward. As a consequence of these contacts, and the appointment of Koča Popović to succeed Edvard Kardelj as Yugoslav Foreign Minister in 1953, Yugoslavia adopted a foreign policy of neutralism similar to that of Finland in its relations with the USSR. Simultaneously, as already noted in Chapter 2, in 1953 Urho Kekkonen served as both Foreign Minister and Prime Minister in separate governments between 1953 and 1954 under President Juho Kusti Paasikivi, his partner in guiding a Finnish policy of neutralism. Kekkonen was instrumental in solidifying Helsinki's bargain of neutralism with Moscow. His focus on Finnish-Soviet relations is also an element that attracted the Yugoslav Ministry's attention.

Subsequent exchanges between the two foreign ministries demonstrate that first Finland, and then Yugoslavia, situated along the border of the Soviet bloc found Stalin's death to be an opportunity to improve their relations with Moscow. Already in June 1953, Yugoslavia re-established diplomatic relations with the Soviet Union.[9] In 1955, the Soviet-Yugoslav rapprochement liberated the Yugoslav Foreign Ministry from its previous concentration on monitoring the Soviet's anti-Yugoslav propaganda acts and deflecting military threats. The Ministry could now pursue international bilateral contacts outside the Soviet bloc with its extensive network of embassies.

Instead of a military takeover, Lavrenty Beria and Georgi Malenkov nearly succeeded in taking over Soviet foreign policy.[10] Beria and Malenkov initially vied with Vyacheslav Molotov and Khrushchev for the political leadership of the Soviet Union. But the feared Beria was soon executed and Khrushchev then defeated all other political competitors, including the hard-line Molotov. Khrushchev's rise to power incorporated political concessions to Finland and Yugoslavia, far from the dire expectations first reported from Moscow.[11]

Helsinki's Predictions for Soviet Foreign Policy in Europe

Finnish newspapers initially reported that the death of Stalin was a threat to world security and especially to Finland's. It was feared that Molotov— 'publicly known for his unfriendly attitude towards Finland'—would eventually come to power. Molotov had served as Soviet People's Commissar and Minister of Foreign Affairs from 1939 to 1949, from the Second World War through the Tito-Stalin split. The Finnish public remembered him as the leading figure in the Soviet attack on Finland in 1939–40 and the 1944 offensive, dubbing the most effective new Finnish weapon the 'Molotov cocktail.'[12] Similar fears were put forward in the Belgrade popular press, where Molotov's role in the expulsion of

Yugoslavia from the Cominform in 1948 as Stalin's then most trusted foreign advisor remained infamous. Yet early on—contrary to the international speculation of the dangerous future of Soviet foreign policy in Europe—the Finnish Foreign Ministry noted signs of a softening of Moscow's foreign policy stance.[13] Its reports saw this relaxation to be the result of three factors: 1) the need to address internal conditions, particularly the low Soviet standard of living; 2) a power struggle among high level Soviet leadership for Stalin's position that was expected to continue for an extended period of time, and 3) external pressures, including problems posed by the emergence of South Korea and West Germany.[14] This information was passed on to Belgrade through its Helsinki Embassy in reports during April 1948. As key evidence, the Finns pointed to the Soviet approval of Dag Hammarsjöld's election as United Nations Secretary General on 10 April 1953. Following the November 1952 resignation of Trygve Lie, whose second term as Secretary General the Kremlin had not supported, the Soviets vetoed several candidates before the nomination of Hammarsjöld of Sweden. His near-unanimous election in early April despite his pro-Western reputation, was interpreted by the Finnish Foreign Ministry as a conciliatory Soviet gesture.

When their trade negotiations with the Soviets reached a standstill in March 1953, the Finnish Foreign Ministry became further worried by the decreased production of metallurgy and fuel in the Soviet Union.[15] While still seeking to pay war reparations to the Soviet Union in full after the death of Stalin, the Finns now refused to accept valueless imports from Moscow. As the deliveries of valued fuel products as well as cotton and wheat became scarce during 1952 and early 1953, the Finns now refused Soviet offers of other imports as substitutes. In order to renew the five-year trade agreement with Finland (originally signed following the Finnish-Soviet Agreement on Friendship, Cooperation and Mutual Assistance in December 1948), the Soviet Union resorted to exports from Czechoslovakia and Poland.[16] Out of a total of 38 billion Finnish marks of imports to Finland, 12 billion originated from the two bloc members.[17] The Finnish foreign ministry took such outsourcing as evidence of serious internal Soviet difficulties already in place by 1952. By early 1953, the Soviet export obligations to Finland were in chronic arrears. The Soviets had been scheduled to deliver 10,000 tons of sugar for January and February but by March had sent only 3,000 tons. In 1952, only 5,000 tons of the cotton from the promised 7,000 tons had been delivered and them at the last minute.[18] The Finnish Foreign Ministry was dismayed over the missing Soviet deliveries, sorely needed in Finland, but equally encouraged at the same time by Soviet economic difficulties. They presented Finland with an opening to ask for concessions in the overall trade agreement, now up for renewal after its initial five year term from 1948.

Unlike the Finnish popular press with its fears of Molotov, the Foreign Ministry, foresaw Nikita Khrushchev as the likely candidate for the leadership position in the Kremlin. In contrast to US predictions, the ministry did not make much of the elevated position of Malenkov as expected heir to Stalin's leadership in the Beria-Malenkov-Molotov troika.[19] As early as April 1953, Finnish representatives in Moscow were telling the Ministry in Helsinki that the status of all three members of the troika was in question and that Khrushchev's rise could be expected. The Finnish Foreign Ministry considered these to be signals as well of a significantly weakened Soviet position in its European relations. By early April 1953, it's reporting judged the position of Malenkov as not consolidated, with no equilibrium in his relations with Molotov and Beria.[20] Beria had replaced Andrei Zhdanov as Stalin's closest associate after Zhdanov's death in August 1948. Malenkov's position had been further weakened by Beria's long tenure as the head of the dreaded secret service (NKVD, now MVD) and by Molotov's re-established control over the Foreign Ministry.[21] Matters were made worse, the reports continued, by Nikolai Bulganin's ability as Defence Minister to strengthen his own position by appointing the key Marshalls Aleksander Vasilievski and Georgi Zhukov as Deputy Defence Ministers. 'If the power balance became any more uncertain for Malenkov,' the Finnish analysis concluded, 'he would give up his position as the Secretary of the Party to Khrushchev; Khrushchev is [Bulganin's] guy and his closest friend.'[22] The Finnish Foreign Ministry considered that these signals made a long, harmonious future for a collective Soviet leadership unlikely.[23] Rather than fearing a military take-over in Moscow, the Ministry calculated that the political power struggle would force a more conciliatory Soviet stance towards Finland. As evidence, the Finnish Embassy in Moscow pointed to the unusually cordial behaviour of Anastas Mikoyan and Molotov in celebrating the anniversary of the Finnish-Soviet Friendship and Cooperation treaty in Moscow in early April 1953.[24]

Finland's Focus on Soviet-Yugoslav Relations

Based on these observations, Finnish Foreign Ministry analysts considered that Yugoslavia's status as a state bordering at least the Soviet bloc could become similar to theirs. They decided that Soviet-Yugoslav relations should be closely watched and could be used to test hypotheses of likely future Soviet positions toward Finland. From April 1953 onward, one of the two architects of the Paasikivi-Kekkonen Line took charge of the Finnish Foreign Ministry. Urho Kekkonen served as Foreign Minister for

1952–53, and in 1954 while acting as Prime Minister 1954–56. As President from 1956 forward, he systematically led the Ministry to pursue Yugoslav contacts in Belgrade, Helsinki and Moscow, questioning them persistently about changes in the Soviet approach to dealing with Yugoslavia. Kekkonen's leadership in the Ministry immediately prior to and immediately after Stalin's death, and his dual role as both Foreign Minister and Prime Minister in 1954 focused the Ministry's analytical work on his special interest in Soviet policy. This strategy promoted talks between Yugoslav and Finnish representatives in East European embassies and at the highest level of Finnish officialdom. Only one month after the death of Stalin, Finnish representative Mäkinen invited Yugoslav representative Božić to a sauna in Moscow and told Božić that he believed Stalin's death would mean a swift improvement in Soviet relations with Yugoslavia. This had been suggested to him indirectly by a Russian representative he would not name.[25] Mäkinen asked Božić directly, 'Has Molotov invited you over yet? Have the Soviets begun contacting you with complete courtesy? Have the Soviets requested re-establishing diplomatic relations or opening an embassy in Belgrade?'[26]

But Božić in Moscow and the Yugoslav Ministry's Soviet desk in Belgrade found Finnish candour initially alarming. They worried about 'the lack of evidence' for the Finnish conclusion, but also the significance of a comment being passed on by a Finnish official in Moscow to a Yugoslav one given Soviet intelligence's interest in such information. The Yugoslav Foreign Ministry contacted Helsinki in disbelief, suspecting that Mäkinen might have become a rogue element, taking initiatives without the knowledge of the Finnish Foreign Ministry. After all, it was possible that the sauna in Moscow was under Soviet surveillance. Despite Božić's cautious reaction, the Finnish Embassy in Moscow continued to press on in the same direction, suggesting that Yugoslavia should consider the death of Stalin as a basis on which to pursue Yugoslav relations with the Soviet Union. Åke Gartz became the new Finnish Ambassador to both Moscow and Bucharest simultaneously in early 1953, as the Bucharest representation was attached to the jurisdiction of the Moscow Finnish Embassy. During his inaugural visit to Bucharest in May, Gartz approached the Yugoslavs directly. Over a dinner, the insistent Gartz asked Yugoslav Ambassador in Bucharest 'whether Božić in Moscow had already been received by Molotov?'[27] The Finnish Foreign Ministry predicted that despite Molotov's promotion of the Tito-Stalin split, he would seek to reopen diplomatic relations with Yugoslavia. Gartz, certain of a shifting mood in Moscow, suggested that 'there are many changes in the latest period in our relations [with Moscow]; we could use this situation' for political gain.[28]

Throughout the spring and summer of 1953, the Yugoslav Foreign Ministry thought it best to officially defer Finnish speculation on Soviet moves toward rapprochement. A report of this conversation with Gartz to Belgrade argued that the Yugoslav Ministry should be cautious in adopting the Finnish advice without hesitation: 'after all, the Finns have no proof of the future.'[29] Yet Gartz and several of his colleagues continued to address Yugoslav officials openly and repeatedly throughout May, June and July, setting out their belief that 'changes are coming in the position of the Soviet Union towards [Yugoslavia]' in the next few months.[30]

According to the Finnish analysis, Yugoslav-Soviet conflict was grounded in the personalities of Stalin and Tito. Stalin's passing meant that 'those relations could be easily and quickly reorganized.'[31] The Finnish Foreign Ministry suspected that if the hypothesis about the Soviet need to relax policy towards Europe along the Soviet-European border as accurate, the Soviet Union would first and foremost seek restoration of Soviet-Yugoslav diplomatic and then trade relations.[32]

Belgrade's Reaction to Stalin's Death and the Finnish Connection

Although hesitating to accept officially or publicly Finnish encouragement for rapprochement with the Soviet Union, the Yugoslav Foreign Ministry had immediately turned, as noted at the start of this chapter, to their counterpart for the Finnish reaction to Stalin's death. Koča Popović had already replaced Edvard Kardelj as Foreign Minister on 14 February 1953. He was most interested in furthering those foreign relations that moved Yugoslavia from ideological arguments with the Soviet party into bilateral trade relations with alternative partners. This appointment also led to significant changes in the role of the Ministry. The Yugoslav Foreign Ministry's First and Second Divisions, under their chiefs Arso Milatović and Aleš Bebler, quickly put forward an argument for a new approach towards the Soviet Union after Stalin's death.[33] As outlined in a communiqué of 6 April, this approach recognized the need to appraise changes in the Soviet Union for their effects on the bordering states.[34] Bebler asked that as a separate matter, Yugoslav embassies investigate in detail all Soviet exchanges with Yugoslav representatives, reporting immediately on all contact with Soviet state personnel officially and unofficially, as well as reporting contact with Soviet bloc members. The Finnish Foreign Ministry had predicted that Soviets would first allow Yugoslav diplomats to attend diplomatic events in Moscow, and that they would subsequently begin to approach the Yugoslavs in a cordial manner. While the Yugoslavs continued adamantly and publicly to deny the Finnish hypothesis of a fast Soviet turnaround in their Yugoslav policy, Bebler and

Milatović took the suggestion seriously. A new, faster delivery network for reports, together with media and news analysis, were set up between Belgrade and a few select embassies, including those in Helsinki and Moscow, in April 1953.[35] London, Washington, Paris, New Delhi and Bonn were also identified as key locations, along with Rome, Stockholm, Helsinki, Tokyo and Tehran.[36] Additionally, if still more information was needed, the Moscow representation was told to seek a permission to travel by train to four key locations: Leningrad, Warsaw, Helsinki and Tehran. The requests were to be made under the pretence of visiting the Yugoslav representation in these four cities. Their real aim was to 'obtain good information throughout travel by private [communications with others] and personal observations' and simply to test whether the Soviet Foreign Ministry would grant a Yugoslav representative a visa for travel across Soviet territory that had been barred since 1948.[37]

The Yugoslav Foreign Ministry instructed the ten key embassies listed above to follow the events resulting from the death of Stalin in light of events in Warsaw and Balkan Pact countries, and Tito's concurrent visit to Britain.[38] In February 1953, Yugoslavia had signed the Tripartite Treaty of Friendship and Cooperation with NATO member states, Greece and Turkey. The treaty outlined cultural, economic and technical cooperation between the three states, but its true aim was to create an alliance to prevent Soviet expansion and influence in the Balkans and the Mediterranean.[39] A formal military alliance was signed in Bled on 9 August 1954, making it officially the Balkan Pact.

Unlike the Finns, who placed emphasis on material conditions within the Soviet Union, Yugoslav analysis paid more attention to 'the reconstruction of the state and the party leadership in the USSR as revealing the further course of Soviet politics.'[40] For Kardelj and Tito, Stalin and Molotov had caused the split. The Yugoslav Foreign Ministry officials were aware of the highly personalised view of Yugoslav-Soviet relations held by the party leadership. Kardelj had left the position of Foreign Minister a mere two weeks before Stalin's death. Despite the independent position Ministry analysts had achieved by 1953, many must have been cautious of departing from the party-political focus. The Yugoslav Foreign Ministry's analysis found it difficult to predict 'the correct place of the Soviet party leadership's position in future relations towards the state apparatus.'[41] Yugoslav analysis expected unforeseeable changes to take place in the Kremlin in the course of the summer and fall of 1953. Unlike the Finns, who considered this intermediate period of uncertainty as an important opportunity to assert pressure on Finnish-Soviet relations, the Yugoslav Ministry cautiously categorized this period as unrepresentative of the future and thus a dangerous time for making policy changes. The Yugoslav leadership of a multi-ethnic, increasingly republic-based yet resolutely one-party state understood the broad impact of the removal of an undisputed leader of both the party and the state like Stalin. More than their Finnish or European counterparts, the Yugoslav Foreign Ministry appreciated the difficulty of foreseeing the internal political consequences of the impending restructuring of the Presidium and the Secretariat.[42] The Yugoslav leadership had faced great difficulties in maintaining an alternative yet still one-party state structure in Yugoslavia after 1948, once the initial Soviet model was no longer appropriate. This included empowering the republic-based party structures, disbanding the apparatus for central economic planning, and forming local workers' councils, all in order to improve on the Soviet model for a Communist state. The republican parties in Croatia, Bosnia, Macedonia, Montenegro, Serbia and Slovenia were to become the basis for socialist democracy and Communist power. The Yugoslav leadership also changed the name of the Communist Party of Yugoslavia to the League of Communists of Yugoslavia (LCY) in 1952, in order to differentiate themselves further. Milovan Djilas explained to the November party congress that Karl Marx himself had envisioned a looser association or a league in place of a hierarchical party.

Any restructuring of the Soviet's own one-party state would doubtless, the Yugoslavs assumed, alter the balance of power between the higher echelons of the party and the army. Its anticipation discouraged the Yugoslav Ministry from commenting on Finnish speculation about betterment of Soviet-Yugoslav relations or even from embracing the Soviets' requests for a normalization of relations until 1955.[43] Rapprochement with the Soviets, although desired by the Ministry, was still considered dangerous to a Yugoslav foreign policy that sought above all to preserve the country's independence. Having survived the tense five years following the Tito-Stalin split, the Foreign Ministry was wary of re-establishing ties that could allow Soviet pressure on Yugoslav affairs.

The Ministry was concerned that the Finnish hypothesis underestimated the significance of ideological differences between Soviet and Yugoslav Communism. For Yugoslavia's elevated significance in Europe to continue after Stalin's death, the differences from Soviet Communism would need continued emphasis.[44] Moreover, Tito and Kardelj, who had orchestrated the highly personal Yugoslav-Soviet diplomacy around Yugoslavia's expulsion, were very likely to resist any renewal of relations with the Soviets. Not only had Stalin and Molotov sought to engineer a regime change in Yugoslavia in 1948 since then Yugoslavia, and Tito and Kardelj in particular, had been the targets of Soviet attacks propagated by Moscow through Eastern Europe. From 1948 to 1953, it was a major task of the Foreign Ministry to gather statistics and accounts of the countless Albanian,

Bulgarian, Czechoslovakian, Hungarian, Romanian and Polish criticisms of Yugoslavia and its leadership in their domestic press, public events, radio and television. The demand for gathering this data from within the Office of the President soon preoccupied the Foreign Ministry. Simply generating counterpropaganda led to diverting the Ministry away from focusing on bilateral relations with non-hostile states.

Koča Popović and the Emergence of an Autonomous Foreign Ministry

Koča Popović (1908–93) became Yugoslav Foreign Minister upon the conclusion of the Balkan Pact and immediately prior to the death of Stalin, on 14 February 1953. He would hold the post for over twelve years until 25 April 1966. He was the longest-serving Foreign Minister in Tito's Yugoslavia. Popović's term is considered one of the most successful in Yugoslav foreign relations, and is even termed by Ranko Petković 'a star-studded time for Yugoslavia.'[45] He is particularly appreciated for the political independence of his position and persona, by which he transformed the Yugoslav Foreign Ministry. Unlike his predecessor, Popović was not one of Tito's inner circle. He was never a member of the Politburo, and unlike Kardelj and Tito, he had spent no time in the interwar Soviet Union.

His background was unusually diverse, but his wartime credentials were unimpeachable. Born into a wealthy and renowned Belgrade family of Vlach origin, Popović spent his childhood in Switzerland, attended high school in Belgrade and studied philosophy at the Sorbonne, graduating in 1932.[46] Popović joined the CPY in Belgrade in 1933 while he was pursuing a career as a journalist and surrealist poet. From 1937 to 1939, Popović served in the International Brigade in Spain as a military officer. In 1939 he was briefly interned in a camp in France. Popović played a crucial role in the Partisan uprising in Serbia in 1941, leading the Kosmaj mountain units close to Belgrade, finally rising to command the First Proletarian Brigade of the Second Yugoslav Army by the war's end. Popović then became the Chief of General Staff of the Yugoslav People's Army after the war's end and remained in that position until 1953.

In the post-war period, Popović was celebrated as a war hero and could have sought out a position more closely connected to the party leadership. 'All or almost all who passed through the Second Yugoslav Army, and without exception all in leading positions,' according to Ranko Petković, 'could also form party careers, most securely and directly climbing the ladder of power. Nearly all became members of the Politburo.'[47] Yet Popović, considered by some of Tito's closest associates to be 'a salon communist' or 'a man who fitted better in a tailcoat than in a uniform,' had no desire to join the Politburo or Tito's circle.[48] Despite his long-held Communist loyalties, Popović considered Tito and Kardelj's approach too full of 'ideologisation,' Marxist rhetoric without practical value for the goals of Yugoslav independence and prosperity which Popović wished to pursue. Moreover, Popović made his general feelings public, leading Radio Free Europe to comment, 'he never hides how proud he has always been of his intellectual brilliance and expert knowledge.'[49]

Tito's naming of Popović as Minister of Foreign Affairs was therefore a major surprise to much of the Yugoslav leadership. Several explanations for Popović's appointment have been put forward, for example that Popović was 'well known by Tito even before the Second World War,' or that Tito and Popović became close during the war. These views tend to support the impression passed from Yugoslav to Western historiography of a foreign policy operating closely under Tito's guiding hand, with the Foreign Ministry in the subordinate position common in other Communist regimes.[50] Yet Popović was already known for his independent persona, which survived first military, then party discipline, always being 'seen to go on his own.' It is therefore, certain that the appointment of nonconformist Popović was significant for the relative autonomy of the ministry, whether intended or not, following Kardelj's departure. The Yugoslav Foreign Ministry did need a leader capable of successfully initiating new negotiations with a wide range of international actors, especially with Western governments. Outside the Soviet bloc, loyalists like Kardelj held less sway than Popović, the Sorbonne-educated intellectual who was more persuasive for not repeating Kardelj-coined rhetoric on Communist ideology. That such a capacity served Tito's purposes seems to be a more likely reason for his appointment.

But there is another likely reason. Kardelj did not want to leave the post to a competitor within Tito's innermost circle, but to a 'lesser,' more remote figure. Those competitors included the then-Deputy Foreign Minister Veljko Mićunović and Vladimir Velebit. Velebit would also have been a Yugoslav diplomat whose skills were appreciated by Western governments, but he could not be considered. He had been portrayed as a British agent by the Soviet leadership in 1948. Leading ideologue Milovan Djilas was already at odds with Tito. Thus, the way was open for Ivo Vejvoda, the Deputy Foreign Minister who had as the Head of Regional Nordic Section in the Foreign Ministry not incidentally been a major figure in establishing Yugoslav-Finnish relations after 1948, to propose Popović as Kardelj's successor to Kardelj personally.[51]

Popović inherited an internally well-organized Ministry that had by 1953 established a wide network of embassies as a significant asset for global communication. Many within the Ministry expected Popović to reorganize its relationship to the State Security Administration which was now ominously located on the fourth floor of the Foreign Ministry. Its head, Aleksandr Ranković, was indeed one of Tito's inner circle. In 1952, Kardelj, had institutionalized the presence and influence of the UDBa in agreement with Tito within two departments of the Foreign Ministry: the Foreign Political Department and the Coordination Division.[52] The UDBa's 'invasion' of foreign affairs was managed by Kardelj's Deputy Minister Mićunović and his associate and head of Coordination, Anton Vratuš.

Kardelj saw some influence for the UDBa within the Foreign Ministry as essential in the aftermath of the Tito-Stalin split. Kardelj, like Tito, feared a Soviet effort to replace them and wanted everyone suspected of Soviet contacts to be observed closely. Membership of the CPY had grown close to a half a million by 1948, and there was no shortage of suspected Soviet sympathizers.[53] Between 1948 and 1949, 27,000 party members, were charged with being 'Cominformists' and 16,000 of then were sent to one of a dozen camps for hard labor.[54] Of these camps Goli Otok is the most infamous one. The importance of UDBa in the state bureaucracy grew exponentially. In the aftermath, Ranković and Kardelj became even closer to Tito. The presence of UDBa was not welcomed by the civil servants in the Foreign Ministry. Popović resented it from the start. It was generally known that he 'did not care very much for Edvard Kardelj, nor did he especially appreciate Aleksandar Ranković,' and he had no interest in interfering in their internal conflicts.[55] Popović did not want the UDBa to become a force above diplomacy in the Foreign Ministry. Thus, many expected him to attempt to move Ranković's offices from the building and thus out of the Ministry immediately. Popović cleverly did not attempt a manoeuvre that was unlikely to succeed in the still insecure atmosphere of 1953. Instead, he simply replaced Vratuš, since UDBa's oversight had depended on his loyalty as the head of the Department of Coordination of the Ministry of Foreign Affairs.

Popović worked from there to institute the kind of discipline and attention to protocol in Yugoslav diplomacy that was common to West European governments. For this, he did not need to directly challenge the UDBa, but simply worked to limit its access to diplomatic reporting and analysis. Already in 1953, Popović was rushing to centralize the analysis of reporting from Yugoslav embassies and to apply this analysis more directly to questions of current state interests. One of Popović's most important legacies remains the Ministry's integrated system for recording information. Unlike the organization of many counterparts, including the US State Department and the Finnish Foreign Ministry, the Yugoslav Ministry's files are organized not only by geographical location or original source, but by the subject under investigation. For example, all information on the topic of Stalin's death, from all Yugoslav embassies, is located in a file titled 'Yugoslavia 1953' in the folder for March, under the topic of Stalin's death. This information is cross-referenced in the files of the Embassy source countries such as 'Finland 1953' and 'the USSR 1953.' Included here are reports of diplomatic chatter on the topic of Stalin's death from Yugoslav embassies in Istanbul, Tehran, Mexico City and every other country where a diplomatic report mentioned the subject.

After his term, Popović was criticized for concentrating solely on diplomatic procedures and failing to remove the UDBa from the Foreign Ministry. According to this argument, Popović had enough authority as a military leader in 1953 to push the security service out. This argument neglects the aforementioned severing of the intimate connection between the Coordination Department and Ranković. There were still complaints from the Ministry's diplomatic personnel regarding the 'incorrect' and crude behavior of UDBa colleagues when traveling to the fourth floor. These complaints were understandable given the stark distinction between UDBa's political police officers, often Partisans from poor rural backgrounds, and the Foreign Ministry's younger, university-educated, diplomatic civil servants, especially those working in the Division of Analysis and Planning or in the Coordination Division. Popović helped the Ministry to work around the existence of the UDBa on its fourth floor until Ranković's purge from power in 1966 (also Popović's final year as Foreign Minister), only then did the UDBa finally move out of the Foreign Ministry. As evidence that their influence had not always been contained, a report of the Investigating Commission at the Fourth Plenum of the Central Committee purging Ranković from his position included the charge that he had replaced two top Foreign Ministry officials with UDBa agents in October 1964 without informing Popović.[56]

Popović's term had begun with the signing of the Balkan Pact, an agreement with Greece and Turkey which he had already been pursuing while acting as the Head of General Staff of the JNA. When named to the Central Committee in November 1952, he was given responsibility for the negotiations with Greece and Turkey. Soon after he became Foreign Minister Popović worked to end the Yugoslav dispute with Italy over Trieste in October 1954. This was a dispute over the Yugoslav-Italian border to the south and east of the port city, which Tito and Kardelj had been reluctant to conclude. Tito objected because of the presence of US troops in Trieste and Kardelj because the border was with his native Slovenia. Popović was required to address the intense post-war tension with Italy already at the end of October 1953, when Tito publicly threatened that Yugoslavia would enter into armed conflict with Italian troops, if they replaced British and American troops in Trieste.[57] A year later, in November 1954 Popović and his Ambassador to Great Britain Velebit persuaded Tito to accept the London Agreement of 1954, which effectively fixed the border and ended potential conflicts between Yugoslavia and Italy.

From 1953 to 1955, it was Popović who turned Yugoslav foreign relations toward a policy of Europe-centered neutralism comparable to that of Finland, but without moving towards non-alignment until 1959–61. Curiously, scholarship dating Yugoslav non-alignment back before these years rarely mentions Popović but focuses instead on Tito's visits to Asia and Africa in 1954 and 1955.[58] These visits did not shift the focus of Yugoslavia's foreign relations away from Europe in general and a modus vivendi with the Soviet Union in particular. Indeed, Popović was not enamoured of the Non-Alignment Movement because of its ideological pretensions and its main concern with advancing the position of formerly colonial, non-European states. Later Popović would comment that he 'never saw in non-alignment a real ideology.'[59]

For Popović, as for Paasikivi, neutralism was not an ideology but a political strategy. In itself, it did not seek political goals beyond independence and avoidance of conflict, here the East-West conflict. Paasikivi only turned to neutralism when independence from the Soviet Union through military defence was no longer possible. Yugoslavia was in a similar position to Finland in the post-1948 period: facing the prospect of Soviet military intervention as the major threat to independence. As Foreign Minister, Popović had the reputation of 'an official who rarely "rose up" from his strategic overview to address the party or act as a political preacher or arbitrator.'[60] Popović understood that in the Yugoslav system of government, large decisions originating 'from above' from Tito were inevitable, but would not in themselves constitute an effective foreign policy. Popović concentrated on improving the Ministry's analytical and administrative capacity. As demonstrated in this chapter and the next, the Ministry also begun to formulate policy that used Finland as a point of reference in the aftermath of Stalin's death.

Popović replaced his old adversary Ranković as Vice-President of Yugoslavia in 1966, and was then a member of the collective Presidency from 1967 to 1972. Popović's appointment as Vice-President prompted Western analysts to note that 'in their efforts to separate state and party functions, Tito and his colleagues are appointing people who have the highest of reputations but are not members of the Politburo.'[61] In fact, Popović was so independent that in 1972 he resigned permanently from the government as a protest against Tito's purge of the liberal leadership of the Serbian party.

Finnish-Soviet Relations and the Yugoslav Perspective, 1953–55

The Yugoslav Foreign Ministry had generally committed itself to not raising anti-Soviet and anti-Warsaw Pact propaganda efforts in Finland between 1948 and 1953. Finland had since 1948 been considered a friendly country facing a problematic geopolitical position in relationship to the Soviet Union similar to that of Yugoslavia. The Yugoslavs had accurately identified the Finnish Communist Party, a faction of the Finnish People's Democratic League, as an organization essentially committed to the distribution of Soviet propaganda and furthering Soviet foreign policy positions in Finland. The Yugoslavs therefore termed the SKP 'Cominformist.' Indeed, the party had spread Soviet propaganda against Yugoslavia since 1948. However, the Yugoslav Foreign Ministry also identified the SKP as hostile toward the official positions of the standing Finnish government, a party that was made illegal in the inter-war period but resurrected in the post-war period to serve Soviet concerns, and in order to conclude the Finnish-Soviet Treaty in Paris. To help preserve the balance in Finnish-Soviet relations, the Yugoslav Ministry had generally not attacked the SKP in Finland. For the Foreign Ministry in Belgrade:

> the basic characteristics of the Finnish political reality demonstrate on one hand loyalty in fulfilling obligations which originate from the Finnish-Soviet Friendship and Co-operation Agreement, and on the other hand in the real and extensive Finnish effort to incapacitate directly and indirectly the influence of the USSR in the internal political development of the country.[62]

In addition to this duality, the Yugoslav analysis also noted a third element, 'the increasing importance of Western and especially American influence' in Finnish economic policy.[63] The Yugoslavs thought that by 1953 if trade with the Soviet Union continued to decline with difficulties in promised Soviet supplies, then Finland would have to increase its trade with the Euro-Atlantic economies. As such a shift did not conflict with the Yugoslav foreign policy goal of political independence from the Soviet Union, Belgrade had refrained from any efforts in Finland for fear of decreasing the overall Finnish ability to counter Soviet pressure. By December 1953, the Yugoslav Embassy in Helsinki admittedly concluded that the 'dialectic of the Finnish foreign policy has succeeded [since 1948] in making free internal development stronger' by accepting limited foreign political obligation to the Soviet Union in order to strengthen the domestic and international political independence of Finland.[64] The Ministry's year-end report shows that, the First and the Second Divisions of the Foreign Ministry, with Milatović and Bebler, as their chiefs, were paying close attention to Finland's relationship with the Soviet Union. Moreover, drawing on the initial authority that went with Kardelj's tenure as its head, the Ministry became a force in itself except in cases like the 1956 Hungarian Revolution, as we shall see in Chapter 4, where Tito himself chose to intervene. There was thus an ongoing incentive to look at Finnish-Soviet relations and to find out, how Finland had been able to manage this relationship since 1948. Undoubtedly, the strong anti-Russian feeling manifested in Finland also appealed to the Yugoslav analysts in the bitterly anti-Soviet atmosphere in which they worked.

The Yugoslav Foreign Ministry's analysis of Finland concluded that despite political bartering, '[the] tendency towards political independence and national sovereignty are related characteristics of the Finnish political reality. Development of these tendencies especially accelerated after Stalin's death.'[65] The Yugoslavs observed that 'the relative reduction in tensions in the world and the strengthening of the idea of collective security [in Europe] together with the reduction of danger from local aggression' made the Finnish position more viable, and perhaps should be applied to Yugoslav foreign policy as well.[66] As evidence, Ambassador Zore in Helsinki observed key changes within the leadership of the Finnish Army in May 1953 that he related to the death of Stalin and the increased stability in Finnish-Soviet relations of which the Finnish Foreign Ministry was convinced, as the General Staff and Ministry of Defence dismissed a number of important personnel. In the summer of 1953 high-ranking officers, among them several colonels had been found in previously non-disclosed internal investigations to have political connections with the Soviets. These officers in fact had been under surveillance since the end of the Second World War. Paasikivi had not ordered their internment (as Tito had of suspected 'Cominformists'). They remained on active duty but under suspicion. Zore observed that 'without a doubt the initiative by [the Finnish political leadership] comes now as a result of the stabilization in the Finnish position in general in reference to Russia.'[67] The Finnish Foreign Ministry, under Kekkonen until July 1953, waited only two months after the death of Stalin to pension off these suspected Soviet informants. Zore was disappointed that they would not be tried but concluded that:

> Without consideration for the manner in which the dismissals were carried out, they still constitute a strong blow [to the Soviets] because their people will in the least be removed; [the Finns] are expecting a reaction from [the Soviet] side...They are expecting that the Russians will not easily accept this and will characterize all eventual changes as further strengthening American influence and pro-American people [in Finland] and will characterize this further as an attack on the

friendly governmental relations between the Finnish and Russian relations.[68]

Building Yugoslav-Finnish Ties from Sports to Trade

Milatović's and Bebler's elevated view of Finnish analysis of the Soviet Union in April, and Zore's reporting of the personnel changes within the Finnish Army in May, helped to reconfigure this Yugoslav Foreign Ministry's view of Finland. By December 1953 Yugoslav Ambassador Zore in Helsinki told Belgrade that 'in these conditions…we need to operate in regard to the propaganda activity in Finland with maximal use of opposition…in our opinion propaganda efforts in Finland should be developed during this stage and direct the center of gravity of our work.'[69] Following Stalin's death, the Yugoslav Embassy now launched propaganda efforts within Finland that had previously been rejected as potentially damaging to Finland's Soviet policy. Yugoslav Embassy reports from Helsinki regarded the period immediately following Stalin's death as a time when 'Moscow wants to make further use of [amicable] Russian-Finnish relations as evidence of Russia's peaceful politics and the possibility of good relations with capitalist states even on their [European] border.'[70] The Yugoslav delegation sought from late 1953 to develop 'various activities in political, economic and propaganda spheres, on organizational matters and work between these countries deepening of the associational relationship [between Finland and Yugoslavia].'[71] Under Zore's leadership, the Helsinki Embassy undertook a renewed effort to 'inform responsible governmental officers and leading political persons of individual parties of [the Yugoslav] foreign policy positions…especially on the Trieste question.'[72] The Finnish position was considered as essentially pro-Western given its trade interests. Under Popović, the Yugoslav Foreign Ministry began to view the unresolved status of Trieste as hindering Yugoslav relations with Western governments. In 1953, Finland was considered 'Western enough' for Belgrade to worry that Trieste stood in the way of improving Yugoslav relations not only with Italy, but the UK, the US and Yugoslav-Finnish relations.

The increased Yugoslav interest in Finland allowed the Foreign Ministry to learn that the Finnish press generally held a very sympathetic view toward the Yugoslavs and their famous resistance to Soviet pressure.[73] Yugoslav representatives also characterised Finland as:

…sports country where almost everyone practices some sport and of course attends sports events. It can be said without hesitation that for [Yugoslavia] the victory over Russia in soccer in 1952 gave Yugoslavia the kind of public popularity from the broad Finnish masses which would not be possible to attain through any kind of propaganda action.⁷⁴

Efforts to increase Yugoslav popularity and importance in Finland in 1953 were therefore focused on athletic exchanges. The Finnish Foreign Ministry enthusiastically responded to the increased Yugoslav interest. In keeping with Finnish neutralism, the cultural and economic spheres were best suited for Finland to develop contacts with states considered hostile by the Soviet Union. Yugoslav track and field stars Ceraja and Mugoše toured Helsinki and smaller towns in southern Finland. All Finnish publications carried stories on the tour, and in Finland 50–60 per cent of each town's population attended these events.⁷⁵ In response to this tour, Finland sent its own delegation of track and field athletes to Yugoslavia along with reporters who prepared a total of three half-hour reports from Yugoslavia that played repeatedly on Finnish Public Radio (YLE) throughout 1953. In pursuit of their anti-Yugoslav goals, the Communist SKP criticised the YLE in their publications for 'granting Yugoslavia lengthy coverage while sending no reporters to either Hungary nor Romania' within the Soviet bloc. The Finnish Foreign Ministry, like their Yugoslav counterpart, was not interested in expanding relations with Hungary or Romania. Relations towards the two Soviet bloc states were formal and properly maintained, but there was no interest in promoting cultural exchanges for political goals.

In July, the Split soccer team 'Hajduk' toured Helsinki, Tampere and Turku, attracting crowds of 15,000 or more.⁷⁶ The Yugoslavs also sent representatives of the Yugoslav railroad workers soccer association, who toured the cities of Kuopio, Kotka and Kemi.⁷⁷ These activities were 'recorded in detail in sports columns of all news sources stressing the high level of sports performance in Yugoslavia.'⁷⁸ In addition to athletes, an eight-person delegation from the Invalid Association of Yugoslavia was sent. Most members, like their Finnish counterparts who they met, were veterans of the Second World War. The 14-day tour included events coordinated with the Finnish Association for Invalids. The delegation's visit was covered in all major Finnish publications with special attention to photographs that could portray the suffering from the Second World War. Press coverage emphasized parallels between Yugoslav and Finnish sacrifices in the war despite the fact that Yugoslavia had fought with the Soviet Union and Finland against it. Symphony conductor Sama Hubada was even sent on a tour of Finland, sponsored interestingly by the Yugoslav Interior Ministry.

Yugoslavia also sent a trade delegation to Finland. It was given the broadest possible publicity within the Finnish mainstream media and was welcomed by Minister of National Defence and later Minister of Economy, Päiviö Hetemäki. His prominence alone made the occasion significant in Finland. At the end of the year, the Yugoslav Embassy in Helsinki concluded that public relations efforts in Finland had been an unprecedented success. Due to these efforts, Zore calculated that by the end of 1953 'there was hardly a day when the Finnish publications did not give attention to Yugoslavia in at least in one of its agencies' news, columns, reports, travel accounts, tourist reviews or foreign affairs reportage.'[79] According to Yugoslav calculations Finnish newspapers wrote about Yugoslavia one hundred times more than coverage of Finland received in Yugoslav newspapers. Zore suggested to Belgrade that 'by copying similar sports events we can achieve in Finland coverage writing and discussion about [Yugoslavia].' Thus, he added, it is not only the sports achievements of the United States and the Soviet Union that receive attention in Finland. Further, 'on the whole the position of publications and radio towards Yugoslavia [in 1953] was positive, well intentioned and sympathetic,' excepting only the newspapers of the Finnish Communist Party.

To celebrate the 1953 anniversary of the Federal Republic of Yugoslavia on 29 November, the Embassy invited a total of 350 Finnish guests to their reception in Helsinki. The President of Finland, the Minister of Foreign Affairs, President and Secretaries of Parliament all attended the high-profile event.[80] Yugoslav representatives observed that 'respected political people' in Finland felt that the history of this Second Yugoslavia shared many similarities with the history of Finland. When informed of 'our national liberation, consistent peace-seeking foreign policy, conflict with the Eastern bloc countries and a well-defined stance towards England and America,' the Finns exhibited sympathy towards Yugoslavia.[81] Moreover, the Helsinki Embassy reported to Belgrade that by the end of 1953 'the average Finn knows that [Yugoslavs] resisted the Russians and that we consistently protect our independence, and those are elemental things which the Finns appreciate.'[82] Zore informed Belgrade that he had chosen Päivö Kaukomieli Tarjanne, the highest ranking official in the Balkan section at the Finnish Foreign Ministry to be a trusted confidant, someone with whom 'to exchange political thinking periodically.' Discussions between the two focused on how to 'strengthen [the] political, economic and defensive position of Europe' from the joint perspectives of their countries.

In June 1953 the Finnish Foreign Ministry requested that it's combined residence and representation in Belgrade be upgraded to an Embassy and the Ministry acquired a second residence in Belgrade. After the concerted efforts of Finnish chargé d'affaires Ville Niskanen and his personal negotiations with Vejvoda since 1948, Finnish interest in Yugoslav trade also grew in 1953.[83] In early 1953, the head of the Bank of Finland Sakari Toumioja begun to develop a personal relationship with the Yugoslav economist Bogdan Crnobrnja, the Deputy Foreign Minister with whom Popović had replaced Tito-loyalist Mićunović in February.[84] In June 1953, Finland sent a delegation from the Economic-Political Department of the Finnish Foreign Ministry to Belgrade. The Yugoslavs increased their import of Finnish wood materials for paper production for that year to $200,000 doubling the total value of Yugoslav imports from Finland in the process.[85]

Yugoslavia Tries Turning to Finnish Neutralism

Following Stalin's death, close Yugoslav attention to Finnish analysis of the Soviet Union, the sharp increase in cultural contacts, and the simultaneous arrival of Popović as Foreign Minister combined to lead the Yugoslav Ministry to consider neutralism as an explicit policy. The Yugoslav Foreign Ministry began to recognise the benefits of the Paasikivi-Kekkonen Line as a successful road to a renewed relationship with the Soviet Union. For Finland this neutralism had reduced the threat of armed conflict but left domestic politics to proceed on their own course. For Yugoslavia, such a strategy would leave the still Communist regime free to pursue its separate course and develop its bilateral relations with states outside the Soviet bloc. The Yugoslav foreign policy team in Belgrade under Popović was willing to consider rapprochement, so long as Yugoslavia's Western ties remained in place. Still the party leadership around Tito and Kardelj, whose very survival had depended on the split, were reluctant to consider diplomatic rapprochement with the Soviet Union. Those closest to them, notably UDBa chief Ranković, benefited from maintenance of the status quo. The dependence on UDBa's counter intelligence in determining policy towards the Soviet Union would lessen with the renewal of formal relations. In any case, renewal would come at a price, including the public Soviet admission of wrongdoing against Yugoslavia that Tito and Kardelj considered essential. Negotiations had to include issues especially sensitive to Soviets, such as the Balkan Pact and the Yugoslav decision to abolish their collective farms—all of which the Yugoslavs were adamant about defending.[86] Already in June 1953, Popović won approval for a delegation to be sent to Moscow to discuss the renewal of diplomatic relations. Over the course of the year 1953 and into 1954, Popović pursued a two-pronged strategy: to negotiate with the West as noted above in order to bring the Trieste conflict to an end, while simultaneously seeking the re-establishment of formal relations with the Soviet Union. Although not widely understood in Belgrade, the Yugoslav Foreign Ministry was already pursuing a strategy similar to that of the Finnish Ministry toward the Soviet

Union after Stalin's death—seeking political concessions in return for established, formal bilateral relations.

As a part of its Soviet strategy, the Yugoslav Foreign Ministry asked its Moscow representatives in April to prepare a list of concrete demands with which to engage the Soviet government. They were put forward in negotiations that began in June with Molotov still in place, at least as Foreign Minister.[87] The Yugoslavs demanded among other things that Yugoslav school children trapped in the Soviet Union without exit visas since 1948 be allowed to return. After the conclusion of the Finnish-Soviet Friendship Treaty in 1948, the Finnish Foreign Ministry had made similar efforts to inquire about any Finnish citizens remaining in the Gulag from returnees to Western Europe. When some 52 were identified in April 1953, the Finnish Foreign Ministry requested that the Soviet Foreign Ministry return them to Finland. Surprisingly, the request was granted, and in three separate transfers 50 adult Finnish citizens were returned to Helsinki between July and September 1953.[88] Initial discussion within the Yugoslav Foreign Ministry led some to argue that 'we cannot expect that Russia will change its stance on the question of children,' mostly adults by now, and that there was nothing to be gained from asking for their return. Yet, the contrary view prevailed, and Belgrade continued to request the return of an indefinite number of 'children.'

This was surprising given the significant difference in age and experience between the potential returnees on the Yugoslav and Finnish sides. The majority of Finland's 1953 returnees had voluntarily left the country before or during the Second World War to support the Soviet Union, even to fight against Finland in the war.[89] Why would Tito and Kardelj welcome the return to Yugoslavia of an indeterminate number of people whose parents had been pro-Soviet and managed to flee the wide-ranging purge of such persons following the split in 1948? Why would the Soviet Union allow the children to return and turn against their parents? Apparently some in the Yugoslav Ministry saw the likely Soviet refusal as a good way to delay any rapprochement in Soviet-Yugoslav relations or to test the Kremlin's resolve. Others, believed that 'at the moment [Yugoslavia] should go around all those questions for which [they] knew before hand would sharpen [Yugoslav-Soviet] relations and look for a way by which [Yugoslavia] can take the initiative in questions whose resolution can be accepted by both sides.'[90] As a modest start, Belgrade suggested that its Moscow representation begin by asking for a permit to visit the Crimea, relaxing the restrictions that had confined them like their Western counterparts to one section of the Soviet capital.[91]

Although Yugoslav representatives requested that the Soviets in Belgrade also make 'concrete suggestions to the Yugoslav government,' the negotiations proceeded ahead on the basis of Yugoslav demands.[92] Unrealistically, the Yugoslavs demanded freedom of the press for Yugoslav immigrants in the Soviet Union. They demanded the repatriation of all Yugoslav children. These requests were surprisingly met by the Soviets. Yugoslav citizens were granted amnesty retroactively from three days before the official announcement of the death of Stalin, on 2 March 1953.[93] All those who wished to be repatriated were to be handed over the Yugoslav authorities at the Vojvodina border in Subotica. On 10 June 1953, the Soviets agreed to the repatriation of Yugoslav children identified as 'residents of boarding schools.' The repatriation of course demanded that the Yugoslavs themselves be able to locate their citizens in order to make their request. In exchange, the Yugoslavs granted the Soviets very few concessions. The Soviet request for additional visas for more diplomatic personnel in Belgrade was denied, with only permission to substitute one person for another being allowed. The Yugoslav team in Moscow directly in contact with Popović in Belgrade repeatedly rejected Soviet requests for commercial flights over Belgrade en route from Moscow to Tirana. The Yugoslav leadership did not even reply to several Soviet requests for 'cultural collaboration in various forms.'[94]

As predicted by the Finnish Foreign Ministry's analysis, the Kremlin increasingly demonstrated willingness to work toward rapprochement. Already in June the Soviet Foreign Ministry requested accreditation and exchange of ambassadors.[95] In response, Tito wanted to underline Yugoslav demands. In an official statement in June, he explained that:

> The Soviet Union has recently shown a desire for ambassadors to be exchanged...We shall accept the offer...However, the exchange of ambassadors does not necessarily imply normalization or improvement of the relations between two countries, in so far as the worst enemies exchange diplomats. The harm they did to Yugoslavia will not easily be repaired...We need relations that are normal, if need be formalized.[96]

While the Yugoslavs agreed to exchange ambassadors in June 1953, and Moscow sent Vasilii Valkov to Belgrade in July, Belgrade waited until September to appoint Dobrivoje Vidić to Moscow.

The Yugoslav representation in Moscow reported that each month between April and August 'Soviet publications wrote less criticism of Yugoslavia than in the previous month.'[97] As the Finnish counterparts had predicted, by November 1953 'meetings with Soviet officials [had become] friendly and in fact [the Soviets] were more than warm, in many meetings they are acting as if there never was anything' to a Yugoslav-Soviet split.[98]

Despite the ideological reinforcement and security benefits to Yugoslavia of a possible rapprochement with the Soviet Union, the Yugoslav Foreign Ministry was not able to carry through a full-scale rapprochement while Tito and Kardelj continued to deem it better to wait and see the nature of changes in Moscow before taking further steps.

The Limited Revival of Soviet Relations with Yugoslavia 1953–55

To the Finns, this Yugoslav approach was not optimal. The Finnish Foreign Ministry anticipated a relatively rapid Yugoslav agreement with the Soviets. Finnish predictions failed to account for considerable Yugoslav resistance to the Kremlin's overtures. Tito, hailed as victorious in this conflict by Yugoslavs, remained leader even when Stalin had died. Molotov's position was weakened by late 1953, but he was still present as Foreign Minister. The Paasikivi-Kekkonen Line was based entirely upon the assumption that maintenance of proper foreign relations with the Soviet Union was the best mechanism by which to maintain domestic political independence while avoiding military conflict and economic or diplomatic confrontation. The Finns expected the Yugoslav leadership to arrive at a similar conclusion. The delay caused analysts in Helsinki to question their initial hypothesis of Soviet relaxation following Stalin's death. Explaining their position to the Finns, the Yugoslav Foreign Ministry cited the continuing series of border incidents noted in Tito's speeches in 1953.[99] In November, Bulgarian forces were still occasionally firing across the Macedonian border, acts that were 'not in the spirit of normalization.'[100] Finnish representatives commented on Yugoslav reluctance several times during regular exchanges in the course of 1953. For the Finns, the Yugoslav approach of making the Kremlin demonstrate that rapprochement was *their* initiative did not serve a useful purpose. The Finnish Foreign Ministry relayed to the Yugoslavs that they should remember that 'the pride of large countries does not allow them to say "Pardon, please" and that the Yugoslavs should accept the Soviet response' without further ado.[101] The Finnish Foreign Ministry hoped that the Yugoslavs would alter their attitude to rapprochement because only the re-establishment of viable Soviet-Yugoslav diplomatic relations could lead to Yugoslavia's adoption of a neutralism policy that would be mutually supportive to Finland. Employment in Belgrade of a similar strategy to that practiced by Helsinki could only further Finland's goal of managing the course of its relations with the Soviet Union.

For the Soviet leadership, rapprochement with the Yugoslavs was problematic as well. Molotov had been one of the key architects of Yugoslavia's expulsion from the Cominform and Tito's isolation from the

Soviet camp that had not however, produced the desired outcome of the replacement of the Tito-leadership. Since the Tito-Stalin split the Soviet leadership had followed the Anglo-American exchanges with Yugoslavia and the establishment of Yugoslavia's relations with other Western countries. Khrushchev came to count these ties as a mistake resulting from Stalin's and Molotov's foreign policy. By 1953, Tito's leadership had not only survived but proceeded to form the Balkan Pact. According to Zinjanin, Chief of the Balkan Division in the Soviet Foreign Ministry in 1953, the agreement was a military pact against the USSR 'making normalization of relations especially difficult.'[102] Moreover, Soviet overtures also through the Foreign Ministry's Balkan desk towards re-establishing relations with the Yugoslavs, emphasizing the difficult nature of the Balkan Pact for the Soviets, did not receive a favorable response in Belgrade. The Yugoslav Foreign Ministry, with the Pact's chief architect Popović as its head, insisted on preserving the agreement. At the instructions of the Yugoslav Ministry for Foreign Affairs, Yugoslav representatives defied Soviet requests by raising their alternate option of becoming a member of NATO. The Yugoslavs reiterated that 'against all opposite expectations from many sides [Yugoslavia] has not become a member of NATO,' telling the Soviet leadership in their characteristically confident manner to accept the Balkan Pact as the lesser of two evils.[103]

The tone of most of the Yugoslav officials' responses to Soviet overtures was sarcastic, hostile and suspicious throughout 1953–55. High Yugoslav officials loyal to Tito like Mićunović, refused in 1953 to speak Russian with the newly arrived Soviet ambassador. He mockingly said that he could not speak Russian anymore because of the lack of practice since the Tito-Stalin split, though 'before 1948 [he] often had the opportunity to speak with the Russian representatives.'[104] Undeterred, Mićunović responded to Soviet Ambassador Valjkov's friendly comments (regarding Georgii Malenkov's July initiative to normalize relations with the Yugoslavs), saying the Soviets should know that:

> The maintenance of peace has been the thesis of [Yugoslavia] before 1948, in the last 5 years, and today. With regards to the initiative of Malenkov, we are aware that Malenkov gave the [normalization of relations] initiative, but, also similarly it is true that I do not know who, Mr. Malenkov or one of his predecessors, also took the initiative of 1948 in the infamous politics of the USSR towards Yugoslavia. Regarding that we find it completely natural that also now initiative can only come from your side.[105]

Soviet officials sometimes replied with similar sarcasm and hostility. In the later months of 1953, they often needled the Yugoslavs by evoking their problems with Milovan Djilas. They cited Djilas' publication of views dissenting from those of the Yugoslav party as an embarrassment to the Yugoslav party. In October 1953, Djilas published a pamphlet in which he criticized Stalinist bureaucracy in the Soviet party and said that could be also applied to the LCY.[106] In the party daily *Borba* in November 1953, Djilas stated that in a real democracy there should be no monopoly on ideology of the sort which the LCY in Yugoslavia maintained. The Soviets thereby questioned Tito's ability to control his own party. More generally, the Soviet officials also presented Djilas' critique of the Communist system as hindering the normalization of relations.

The Yugoslav-Soviet dialogue, in its frank and, sometimes, hostile confrontations, differed from Yugoslav communications with Finland and other non-Communist states. The Yugoslavs directly related their European foreign policy to that of the Finnish Social Democrats, as the Finnish Communists had adopted the role of 'Cominformists.' Yugoslav-Soviet communications in 1953 always involved comparisons of their one-party state systems' respective levels of success. With Finland and Western states such comparisons were never made.

The Yugoslav relationship with the Soviet bloc also changed as a consequence of Stalin's death. Anti-Yugoslav propaganda had been heavily distributed through the satellite states. As Moscow now curbed all its anti-Yugoslav propaganda, East European states began overall to improve their relations with Belgrade during the normalization of Yugoslav-Soviet relations. In December 1953, the Yugoslavs exchanged views on the Trieste question with Czechoslovak representatives in Moscow.[107] On Soviet orders, the Yugoslavs began to receive invitations to the diplomatic events in Soviet bloc states abroad and in Belgrade. In December 1953 Yugoslav representatives were invited to the 'Polish Day of the Army' celebration and the Romanian opera *Momcil*, although they chose not to attend the latter. They did, however, attend the football match of Moscow Spartak and Warsaw Doza at the invitation of a Hungarian representative; an event considered more interesting.[108] Overall, the Yugoslav Foreign Ministry took less interest in Eastern European states after 1954. For the growing international Yugoslav diplomatic corps, destinations like Bucharest, Prague, Sofia and Warsaw were considered the least prestigious and desirable destinations, where low-ranking officers or those facing demotion might be sent. Paris and Washington were preferred.

Forming Finnish and Yugoslav Neutralism along the Soviet-European Border

Yugoslavia and Finland scored diplomatic success in being able to extract concessions from the Soviet Union in the early Cold War. The events of 1953 point to the strength that neutralism offered them. Finland was able to better its trade terms with the Soviet Union in 1953. Between 1953 and 1955 Yugoslavia, according to the Finnish model, was able to establish diplomatic relations with the Soviet Union, while maintaining its independent position despite being a competitor amongst Communist states. Most importantly, in 1953, Yugoslavia and Finland were able to establish a mutual dialogue vis-à-vis their relations with the Soviet Union. In December 1953 from Helsinki Zore informed Belgrade that in the period following Stalin's death:

> It should be emphasized that we succeeded in good measure in creating individual trust towards us from the side of the reliable [Finnish] governmental officials and political figures who in general can be characterised by aloofness and caution in making any remarks on delicate international questions. However, [to us] they gave some definite evaluations. By developing friendly activity we succeeded in producing intimate and informal relations in good measure in that competent persons conversed with us with exceptional freedom, directly and with noticeable amount of trust.[109]

The identification of similar geopolitical positions in reference to the Soviet Union strengthened the analyses and positions of both the Finnish and the Yugoslav Foreign Ministries. It had long been assumed that as the leader of a single party emerging victoriously from the Second World War, Tito as President was also primarily responsible for the direction of Yugoslav foreign policy in the 1950s. Here in this chapter, instead, we see the Yugoslav Foreign Ministry beginning to step forward to produce its own independent analysis, and then to consider a policy of neutralism based on that analysis. Tito continued to serve as a decision-maker in Yugoslav foreign policy when he chose to intervene, but after the conclusion of 1953 he no longer took sole charge of its direction. His closest collaborator Kardelj had moved on to tackle domestic questions relating to the republic-based form of Communism now pursued in Yugoslavia. Both Yugoslav and Finnish ministries were equally interested in trade relations with Western states: both wished to remain independent of Soviet influence. The example of Finnish-Soviet relations after the establishment of the Paasikivi-Kekkonen Line in 1948 demonstrated to the Yugoslavs that this could best be achieved through formulaic diplomatic relations which made use of analysis of Soviet politics. When situations such as the death of Stalin presented themselves in Soviet politics, Finland could through its bilateral relations seek gains. Although on the one hand Yugoslavia and Finland would face a high likelihood of Soviet invasion upon trying to join NATO, their position on the border could at times of foreign policy relaxation contain crucial strength. In the end, the Kremlin was both unwilling and unable to give up East Berlin or their military positions within Eastern Europe. Strategic thinking on Soviet defence as bound to Eastern Europe would not allow any military concessions. For Finland and Yugoslavia the post-Stalin Soviet Union seemed increasingly inclined to equate satisfactory diplomatic relations with sufficient military security. However, for the Yugoslav Foreign Ministry's commitment to Finnish neutralism to prevail, it would take Khrushchev's visit to Belgrade in 1955 to bring Tito along. Chapter 5 considers that final turn, along with evidence from the Hungarian Revolution of 1956 that neither Yugoslav nor Finland were prepared to promote their neutral separation from the Soviet Union as a model for regimes within the Soviet bloc.

5

KHRUSHCHEV, TITO AND YUGOSLAV/FINNISH NEUTRALISM: SURVIVING HUNGARY 1956

On 23 October 1956, Hungarian protestors staged large-scale demonstrations in Budapest to support the new reformist leadership in the Polish Communist Party. By that evening a growing crowd was pulling down a statue of Stalin and demanding the return of reformist Communist Imre Nagy to power. The following day, a shaken Politburo appointed Nagy Prime Minister after making him a Politburo member. That same evening Soviet tanks entered the streets of Budapest in an attempt to crush the demonstrations. Locally garrisoned Soviet tanks were met with defiance by the Hungarian crowds who fought them to a standstill until Soviet troops were withdrawn by Moscow on 28 October. Thus began a series of events that would challenge the post-Stalin balance of Yugoslav and Finnish relations with the USSR.

On 30 October, Nagy announced the discontinuation of the one-party system. The Soviet Union now sent additional troops into Eastern Hungary and Nagy responded by declaring Hungary's neutrality, threatening Hungarian withdrawal from the Warsaw Pact and requesting help from the United Nations in resolving the crisis in Hungary.[1] On 4 November, the reinforced Soviet troops remobilized against the demonstrators in Budapest and in other Hungarian cities and suppressed the demonstrations in a bloody conflict that lasted over a week. The Yugoslav Embassy in Budapest offered Nagy and more than a dozen officials asylum, which they accepted. This offer, according to Charles Gati's newly documented account, was 'made in collusion with the top Soviet leadership, [and] was intended to trap and neutralize Nagy's government.'[2] The Soviets simply installed a new, pro-Soviet government under János Kádár and Ferenc Münnich. During the conflict, 2,500 Hungarians died and over 19,000 were wounded.[3] Soviet losses were 720 dead and over 1,500 wounded. 182,000 Hungarians fled the country.[4] In the aftermath of the crisis, more than 100,000 were arrested and nearly 26,000 sentenced to prison.[5]

The events of 1956 in Hungary came to dominate Eastern Europe's self-perception of its political relationship with the Soviet Union for the next three decades. Soviet documents suggest that Nikita Khrushchev would have tolerated the Hungarian uprising had Nagy confined its demands to additional autonomy to reform the Communist party, as Władysław Gomułka had done in Poland.[6] In the long run, the Soviet crushing of the emerging Hungarian revolution demonstrated to Eastern Europe itself that neutrality might be possible on the borders of the Soviet bloc but not inside it, as the Soviet military withdrew from Austria after 1955. Tito could keep his own road to socialism after rapprochement with the Soviets that same year. Finland could pursue neutralism. But the Soviet-installed leadership of the Warsaw Pact nations could not seek independence from Moscow. Through images widely disseminated on television screens and in newspapers everywhere, the events demonstrated that reform Communism independent from the Kremlin's control would remain impermissible for the foreseeable future. In the short term, the Soviet suppression of the Hungarian revolution also triggered serious concern within the states bordering the Soviet bloc, primarily in Finland and Yugoslavia. The Yugoslav Foreign Ministry noted with particular interest Finland's strong reaction to the Soviet invasion. Yugoslav Ambassador to Finland Slobodan Sardelić reported from Helsinki on 13 December 1956:

> All political parties with the exception of the Finnish Communist Party have made great efforts to collect aid for Hungarian refugees through schools, across large sections of the public and the working class organizations…the donation of aid was not the only demonstration of sympathy—meetings, lectures and parliamentary assemblies were put to the same purpose…within the highest leadership circles a similar feeling and same emotional reaction of can be observed…several reasons to 'justify' this type of a reaction can be heard in Helsinki, for example, similar ethnic origin, respect for traditional Hungarian liberalism, the right of the people to revolution, etc…Also, before the second intervention of Soviet troops on 2 November, [President] Kekkonen talked to me with an embittered tone only about the presence of those [Soviet] troops and saw nothing positive in their presence in Hungary thus far.[7]

Since Sardelić and the Yugoslav Foreign Ministry expected that the Finnish position would be concerned mainly with the country's own security and any role the Soviet troops might play on Finnish soil in the future, they were taken aback by the openly critical Finnish reaction. The Yugoslav Foreign Ministry was surprised that at private discussions Urho Kekkonen, now President, was critical of the Kremlin since he had carefully constructed a conciliatory attitude towards the Soviets, as Foreign Minister in 1953 and as co-founder of post-war Finnish neutrality.

For Tito and Kardelj, their reaction to the events in Hungary was personal. In 1953, Imre Nagy, had become the Prime Minister of Hungary, heading the new collective leadership that favored relaxed controls in the spirit of post-Stalinism. It is true that Nagy had cooperated with the Soviet secret police in Moscow in the 1930s, and it was the Soviet Politburo that had both approved his appointment as Prime Minister in 1953 and dismissal from the post in 1955. Nagy nonetheless was a reformist. Tito and Kardelj favored Nagy for his reported interest in Yugoslav-type workers' councils. Nagy was personally well disposed towards Yugoslavia. After his ousting in 1955, Nagy had sent copies of his plans for reform Communism to Tito through a personal contact at the Yugoslav Embassy in Budapest.[8]

In February 1956, Khrushchev's secret speech at the twentieth Party Congress of the Soviet Communist party announced the start of official de-Stalinization.[9] By the spring and summer of 1956, intellectuals, students and industrial workers began to form groups demanding change. In June 1956, Nagy's successor Mátyás Rákosi was dismissed by the Soviet leadership in part at Yugoslav urging during Tito's first state visit to the Soviet Union since the Tito-Stalin split.[10] Tito and Kardelj resented both Rákosi and his immediate successor Erno Gerö for their virulent attacks on Yugoslavia during the Tito-Stalin split and afterwards as part of a Soviet anti-Yugoslav campaign from 1948 to 1953.[11] Tito and Kardelj had been disappointed to see Nagy ousted in 1955. Even in the political context of Yugoslav-Soviet rapprochement, Kardelj and Tito made public speeches calling Rákosi and Gerö Stalinists while emphasizing their anti-Yugoslav views.[12]

The Hungarian events also increased public awareness of the proximity of Soviet troops to Finland, the ubiquitous Cold War dynamic, and the Soviet control over Warsaw Pact states and their citizens. The memory of Hungary 1956 would not quickly fade in Helsinki. In the press, photographs of the Hungarian uprising and the Soviet invasion showed bodies hanging from trees and Soviet tanks firing into buildings, emphasizing for the Finnish public the individual's helpless position against the state at their own doorstep.[13]

The Hungarian uprising and its Soviet suppression are well recorded in the literature of the Cold War. Little attention, however, has been paid to Finland and Yugoslavia, two states whose growing connections as independent but neutral while bordering the Soviet bloc were challenged by the Soviet intervention in Hungary. Their initial reactions were contradictory. Despite the December condemnation passed on privately to the Yugoslavs, Kekkonen and his Agrarians' Party worked to curtail public Finnish condemnation of Soviet military measures in Hungary. Foreign Minister Ralf Törngren evaded the actual issue of Soviet intervention in Hungary by speaking mainly of the goals of Finnish neutralism in terms of ending of superpower conflict in Europe, refraining from direct statements on the events in Hungary.[14] In his speech in London at the end of November he stated that:

> As a member of the UN, Finland purposefully sought further to remain out of conflicts of the great powers. Her efforts are known and acknowledged. Her intentions are to carry out independent and neutral politics. In view of Hungary, Finland consistently supports measures which can facilitate the improvement of the tragic state of things. Naturally we cannot reconcile with resolutions which would only intensify conflict between great powers, and would not contribute to a peaceful solution of the Hungarian question. I believe that when the positions which we took are considered as a whole, it will be seen that they are in most part in agreement with [Finland's] foreign policy orientation which is accepted from us by all.[15]

After initial sympathy and support for Nagy, Tito even sanctioned Soviet military action in Hungary after Khrushchev visited him on 2 November. This was two days after the Soviet Politburo had decided to crush the Hungarian revolution, and two days before they did it on 4 November.[16]

Subsequent Finnish and Yugoslav policy returned to the common ground of assertive neutralism. Their analysis of each other's reactions to the Hungarian events restored their common ground in the post-1956 period. Each had by 1956 bargained for its status through hard negotiations, which involved guaranteeing the Soviet Union's security along its bloc borders, and through trade relations with the Soviet Union. In the aftermath of the Soviet invasion of Hungary, both states feared a possible retreat from Khrushchev's foreign policy of accepting Finnish and Yugoslav independence on its own terms. When the Soviet Union did not, after all, retreat from its accommodation after the Hungarian uprising, both states continued to pursue unaltered security guarantees and economic exchange with the Soviet Union.

This chapter will move from an analysis of Khrushchev's post-Stalinist foreign policy as it applied to Finland and Yugoslavia to the Yugoslav Foreign Ministry's analysis of Finland's Soviet policy in 1955 and 1956. Prior to 1956, Finnish analysis of the Yugoslav-Soviet rapprochement concentrated on trade relations. As we shall see, however, the Ministry discovered that Tito, Kardelj and the Yugoslav party had a different, ideological role to play in rapprochement from that of the Yugoslav Ministry. The Ministry sought formal, not extensive relations with Moscow similar to Finnish-Soviet relations. How that approval survived Tito's ideological support for and subsequent opposition to the Hungarian uprising concludes this chapter and introduces the next one.

Neutralism and Soviet Foreign Policy in 1955–56

Soviet foreign policy after the death of Stalin and the consequent rise of Khrushchev as the Soviet leader did not anticipate a Hungarian intervention. Domestically, Khrushchev was initially interested in introducing more flexibility into the Soviet system. He sought to relax trade regulations within the bloc in order to diversify the Soviet economy.[17] Political detentions were curtailed, and some social space freed up.[18] Khrushchev's main foreign policy goal in Europe was to consolidate the Soviet bloc. To that end, Khrushchev was also willing to explore a wider set of regional relations along the bloc's border. Khrushchev's Kremlin was engaging in political negotiations in the north with the Scandinavian countries and in the south with Yugoslavia.[19] True, the Warsaw Pact was formally concluded with the bloc members in May 1955. But overall, the goal of the Pact and this wider regional policy was to strengthen European security for the Soviet Union.

Khrushchev launched his new regional policy by publicly admitting in June 1955, even before his Secret Speech in February 1956, that the expulsion of Yugoslavia from the Cominform was a mistake resulting from the excesses of Stalinism. To underscore this new direction, Khrushchev traveled to Belgrade in 1955. Hardliners within the Soviet foreign policy establishment such as Molotov were incensed. Given the preponderance of Soviet military power, Tito should have traveled to Moscow. During his visit to Yugoslavia, Khrushchev publicly lamented the mistakes resulting from the split. He expressed his regrets broadly on behalf of 'the Presidium of the Supreme Soviet of the USSR, of the government of the Soviet Union and of the CC of the CPSU, on behalf of the Soviet people.'[20] Upon his arrival at the Belgrade airport, Khrushchev stated that the heroic, anti-Fascist wartime collaboration and friendship between the Soviet Union and new Yugoslavia had been 'disturbed in the years that followed,' finally apologizing unequivocally: 'We sincerely regret that, and resolutely sweep aside all the bitterness of that period.'[21] Tito and Kardelj had in fact demanded that Khrushchev apologize, and that he do that upon his arrival at Belgrade airport. Khrushchev, however, was willing to accept even this stipulation in order to establish his new policy.

In the Belgrade meetings, Khrushchev did most of the talking. Tito guided the conversation by making short comments such as 'at first, we will discuss international affairs and, then secondly our bilateral relations. I give the floor to Comrade Khrushchev.'[22] After his apology, Khrushchev instead engaged several issues of the past by referring to people and events while circumventing any direct statements:

> How should I say it, Russian Communists, and the Communists of the USSR wish at the moment to be blocked away from [Beria] and Abakumov [who were responsible for Yugoslavia's expulsion from the Cominform], but where were you? Yes, we are comrades; we were there where you knew we were. Comrade Kardelj [pointing to Kardelj], when you were in the USSR in 1937. Oh, that is not protocol. From then onwards we lost much and many good people. And then what happened?...we are some of those people, and in that majority who returned and again recently returned to the party. And therefore, after the death of Stalin, when that activity [of Beria] was developed, recently, those people returned to the party.[23]

Khrushchev first placed over all blame on Beria for executing the anti-Yugoslav campaign of the past, and then reminded Tito that they had fought on the same side in the Second World War. Khrushchev went on to separate himself from the party of the past, which had had the conflict with Yugoslavia. He also suggested that only now had he, and Tito, returned to the respective correct policies. Khrushchev seems to have not understood the fact that Kardelj's pre-1945 cooperation with Soviet Communists was no longer a merit in Yugoslavia after the commencement of the Soviet anti-Yugoslav campaign.

At the time of Khrushchev's visit, Tito and Kardelj, under prodding from Koča Popović and his Foreign Ministry, were willing to re-establish economic trade relations and some limited cultural cooperation between the two states. Close to two years had passed since Belgrade and Moscow had exchanged ambassadors in September 1953 as we saw in Chapter 3. The Foreign Ministry needed formal relations if it was to pursue a policy of neutralism. Creating relations globally outside of the Soviet bloc was underway, but for neutralism to work as a policy, relations with the Soviet Union needed to be stable and established. Tito and Kardelj were focusing on the visit as primarily an occasion for a Soviet apology to the Yugoslav

Party leadership. They were not yet willing to renew relations between the Yugoslav and Soviet Communist parties. Khrushchev's visit did however result in the signing of an agreement between the Yugoslav and Soviet states.

This Belgrade Agreement, signed in June 1955, asserted on Tito's terms the that bilateral cooperation between Yugoslavia and the Soviet Union could only proceed upon the establishment of 'mutual respect and non-interference for any reason in internal affairs—whether of an economic, political or ideological nature—since questions of the internal structure, differences of social systems and differences of concrete forms in developing socialism exclusively were to be a matter for the peoples of the different countries.'[24] By April 1956, Khrushchev further agreed to disband the Cominform, the institution from which Yugoslavia's formal expulsion in 1948 had marked the start of the Soviet campaign to further Soviet military threats to Yugoslavia's borders as staged from Bulgaria and Hungary between 1948 and 1953. These runs at the Yugoslav border were also disavowed.

After Khrushchev's visit to Belgrade, which was interpreted as a sufficient Soviet apology, Tito promised to visit the Soviet Union to renew ties between the two Communist parties. This he did in June 1956. The Moscow visit resulted in the signing of two declarations: one between Prime Ministers Tito and Nikolai Bulganin and a declaration between the Party Secretaries Tito and Khrushchev. Reaffirming Yugoslavia's independent position as agreed in the previous year, the governmental document declared that 'the principles of the Belgrade Declaration signed 2 June 1955 will be applied to the official policies of Yugoslavia and the Soviet Union.'[25] However, it also stated that 'because there have been formed two sovereign states over the German territories, negotiations between these two states are necessary for finding a solution to the German question. Both signatory states insisted, that other states and especially the Great Powers adopt this position.'[26] The document balanced Yugoslav independence from the Soviet bloc with the obligation to support the Soviet Union on key questions such as the division of Germany and support for Communist China.[27] The second document correctly identified as 'the Moscow declaration' re-established ties between the two parties. As an additional concession to Tito, the former Foreign Minister and major adversary Molotov who had in 1948 worked with Stalin to expel Yugoslavia from the Cominform was even made to resign from his post as Soviet Foreign Minister during Tito's state visit.[28]

Finnish analysts of the Yugoslav-Soviet rapprochement were particularly impressed both with the length of Tito's 1956 visit to Moscow, from 1 to 23 June, as well as with the high level of attention he received from the

Soviet hosts. Tito visited Leningrad in the north and the Black Sea in the south during the stay. Ambassador Eero Wuori reported to Helsinki that 'out of the state visits I have had the opportunity to follow here [in Moscow] Josef Broz Tito's was—perhaps with the exception of Nehru's visit last year—staged with the most elaborate trappings.'[29] The Finnish reporting of the visit underlined the general enthusiasm of the Soviet public in receiving Tito. His wartime reputation as an anti-Fascist leader seemed to have survived the Soviet propaganda attacks in the aftermath of 1948. Public enthusiasm, even if in part the result of official Soviet efforts to require participation in Tito's reception in Moscow, illustrates Khrushchev's strong desire to renew relations between the governments and two parties in order to pursue his new foreign policy.[30]

In a grandiloquent manner, the Soviet leadership held a large public peoples' ceremony in honor of Tito in Moscow's Dynamo football stadium. Khrushchev assured the crowd that 'already last year, when we were in Yugoslavia we had a friendly and open exchange of opinions. The spirit of the conversations is even more open and friendly now [than] when Comrade Tito and his friends are in the Soviet Union.'[31] The international diplomatic corps in Moscow speculated that the rather unfriendly Soviet-Yugoslav relations which had in fact continued to prevail behind closed doors during the previous year's Belgrade visit of Khrushchev and Nikolai Bulganin had now improved.[32] It is more likely that by elaborately staging Tito's visit, Khrushchev wished to do more than show the outside world that the Soviet-Yugoslav rift was over. He wanted to match Tito's and Kardelj's dramatic demand that Khrushchev apologize upon his arrival at Belgrade airport without proceeding further. Khrushchev brought Tito before a Soviet crowd at the Dynamo stadium considerably larger than any stadium in Belgrade could accommodate.

Khrushchev made several key changes in Finnish-Soviet relations in 1955, which paralleled the 1955–56 shift in Soviet-Yugoslav relations. Following Khrushchev's June visit to Yugoslavia, President Juho Kusti Paasikivi and Prime Minister Urho Kekkonen visited Moscow together in September 1955. Although the Kremlin insisted on the extension of the Finnish-Soviet Agreement on Friendship, Cooperation and Mutual Assistance for an additional 20 years, Finland received the Porkkala Naval Base back from the Soviet Union 37 years ahead of the lease's scheduled end. Both Paasikivi and Kekkonen considered this a major achievement for Finland as they believed that Soviet access to the Finnish naval base had violated Finnish sovereignty. In the opinion of its founders, the Paasikivi-Kekkonen Line had already restored Finnish state sovereignty by 1955. Moreover, Khrushchev lifted the Soviet objection to Finland's membership in the Nordic Council, stating that 'the admission of Finland to the Nordic

Council is the internal affair of Finland in which [the Soviet Union] does not interfere.'[33] From the inception of Finnish neutralism, Paasikivi had envisioned a focus on bilateral trade with other Scandinavian countries and welcomed the parliamentary cooperation that the Nordic Council was formed in 1952 to promote. Finland was admitted in November 1955 and became a member of the United Nations in December 1955.

Khrushchev's new foreign policy also allowed Finland and Sweden to engage in promoting the Scandinavian regionalism as already endorsed by Norway, Denmark and Iceland. Khrushchev's acceptance of Scandinavian regionalism in the north established the Nordic countries as gateway partners by which goods available in the West could be obtained for the Soviet Union without significant political compromise. This harmonized with the Paaskivi-Kekkonen Line, which wanted to avoid Communist intimidation in Finland, but seek trade with the Soviet Union as well as with other Nordic countries. What did the Soviet Union have to gain? If the Nordic states could be considered a group promoting neutralism of some kind, Soviet-Danish and Soviet-Norwegian trade would be viewed as trade between the USSR and two Nordic states rather than with two NATO states.

As the Yugoslav Foreign Ministry noted about Finland, 'the characteristics of Soviet politics towards Scandinavian countries until Stalin's death were underlined by pressure and intimidation, calculated to separate these countries from the West and leave them to Soviet dominance.'[34] Stalin opposed the mutual association of the Scandinavian countries, 'characterizing the Nordic Council as an intimate part of NATO,' and pressured Finland to abstain from joining.[35] After Stalin's death, Khrushchev instituted a series of new efforts in 1955 to improve relations with the Scandinavian countries as a whole. He sought to reestablish friendly political and trade relations, calculating that these would weaken Western political influence in Scandinavia. Regarding Khrushchev's intentions, the Yugoslav Foreign Ministry concluded that 'the independence of these countries from the influence of the West and the independence of their politics in relations with the West' would serve Soviet foreign policy best, since subjugation to Soviet control was unattainable.[36] By 1955, the Yugoslav Foreign Ministry had been largely independent of Tito's and Kardelj's LCY Politburo for two years. The leadership of Koča Popović, was thus able to pursue increased Yugoslav bilateral trade and other contacts with states outside the Soviet bloc. If Finland was allowed to trade freely and associate with other Nordic countries, Yugoslavia might also use normalization of relations with the Soviet Union to advance its contacts with West European states. Khrushchev had encouraged the strengthening of the Nordic Council, calculating that the organization could 'help its

Scandinavian countries to carry out independent politics in relations of the West.'³⁷

The new Soviet policy saw the non-threatening aspects to Scandinavian membership in NATO as an asset, whereas Stalin's foreign policy had only perceived such a threat. Norway and Denmark had since 1953 refused to accept NATO military bases on their territory, and all Scandinavian countries had since reduced military budgets despite NATO requests for their expansion; public opinion in Denmark and Norway generally rejected military engagement.³⁸

Just as he had apologized for Stalin's offenses to Yugoslavia, Khrushchev began to institute his new regional Scandinavian policy with similar expressions of regret. During the visit of the Prime Minister of Norway Einar Gerhardsen to Moscow in November 1955, Khrushchev declared that 'the Soviet politics had made many mistakes towards Norway and that the USSR is also responsible for the circumstances that could naturally lead Norway into NATO.'³⁹ Gerhardsen, a member of the Labor Party of Norway, had been a socialist in the inter-war period and took part in the gradual conversion of the Norwegian labor movement into a Social Democratic party. By 1956, all Scandinavian governments except Iceland's were led by Social Democratic prime ministers.⁴⁰ Khrushchev was especially interested in seeking cooperation with such parties. They focused on the creation of a welfare state. These parties also opposed the expansion of NATO from Denmark and Norway to Sweden and favored more Nordic integration.⁴¹ Khrushchev proceeded to establish trade relations with each of the Scandinavian countries, visiting Norway, Denmark and Iceland personally in August 1956 (in between Tito's visit to Moscow in June and the Hungarian uprising in November) seeking to expand trade through Scandinavia with Western Europe in order to help the Soviet economy.

Despite Finnish requests to be included on his itinerary, Khrushchev opted not to visit Helsinki. This decision indicated that his foreign policy did not yet envision parity between Finland and the other Scandinavian countries. But acquiring equivalence with the other Nordic countries was Finland's next foreign policy goal in 1955, after stability in Soviet relations had been followed by Soviet troops leaving Porkkala. Since Finland could not join NATO, Nordic regionalism offered the best option to build a strong relationship with Western Europe. While Khrushchev sought to promote Nordic regionalism as a tool to divide Scandinavia from Western Europe, the Finnish leadership of Paasikivi and Kekkonen saw it as an opportunity to extend ties with the West. As Yugoslav analysis of Finland in 1956 noted, 'The Finns are interested in [Khrushchev's] visit because it would be in the framework with the other Scandinavian countries; Finland would not be treated as separate.'[42]

Khrushchev's Scandinavian regionalism in fact reflected the favorable experiences of the Soviet-Finnish relations 1948–55. Because Finland and the Soviet Union shared a long border, the Soviet interest in connecting Finnish neutralism more tightly to Moscow persisted, even under Khrushchev's new more flexible regionalism. The Paasikivi-Kekkonen Line still guaranteed the security of the border for Finland. While the Finnish Social Democratic Party (SDP) was still the more desirable political partner for the Yugoslavs, the conservative Agrarians' Party with Kekkonen at the helm was the most important connection for the Soviets in dealing with Finland, even under Khrushchev. Kekkonen could be trusted by the Kremlin to maintain the Kekkonen-Paasikivi Line even when less Soviet pressure was applied in 1955's atmosphere of rapprochement.

Khrushchev's policy of improving relations with Western Europe faced a variety of criticisms. The Western governments were suspicious of his underlying intentions toward Scandinavia and Yugoslavia. Khrushchev's political flexibility was also criticized by the hardliners in the Kremlin and the East European party leaderships that had been installed during Stalin's time. These groups feared that they would lose their positions. As early as 1955, the new Soviet leader's criticism of Stalin extending from the cult of personality into his foreign policy was rejected at first by Khrushchev's former supporters in the Presidium Vyacheslav Molotov, Lazar Kaganovich, and Kliment Voroshilov. They considered that 'to investigate Stalin's activities would mean revising the results of the entire great path of the CPSU!'[43] They asked Khrushchev in exasperation: 'Who would benefit from it? What purpose would it serve? Why stir up the past?' One view suggested that rapprochement with Yugoslavia could be interpreted as a relaxation in the role of Soviet troops in holding the Warsaw Pact together.[44] Hardliners could also link Khrushchev's vulgar and unpredictable, on at least one occasion drunken, behavior during the Belgrade visit of 1955 with the notion that Khrushchev had mistakenly given too much away to Tito.

The importance to Soviet security of Khrushchev's reformulation of relations with Yugoslavia became clearer however, during the sequence of Hungarian events. Tito's reciprocal visit to the Soviet Union in June 1956 had completed initial Yugoslav support for the new policy with the re-establishment of relations between their two Communist parties. In order to counter Tito's initial support for Nagy, Khrushchev visited Tito on his island resort of Brioni on 2 November 1956. There, Khrushchev managed to secure Tito's tacit support for the decisive Soviet military intervention in

Hungary. Yugoslav Ambassador to Moscow Veljko Mićunović recorded the conversation between the two leaders:

> We explained that we the Yugoslavs were also concerned at the swing of events to the right, towards counterrevolution, when we saw Nagy's government allowing Communists to be murdered and hanged. There would have to be intervention if there was counterrevolution in Hungary, but it should not be based exclusively on the weapons of the Soviet Army.[45]

Foreign Minister Koča Popović did not participate in the Brioni meeting, nor is he mentioned by Vladimir Dedijer or Mićunović, who have provided the most frequently quoted accounts on the meeting.[46] Mićunović had hoped to become Foreign Minister in 1953. As noted in Chapter 3 he was part of Tito's inner circle. According to post-Communist Yugoslav scholarship, 'the position towards the events in Hungary was dictated by the Politburo, and theoretically justified by Edvard Kardelj. He called the first phase of Soviet intervention unacceptable but justified the second for preventing of a counter revolution.'[47] Khrushchev left Brioni on 3 November, and the following evening Soviet tanks attacked the Hungarian rebels in Budapest and in other smaller Hungarian cities. Tito apparently feared an anti-Communist government in a former one-party state on Yugoslavia's physical border more than a Soviet-governed Communist regime. Following the Soviet intervention, Nagy nonetheless sought refuge in the Yugoslav Embassy in Budapest. According to Kardelj's later memoirs, Nagy requested asylum and was granted it by Ambassador Dobrivoje Vidić without the authorization of the party leadership.[48] The role of Popović in the events has not been made clear in the scholarship that rarely mentions the Foreign Minister, but it appears that Vidić was a closer to him than to the party leadership. On 7 November, Khrushchev informed Mićunović that Nagy should be handed over to the Soviets.[49] On 23 November, the Yugoslav officials discharged Nagy from the Embassy under an improbable agreement with the Soviets that Hungarian authorities would return him to his home. Nagy was immediately seized by Soviet security personnel and moved to Romania. In June 1958, Soviet newspapers published the information that Nagy had been executed following a trial in Hungary.[50]

The strong Finnish public and official Western reactions to the Hungarian intervention would have been still more damaging for Soviet foreign policy without the agreements in place which Khrushchev had established in 1955 with Finland and in 1956 with Yugoslavia. Kekkonen in particular had appreciated the very early return of Porkkala to Finland, and the country was in a better position having gained membership in the Nordic Council and UN in 1955. However displeased he was with the Soviet military measures, he would not jeopardize the Paasikivi-Kekkonen Line over the events in Hungary.

While the Soviet Union benefited from Tito's sanctioning the suppression in Hungary, the Yugoslav Foreign Ministry expressed serious misgivings about the return of the party and ideology to the forefront of decision making in the matter. The active engagement of Tito and Kardelj in foreign affairs led to the renewal of rhetorical conflicts between the Soviet and Yugoslav parties. These did not serve the purpose of Yugoslav policy of neutralism. The Foreign Ministry's specific objections are the subject of the next section.

The Yugoslav Response to Khrushchev's New Foreign Policy

The reformulation of Soviet-Yugoslav relations would not have been possible without public overtures to Belgrade by Moscow. Tito and Kardelj demanded them, not only for personal vindication but also as domestic currency in consolidating the one-party but multi-national state, just celebrating its first decade in 1956. However by 1956 Yugoslav foreign policy was directed chiefly through its Foreign Ministry, with Tito asked to do the hard bargaining when needed. Kardelj was still drafting Tito's speeches when the party's ideological position was the main concern. Popović's Foreign Ministry on the other hand paid attention to how Western Europe and the United States perceived Yugoslavia to be ready for them as diplomatic partners to support Yugoslav independence.[51] The ideological contest with the Soviet Union received much less attention.

Instead, by the end of 1956, the Foreign Ministry had come to concentrate on the position of Finland in relation to that of the Warsaw Pact countries in its analysis of the Soviet Union.[52] Uninterested in pursuing direct diplomacy with Moscow, the Ministry was trying to create a space for itself outside the Soviet bloc similar to that afforded to Finland through neutralism. Re-establishment of permanent relations with the Soviet Union was needed for this goal, but here Tito, Kardelj and Popović's Ministry were all agreed on rejecting any Soviet attempt to incorporate Yugoslavia into the Soviet bloc.

Khrushchev's conciliatory position made the assumption that the Yugoslav leadership welcomed, or at least would publicly embrace rapprochement with the Soviet Union. The reconciliation contained several clear benefits to Yugoslavia. The Belgrade and Moscow Declarations were not however intended by the Yugoslavs to rebuild a close political relationship with Moscow. Instead, as the Yugoslav Foreign Ministry noted in its analysis of Tito's 1956 state visit to the Soviet Union, the two agreements 'reflect the development of our bilateral relations and worked in the sense of neutralization [of previous conflict] to establish and freeze the status of our concrete stance and our principles as stated precisely in both documents.'[53] In 1955 and 1956, the Foreign Ministry together with Tito's Presidential Office sought to ratify the status quo with the Soviets over foreign policy. The Yugoslav Foreign Ministry hoped to direct Yugoslav bilateral relations away from the Soviet sphere and toward the rest of Europe.

The Yugoslav leadership remained collectively critical and suspicious of the Kremlin and its political goals. The Foreign Ministry surveyed Soviet relations in December 1956 with problems highlighted under the heading 'some negative tendencies in bilateral relations between Yugoslavia and the USSR.'[54] The first and the most important problem was 'the ignoring of the Moscow [Declaration] documents in official statements and in Soviet propaganda immediately after their signing.'[55] The Foreign Ministry noted that 'internal and important statements of the Soviet leadership (Khrushchev in the [the Dynamo] Stadium, [Mikhail] Suslov and [Anastas] Mikoyan in Hungary, Suslov in the Congress of the Communist Party of Finland, [Nikolai] Bulganin in Poland etc…) in general did not mention the Moscow documents' at all.[56] The Yugoslav analysis concluded that 'Moscow's complete silence on the party document is also not possible to explain by its campaign-style of work.'[57] Instead, Moscow's suppression of the document and therefore recognition of the full independence of the Yugoslav party was felt to be intentional.

The Yugoslav Foreign Ministry found other signs that Moscow was not committed to upholding and establishing the Moscow Declaration on party independence. According to Yugoslav sources from Poland, 'The Central Committee of the Communist Party of the Soviet Union explained to the Central Committees of the Eastern Bloc that the Party Declaration between Tito and Khrushchev relates exclusively to relations between the Communist Party of the Soviet Union and League of Communists of Yugoslavia.'[58] This letter was meant to have been secret and confidential. More worrying still, the Yugoslav analysis found that several representatives of the old guard from the Soviet bloc countries:

> placed pressure on the Russians and expressed their own dissatisfaction with the development of Soviet-Yugoslav relations and with the manner of Comrade Tito in Moscow (remarks of Czechoslovak Ambassador I.T. Grishin that the cordiality towards Tito was exaggerated; open criticism of Josef Revaj in the plenum of the Hungarian Communist Party about 'Soviet stance towards Titoism', in Bulgaria remarks that Khrushchev is a 'traitor'…).[59]

The Yugoslav Foreign Ministry thus concluded that the Soviets would seek to restrain East European regimes from forming contacts with the West through renewed relations with Yugoslavia. They also saw that Khrushchev could try to limit Yugoslav bilateral relations with Western and other governments in the future—a possibility highly incompatible with the political goals of the Yugoslav Foreign Ministry. Moreover, the Yugoslav Ministry suspected that the Soviet leadership was wary of resistance from the old guard within the East European Communist party leaderships, as evidenced by their reaction to the endorsement of Rákosi earlier in 1956.[60] This wariness might have been another factor in the Soviets' wilfully ignoring the Moscow Declaration in particular. At the end of 1956, then, the Yugoslav Foreign Ministry concluded that Soviet politics 'give the impression that the Russians comprehend the [Moscow] Declaration as a temporary document which needs to be utilized to bring Yugoslavia closer to the bloc as quickly as possible.'[61] The re-establishment of Yugoslavia's diplomatic relations with Soviet bloc countries thus raised fears in the Foreign Ministry that this might lead to a comparably subservient relation to the Kremlin. Both the Yugoslav Foreign Ministry and Tito's Office of the President, remained suspicious of the old guard within Bulgaria, Czechoslovakia, Hungary, Poland and Romania, which had actively worked to place pressure on Yugoslavia after its expulsion from the Cominform. Whether such suspicions were real as in the case of Rákosi, or imagined, they prevented close collaboration with these states in the near future.

Looking for evidence of the Soviet intention to include Yugoslavia within the Soviet bloc, Yugoslav diplomats observed the placing of Yugoslav books in the windows of bookstores alongside materials from the Soviet bloc countries in Moscow and reported this as Soviet preparation for subjugation.[62] The Yugoslavs were even more angered by the placement of Yugoslav news in the section with articles on Eastern bloc countries in the major Soviet newspapers *Pravda* and *Izvestija* after Tito's 1956 visit.[63] The Kremlin was then reluctant to publish news from Yugoslavia after the signing of the Moscow Declaration. The Yugoslav Foreign Ministry counted this as another sign of Soviet intentions to suppress the significance of Yugoslavia and its independence. The Ministry complained that occasions underlining Yugoslavia's important role in the Balkans such as the arrival of Dag Hammerskjöld in Yugoslavia and Tito's stay in Greece were only noted briefly in the Soviet press.[64] The visit of Nasser and Nehru to Tito on Brioni was published as a note without comment on the meeting.[65] Except for the statement of Tito on the Suez conflict (which seems to be the reason the Brioni meeting was mentioned at all), Soviet publications omitted any citation from the Yugoslav press in the months following the Moscow Declaration. Moreover, the Soviets attempted to downplay the Yugoslav slogan 'independent roads to socialism' by frequently featuring the phrase 'leading the way in the class struggle' to Yugoslav displeasure.

Soviet journals reported on Yugoslavia in short pieces without analysis of internal developments. The Soviet Union did continue to publish some original materials from Yugoslavia, including pieces on legal regulations and textbooks on the economy.[66] *Izvestija* and *Pravda* did occasionally republish editorials from Yugoslav papers. This was the one aspect of the Soviet approach the Yugoslav Foreign Ministry regarded positively in that it offered 'an "objective" treatment of Yugoslavia within the Soviet press.'[67] Republished editorials enabled the Yugoslav party to communicate its views within the Soviet Union in an unaltered form. On the whole, however, the Soviet Union desk in the Yugoslav Foreign Ministry concluded that the Soviets were continuing their efforts to play down Yugoslavia's role within the Communist movement; too little was published, and what was published was placed alongside Soviet bloc material.[68]

To make matters worse from the Yugoslav perspective, the Soviets kept pressuring them to adopt the same easy and low-cost visa regime imposed on the East European states by the Soviet Union.[69] This was not beneficial for Yugoslavia, which had established its own visa regimes for Western Europe and many other regions of the world where by now over 80 of its embassies were located. According to the Soviet proposal Yugoslavia would be obliged to grant inexpensive, easily obtained visas to tourists from Soviet bloc countries. In addition, Yugoslavia would most likely lose its existing visa regimes with several Western states if it adopted the Soviet proposal.

After the Moscow Declaration, the Soviets or their East European satellites even asked the Yugoslavs to participate in intra-bloc negotiations in a few instances. For example, the Yugoslavs were invited to an August 1956 meeting of the Foreign Trade Ministers to discuss the coordination of export and import to Asia and Africa.[70] The Yugoslav Military Attaché received a Romanian invitation to follow its naval exercises and those of the bloc countries.[71] Moše Pijade, then the President of Skupština, was invited again by Romania to participate in a secret meeting of Communist countries' representatives for the Interparliamentary Union to coordinate strategies for an upcoming Bangkok conference.[72]

The Yugoslav Foreign Ministry concluded that such invitations had ulterior motives and noted that:

> Internally, the Russians do not treat us without reservation and prejudice in regard to our foreign and domestic policies, but they want to neutralize our experience and our relations with socialist countries, while publicly they wish to treat us, in the eyes of the West

and also those of other socialist countries [as inside the bloc]—in order to revive suspicion of westerners in the independence of politics of Yugoslavia.[73]

Still, the Ministry welcomed such Soviet attention: 'this tells us that at least the Russians still classify Yugoslavia as an independent socialist country in relation to the Eastern bloc.'[74] The Yugoslavs hoped that the Kremlin would continue to fear their influence on the Soviet bloc countries. This signalled the existence of continued recognition of some independence for Yugoslav foreign policy vis-à-vis the bloc, similar to what Khrushchev had granted Finland vis-à-vis the Nordic Union.

Under these circumstances, the Yugoslav Foreign Ministry advised state organs that 'it seems to us inopportune to silence our publications about the Belgrade and the Moscow Declarations in particular. Our journalism could conveniently dedicate some serious studies to them (especially within party journals), providing documents for us to call upon often as reflecting the foundation of our relations with the USSR.'[75] It is important to note that by the end of 1956 (unlike in 1948), instructions regarding Yugoslavia's Soviet policy no longer originated from Tito and Kardelj alone. Nor were they kept secret from most of the Yugoslav state organs. Instead, they were drafted by the Foreign Ministry, originating with its team of Soviet analysts. Tito and Kardelj influenced the extent to which these recommendations were carried out, but they intervened only on matters pertaining to their own persons or the Yugoslav party's profile.

The Yugoslav Ministry remained frustrated with the Kremlin in that 'many dealings which normally need to be completed between the Yugoslav Embassy [in Moscow] and the Soviet Ministry of Foreign Affairs, including invitations to events, were conducted in Belgrade instead.'[76] The Soviets tended to work around the Yugoslav Foreign Ministry and its representatives in Moscow, instead contacting directly and separately the various Yugoslav state institutions and establishing contacts on the highest levels in an effort to reduce the presumably unsympathetic Ministry's influence. Khrushchev wished to continue dealing with a few key leaders, i.e., Tito and Kardelj alone, just as in Finland he preferred to deal exclusively with Kekkonen. Between 1948 and 1953, the Kremlin had been best able to execute its agenda in Finland through the Finnish Foreign Ministry (which had agreed to curtail anti-Soviet propaganda in order to preserve the Paasikivi-Kekkonen Line). But it quickly became clear that the Yugoslav Ministry in 1956 was not interested in heeding the Kremlin's suggestions or in advancing Yugoslav-Soviet relations beyond limited diplomatic exchanges that did not include, for example, the Soviet suggested visa regime. While Stalin had wished to replace the Tito-Kardelj-

Djilas leadership in 1948, Khrushchev in 1956 wanted to keep Tito and Kardelj in charge of Yugoslav foreign policy and thus to undermine the emerging initiative of the Foreign Ministry. A well organized, ably staffed and relatively autonomous ministry would serve to further the execution of independent diplomatic ties between Yugoslavia and non-Communist states. These ties effectively weakened the Soviet ability to cordon Yugoslavia off from gaining further significance as an independent Communist state outside the Soviet bloc on Europe.

The Yugoslav Foreign Ministry and Finland, 1955–56
The Yugoslav Foreign Ministry was particularly interested in the conduct and success of the Paasikivi-Kekkonen Line in the context of Khrushchev's new foreign policy. Ministry documents analyzing Finland multiplied between 1955 and 1956. Separate studies were written on 'Karelia,' the Finnish territory taken by the Soviet Union at the end of the Second World War, and on Finnish Soviet relations in general from 1948–56.[77] These files featured analysis on topics such as 'Tendency of the Communist party of the Soviet Union for integration with the Socialist Parties of Western Europe' and 'Opinions of the twentieth Party Congress of the CC or the USSR towards Scandinavian countries.' The Yugoslav Embassy in Moscow already noted in its January 1956 report that President Paasikivi's New Year's speech 'reflected in certain manner the stronger international position of the country.'[78] The President, in addition to citing 'the development of good relations with the Soviet Union' for the successes of Finnish foreign policy in 1955, emphasized equally the Finnish commitment to Western economic practices: 'as the American practice has also proved, the successes in the fields of trade [in 1955] prevented the necessity of state intervention [in the economy] as the only means of reducing crises.'[79] The Yugoslav Foreign Ministry's 3rd. Regional Section for Europe was anxious to find out whether 'Finland's membership in the UN and the Nordic Council led to the development of intensive relations and collaboration with the West' in 1956.[80] Both memberships had become possible through Finland's approved distance from the Soviets. Such possibilities were of interest to the Yugoslavs, who were considering further rapprochement with the Soviets on just those terms in January 1956.

Yugoslav analysis of Finland found it curious but instructive that Paasikivi—a conservative member of the National Coalition Party—supported Kekkonen—the leader of the Agrarians' Party—for President very publicly on numerous occasions that year, and even in his New Year's speech.[81] By 1955, and increasingly in 1956, the Paasikivi-Kekkonen Line came under criticism from the ranks of the Social Democrats and also from Paasikivi's own NCP. Critics portrayed overtures made toward the Soviet

Union, such as the Agreement on Friendship, Assistance and Mutual Cooperation of 1948 (renewed in 1955) as conciliatory appeasement. Early in 1956 both the Social Democrats and the Conservatives began to advocate closer trade ties with the United States. The Yugoslav Embassy surmised that the SDP, seeking a new coalition with the NCP in 1956, was in a political battle with the AP. In the context of this power struggle, the SDP and the NCP challenged the Paasikivi-Kekkonen Line, the foreign policy most closely associated with Kekkonen. Yugoslav analysis of Finland appreciated 'the united stance and harmony of Paasikivi and Kekkonen in holding on to this policy tenaciously' in 1956.[82] If the Paasikivi-Kekkonen Line faltered, so would this model of neutralism for the Yugoslav Ministry, balancing correct but limited diplomatic relations with Moscow with the cultivation of ties outside the Soviet bloc.

Yet the Yugoslav Foreign Ministry also found the SDP's pro-Western coalition with Paasikivi's conservative party acceptable. Of course, the SDP 'could not become stronger and a more decisive political factor in the country without the additional growth of the working class.'[83] In addition, the SDP, despite its strong ties to the Trade Union movement, did not desire collaboration with the Finnish Communist Party and this the Yugoslav Ministry welcomed. In fact, according to 'reliable internal sources', the SDP sought to abandon some of its previous 'methods of "radical" agitation, including general strikes, for example, that could alienate [the middle] classes from the Party.'[84] According to its own internal analysis, the SDP needed to 'further strengthen its influence among the middle classes…in striving to reach its goals, SDP needs to collaborate with the more liberal wing of the National Coalition Party, which is interested in the industrialization of the country; with them it is possible to reach an agreement on a number of questions which the Agrarians will not entertain.'[85]

The Yugoslav Foreign Ministry predicted that the result of SDP and NCP collaboration would not be the much-feared increase of Soviet influence on Finnish foreign policy but that instead its 'most likely consequence would be an increase in pro-Westernism,' which would still present a domestic challenge to the Paasikivi-Kekkonen Line.[86] Curiously, for a Communist state which had just concluded rapprochement with the Soviet Union, the Yugoslav Foreign Ministry's analysis seemed to favor the SDP's approach on Western trade. The Yugoslavs projected its possible success under the influential Väinö Leskinen, who had served as Minister of the Interior in Kekkonen's fifth government, 1953–55. Leskinen had by the mid-1950s incurred the disfavor of the Soviet Union and the Finnish Communist Party. The Yugoslav analysis felt Leskinen was in the most favorable position to deliver a victory for the SDP, because 'he both fought against the Soviets [in the Second World War] and there acquired a series of friends who are today very influential politicians in the NCP.'[87] Leskinen was in fact known for his thoroughly patriotic stance during the post-war period. He had served in the famous *Ässärykmentti* (Aces-battalion), composed of draftees from Helsinki's two major settlements of industrial working-class sections, *Sörnäiset* and *Kallio*. He was one of the influential SDP members who founded the so-called *Asevelisosialistit* group (brothers-in-arms-socialists), a subdivision of the *Aseveliliitto* (union of brothers-in-arms), a union dedicated to the conservation of the memory of the Winter and Continuation Wars. This union was however banned in 1945 and condemned by the Finnish Communist Party as a Fascist organization. Leskinen's profile combined a commitment to social democracy with patriotic Finnish nationalism, most often reserved for upper class conservatives. He was also pro-Western, and this combination made him a significant political figure in the view of the Yugoslav Ministry.

The Yugoslav analysis commented critically on the opposition to Leskinen's group in the SDP. The opposition's leader Eero Antikainen, the President of the Finnish Trade Unions 'thinks that it is possible to collaborate with the Communists on certain questions (concretely on a general strike).'[88] The Trade Unions were facing 'an offensive…reducing the force and authority of the Trade Union, an offensive which is supported also by a side of the current Government, a part of the Social Democratic Party, [with which] Antikainen thinks collaboration on concrete questions [with CPF] can accomplish' some goals of the working class.[89] In 1956, Antikainen still 'argued for the nationalization of energy sources, banks and Pharmacies.'[90] The Foreign Ministry's 3rd Section specifically asked its Helsinki diplomats to investigate 'how strong the tendencies towards nationalization of branches of the economy are within the [Finnish] labor movement', whether Antikainen's above-noted goals had 'received the character of an "action program" in the practical politics of the trade unions and how much support such initiatives could find within the Social Democratic Party.'[91]

The Yugoslav ministry obviously feared any development of influence from the Finnish Communist Party. The Yugoslavs had since 1948 identified the party as entirely loyal to the Soviet Union; all party positions, were considered detrimental to Yugoslavia's ability to maintain its neutral position outside of the Soviet bloc. The Yugoslav Foreign Ministry asked its representative in Helsinki to ascertain whether the more conciliatory stance of the trade unions towards collaborating with the SDP was 'a symptom of collaboration on the level of some concrete questions' between the SDP and the KP, or whether the SDP could have fallen under Moscow's influence.[92]

The conflict and competition between the Finnish political parties heavily influenced the Finnish political response to the events in Hungary. The conservatives had not followed Paasikivi after his personal support of Kekkonen since 1948. In this context, the AP had been the political winner. Kekkonen had formed governments in 1950–53 and 1954–56 as Prime Minister to Paasikivi and was subsequently elected President, beginning his term on 1 March 1956. The events in Hungary gave the Social Democrats the much-needed opportunity to challenge the Paasikivi-Kekkonen status quo. SDP's Prime Minister Karl-August Fagerholm stated that 'Finland as a small country cannot allow for the use of force as a method for solving international questions. All aggressive measures in that view are similar and need to be condemned. Our obligation is to contribute to the ending of conflicts and the cessation of bloodshed. In all international questions the basic task we have is to place the preservation of our nation first.'[93] Not only did Fagerholm as a Social Democrat condemn the Soviet invasion in terms of the lives lost. He also commented on it on security grounds for Finland. Antikainen was even more critical, as the President of the Trade Union's he declared on Finnish radio 'that workers are coming to work on the day of a state holiday, and in that way earn overtime wages given as donation to Hungarian refugees.'[94]

Concurrent with the Soviet intervention in Hungary, Ministry cables pressed Yugoslav diplomats in Helsinki 'to extend your reports to a more complete analysis of events which characterize domestic development and foreign policy of Finland.' [95] In response, the embassy submitted a full 12-page analysis of the Finnish response to the Soviet invasion of Hungary.[96] It noted that in the aftermath of the Soviet invasions, 'President Kekkonen thought that the government needs to oppose the earlier described [aid] campaigns [for Hungarian refugees] and criticism of Soviets, despite the mood of the country and to replace the critical press coverage with a passive attitude toward the Soviet government.'[97] Moreover, Soviet Ambassador Vladimir Lebedev's visit to Fagerholm on 19 November 1956 was 'interpreted as an effective warning and pressure on the government, against its views [expressed] in the [United Nation's] General Assembly, and also in relation to the [aid] campaigns in the country which actually have an anti-Soviet character.'[98]

The Yugoslav Ministry noted that the positive effects of restored sovereignty over Porkkala in 1955, as well as UN representation for the Paasikivi-Kekkonen Line, were quickly counterbalanced in 1956 by Soviet military action in Hungary and the formation of the Conservative-Social Democratic opposition coalition. Kekkonen was elected President in 1956, but the legitimacy of the Paasikivi-Kekkonen Line was nevertheless questioned in Finland—so significant were the political consequences of the Hungarian revolution itself. In Finland, popular opinion associated images of the Soviet military action in Budapest with those of Finland in the Second World War. Soviet military intervention was perceived as abhorrent and morally wrong. Kekkonen himself had regarded Finnish passivity as a necessary compromise, only privately expressing his displeasure to the Yugoslavs. After Hungary, Kekkonen had to face a united SDP-NCP opposition that was building ties with Congressional representatives in Washington. In 1956, the Yugoslav Foreign Ministry still considered the Paasikivi-Kekkonen Line its primary Finnish political ally. But after the death of Paasikivi in 1956, the Ministry felt less comfortable with Kekkonen and considered closer cooperation with the Social Democrats, who by this time were also seeking closer Finnish trade relations with the United States.

Finnish Foreign Policy and Yugoslavia, 1955–56

Rather than focusing on political analysis of the Yugoslav League of Communists, the Finnish Foreign Ministry was paying more attention to Yugoslav-Soviet trade relations. Prior to the events in Hungary, the ministry had been observing the growing Soviet-Yugoslav trade and contrasting it with Finland's own prospects with the USSR. The Finns estimated that the Soviet-Yugoslav trade would by 1957 constitute approximately $70 million in exports and imports.[99] The contrast with earlier years was striking. While in 1955 Soviet trade had ranked 8th in Yugoslav exports and 14th in Yugoslav imports, by the first quarter of 1956 it had risen to fourth place in both. The Yugoslav-Soviet financial relationship was also changing. According to the analysis of the Finnish Foreign Ministry, in 1956 the Soviets cancelled the $90 million Yugoslav debt and granted Yugoslavia a $30 million loan in Western currencies at two per cent interest, with a further $54 million credit for part of the remaining debt. The rest was due only over a 10-year period starting in 1959. In addition, according to the Finnish data from Moscow, Yugoslavia was granted an additional $110 million credit for building three factories and mines. All of these sums are modest in the face of US authorizations of aid and credit that averaged $300 million a year from 1956 to 1959.[100] However, in the eyes of the Finnish Foreign Ministry in 1956 these sums were significant, and the reporting of the ministry emphasized them as Yugoslav gains from having reformulated diplomatic relations with the Soviets.

These figures as projected by the Finnish Foreign Ministry may well have been inflated, as their sources were Soviet projections from Moscow. Their importance, however, lies in the fact that Finnish analysis expected Yugoslavia to carry out their economic agreement, within the context of rapprochement, as Finland had done first in 1948 and secondly in 1955.

The international diplomatic corps in Moscow regarded Soviet economic assistance to Yugoslavia as significant by 1956 and expected it to continue.[101] Finnish analysis cited articles in the Soviet press, as in the May 1956 issue *Kommunist*, that emphasized that Yugoslavia's economic difficulties. The Soviet press advanced the view that rapprochement would be mutually beneficial. While Soviet foreign policy needed some agreement with Tito and Yugoslavia, the Yugoslav economy supposedly required Soviet investment in order to expand its industry and raise living standards.[102] For Khrushchev's foreign policy, such economic ties would counteract the image that the Scandinavian countries and Yugoslavia were turning towards the West for assistance instead of the Soviet Union. Trade relations with the Soviet Union that obliged the acceptance of low-quality bloc imports were part of Finland's political compromise, accepted under the Paasikivi-Kekkonen Line. Finland projected similar terms of economic rapprochement for Yugoslavia.

The Finnish trade analysis was framed in light of the Moscow Declaration. The 1956 agreement was interpreted in Finland as setting out to define the policy of 'Titoist neutralism.'[103] This policy was presumed to combine with the previous year's Belgrade Declaration of Yugoslav state independence from the Soviet bloc with a limited commitment to support the Soviet party on certain international key questions vital for international Communism. But according to the Finnish analysis, this 'Titoist neutralism' did contrast with Finland's relationship with the Soviet Union in its accommodation with Soviet party positions laid on the Yugoslav party in reference to issues such as the support of East Germany. The Finnish analysis questioned whether the compromise spelled out in the Moscow Declaration between independence of the state from and party support for the Soviet bloc could be tenable. At the same time, 'Titoist neutralism' highlighted the independence of Yugoslav foreign policy. The Yugoslav government called its policy 'active coexistence.'[104] This term was coined to distinguish Yugoslav from Finnish neutralism, and in order to portray Yugoslav political commitments towards the Soviet Union as a matter of 'active' Yugoslav responsibility. Ambassador Wuori in Moscow reported that 'according to the explanations of Tito, this does not mean passive, peaceful neighbourly relations but the further development of relations between the two states.'[105] Wuori was unaware of the sharply divergent perspectives that had come to divide the Yugoslav Foreign Ministry and Tito's Presidential office. The Ministry sought stability in Soviet relations that would allow ambitious bilateral relations with other nations. Tito, on the other hand, was uncomfortable with diplomacy which might portray passivity or fail to clearly demonstrate his own agency.

The Finnish Foreign Ministry noted that for the Kremlin only the part of the Moscow Declaration that addressed the common support of the two Communist parties for a divided Germany and Korea was really valid.[106] The Party Declaration seemed to support Khrushchev's new position announced at the twentieth Party Congress in February 1956 which proclaimed that the Soviet Communist Party would expand its relationship with Socialist parties across Europe, including even Social Democratic parties.[107] The prelude to the Party Declaration enumerated the officials who would take part in negotiations between Yugoslavia and the Soviet Union. But they were identified by their party affiliation rather than their governmental positions, highlighting dialogue between two one-party states. In the process, this identification pushed aside the importance of the Yugoslav Foreign Ministry. The Soviet party document underlined the necessity of having contacts between the two parties 'as the cooperation of all progressive and peace loving forces has to be furthered as widely as possible.' Yet, the Finnish Foreign Ministry was surprised that the cooperation between the Yugoslav and Soviet parties was to be carried out by 'personal ties, exchanges of written and oral opinions, through sending visiting delegations and when needed joint negotiations' noting that no permanent organ for the maintenance of cooperation was to be established.[108] The Ministry had expected that the Soviet side would have wanted a permanent body of some kind, especially as rapprochement with Tito had required the termination of the Cominform.

Ambassador Wuori wrote to Helsinki, 'It will be interesting to see how this, "Titoist" neutralism will succeed. Undoubtedly it has prospects for success; as international tensions are reduced the opportunities not only to get on speaking terms but also to agree on certain important questions between the two current camps have increased.'[109] While Tito's terminology of 'active coexistence' sought to distinguish Yugoslavia from Finland, the 1955 and 1956 Declarations actually made the positions of the Finnish and the Yugoslav neutralism policies more comparable. Both Finnish and Yugoslav relations with the Soviet Union emphasized economic cooperation as addressing political differences. Both sought to build on existing ties with the Western economies, and both emphasized independent foreign policies in the framework of not challenging the geographic or political borders of the Soviet Union and the Soviet bloc.

According to the Finnish analysis the Soviet Union also benefited from Tito's visit of June 1956 and rapprochement with Yugoslavia in general in that:

> it provided the USSR with another witness for the honesty of its peaceful goals [in addition to Finland]. After all, during the conflict

with the Soviet Union, Tito was made into a hero in the West and his pronouncements were given authority. In order for his interpretation that the Soviet Union truly seeks peaceful goals to be painted false, Tito would also have to be considered a liar or something like that. However, this probably cannot be done as longs as the fight for Yugoslavia's position and 'soul' between the two blocs continues.[110]

The Soviet incursion into Hungary soon overshadowed the optimistic Finnish analysis of Tito's visit to the Soviet Union. The events in Hungary directly challenged the Soviet military establishment, which did not share Khrushchev's conciliatory approach to foreign policy. The military command took the events in Budapest as a provocation. Moreover, the invasion of Hungary weakened the credibility of Khrushchev's claims to a foreign policy based on the idea of 'peaceful coexistence', already being questioned in the Western press. In November 1956, Wuori commented vaguely that 'it is important and also from the Finnish point of view interesting to see whether the Soviet Union will have to change, possibly significantly, its until now maintained position which is based upon "peaceful coexistence"—and especially after the negotiations that were held with Tito—the principle, that "it is possible to strive towards socialism via different paths" while taking into consideration the different factual conditions of each country.'[111] Finnish analysis of Soviet reactions to events in Hungary noted that 'a certain hesitation by the Soviet Union to interfere in the events in Hungary in the beginning stages is explained by the fact that it is not easy for the Soviets to reverse their position.'[112] The Belgrade Declaration established the Kremlin's acceptance of neighboring Yugoslavia's independent road to socialism. This was purported to establish the credibility of Soviet foreign policy's peaceful goals. Intervention in Hungary interfered with this purpose.

But Hungary was a member of the Warsaw Pact, and a falling out between the Soviet Union and Hungary endangered the Pact's integrity.[113] According to Finnish analysis, it was clear from the beginning of the unrest in Budapest that the Soviet regime 'could absolutely not allow Hungary to return to her "capitalist" system.'[114] This analysis of the events in Hungary did, however doubt that a change was coming for Soviet policy outside the Warsaw Pact membership, concluding that:

> It seems that the Soviet Union however seeks to maintain its previous foreign policy line established in the twentieth Party Congress. At this point, there is no essential need to speculate that the Soviet Union would withdraw back to the Stalinist hard-line in domestic or foreign

policy. For this type of change to take place there would have to be major changes carried out within the highest Soviet leadership.[115]

Beyond the Ministry's concern with the future direction of Soviet policy, it was interested in the Yugoslav insight into the Hungarian events. Wuori went on his own initiative to meet with the Yugoslav Ambassador Veljko Mićunović in Moscow on 13 November 1956 concerning the Soviet intervention. Wuori considered this to be crucial since 'Mićunović is not only a well informed man but is also a member of the Central Committee of the Yugoslav Communist Party.'[116] By this, Wuori meant that Mićunović was Tito's confidant. Wuori and Mićunović agreed that the Soviet decision to replace the Stalinist leadership of Rákosi had been made too late.[117] An earlier and successful reform of the Communist leadership, they concluded, would have prevented a large-scale uprising. For Finland and Yugoslavia, Soviet military action in Hungary was however setting a dangerous precedent. Both states would have preferred a stable, Communist government in Hungary, even if it had to be Soviet-led. Mićunović and Wuori agreed that 'it was a completely mistaken expectation in the West that the Soviet Union would have allowed Hungary to be captured by an anti-Soviet leadership.' According to the Finnish and Yugoslav views, this was a sheer impossibility as it 'was against the interests of the Soviet state.'[118]

The Finnish analysis was mostly interested in whether the Yugoslavs found Janos Kádár's leadership to be an acceptable replacement. Mićunović relayed the view to Helsinki that as an anti-Stalinist who had been imprisoned for his views, he was popular as an opponent of Rákosi and someone whom the Yugoslavs considered to be 'a good man.'[119] 'A good man' in this context meant that Kádár had not insulted either Tito or Kardelj nor had he participated in the anti-Yugoslav campaign in the aftermath of the Tito-Stalin split. But from the perspective of the Yugoslav Foreign Ministry, Kádár could be 'an adequate man' at best, as his policies neither included enthusiasm for Yugoslav-type reform Communism important to Tito and Kardelj nor for Western economic ties crucial to the goals of the Yugoslav Foreign Ministry.

Mićunović explained to Wuori that Tito and Kardelj viewed the subordinate position of the Soviet satellites to be based on the close connection between the Communist parties, which made Yugoslavia more vulnerable than Finland. Although during Tito's visit 'the Yugoslavs had had an easy time agreeing with the Soviets over foreign policy, the Yugoslavs found it difficult to reach cooperation between the two parties.'[120] Mićunović further added that 'the Yugoslavs were insulted that after Tito's visit the Soviets sent out a secret memorandum to the

Communist parties of Eastern Europe.'[121] Although, Mićunović was unwilling to reveal the specific content of the letter, he commented that it represented different facts than those agreed upon in Moscow between Tito and Khrushchev.[122] Later Finnish reports from Moscow to Helsinki detailed the content of this letter as consisting of a broadly phrased criticism of the Yugoslav road to socialism and a warning to other East European parties against imitating Yugoslav policies.[123] News of the Soviet secret memo to Eastern bloc states that Yugoslav independence, as outlined in the Moscow Declaration, did not apply to them led to Tito's outburst against Khrushchev in November 1956. Tito found this weakening of the Yugoslav position unacceptable.

Tito and Kardelj's Second Response to the Events in Hungary
The events in Hungary forced the Yugoslav party leadership to seek ways to distance itself from Soviet actions in both the domestic and international arenas. The official Yugoslav response, by way of Tito's speech in Pula on 11 November 1956, was far more defiant in tone against the Soviets than Prime Minister Fagerholm's statements in Finland. The first half of the speech contained several sharp criticisms of the Kremlin and was thus welcomed by several Western newspapers, including some from the Finnish press. It elicited a polemical response in *Pravda*. The harshest criticism was directed at Tito's view that the Belgrade and Moscow Declarations:

> should in fact be significant not only in our mutual relations but also in relations among all socialist countries...in our opinion, [the Declarations] are intended for a wider circle than Yugoslavia and the Soviet Union. We warned that those tendencies which once provoked such strong resistance in Yugoslavia existed in all countries, and that one day they might find expression in other countries too.[124]

Inserted here in Tito's speech on the urging of the Foreign Ministry analysts, were as many references to the Belgrade and Moscow Declarations as possible. Here, in 1956, was an example of Tito allowing the Foreign Ministry analysis to influence his statements.

Although the speech ultimately concluded that the second Soviet intervention was necessary, Tito began his lengthy exposition by openly comparing events in Hungary to Yugoslavia's expulsion from the Cominform in 1948. While Yugoslavia in 1948, like Hungary in 1956:

> desired to build up her life and socialism in accordance with the specific conditions in her country...it did not then come to armed

intervention because Yugoslavia was already united. Various elements were not able to carry out various provocations because we had liquidated their main forces already during the People's Liberation War.[125]

Tito further explained that he himself had informed the Soviets of the dangers of the Rákosi government while in Moscow in June 1956: 'We said that Rákosi's regime and Rákosi himself had no qualifications whatever to lead the Hungarian state and to bring about inner unity,' especially after the Rajk trial of 1949, where the charges against him featured his Yugoslav contacts before the Tito-Stalin split. Tito proclaimed, 'these are the most dishonest people in the world to me.' According to Tito's speech, the Soviets reacted too late in removing Rákosi and made an even bigger mistake by replacing him with Gerö, 'who differed in no way from Rákosi.' Despite his scathing account of a series of Soviet mistakes, Tito eventually arrived at the blasé conclusion that 'there is no point now in investigating who fired the first shot.'[126]

According to Tito's account of events, while 'it is a great mistake to call in the army of another country to teach a lesson to the people of that country,' Gerö was still primarily to blame, since it was he who called in the Red Army. Domestically, Tito's speech served as a defence against rumors that Tito had sanctioned the entrance of the Soviet troops in a neighboring country. This Tito vehemently denied, swearing that 'you can rest assured that we have never advised them to go ahead and use the army. We never gave such advice and could not do so even in the present crises.' In Pula, Tito ultimately condoned the Soviet response, explaining that while the initial uprising against the Cominformist Rákosi was justified, after the initial entry of the Soviet troops 'reactionary elements got mixed up in the uprising…The justified revolt against a clique turned into an uprising of the whole nation against socialism', which is why the second deployment of Soviet troops was justified. Tito concluded that 'if it meant saving socialism in Hungary…although we are against interference, Soviet intervention was necessary to vouchsafe the new Hungarian government…' In an increasingly conciliatory tone, Tito also vouched for the new Hungarian government: 'I can say to you Comrades, that I know these people in the new Government and that they, in my opinion, represent that which is most honest in Hungary.'

In December 1956 Kardelj gave a speech devoted to the events in Hungary at the Yugoslav Skupština. Kardelj defended Yugoslavia's foreign policy and its rapprochement with the Soviet Union by arguing that if Hungary would have followed Yugoslavia's example in building its socialist system, then the events in Budapest would never have taken place. Kardelj's outburst stated that:

> instead of making fruitless attempts to restore capitalism and other political parties, the progressive socialist forces in Hungary should have fought during the past revolutionary days for the victory of the principle of direct democracy by creating united workers councils and self-governing communes as basic foundations for a new socialist regime.[127]

Kardelj's speech highlighted the superiority of the Yugoslav Communist model with its use of workers' councils and other 'democratic' forms of social administration. The speech like Tito's was intended to dispel rumors of the Yugoslav leader's involvement in the Hungarian events and to portray the Hungarian events as mistakes typical of the prior Soviet policy of intolerance towards independent Yugoslav socialism. Like Tito's outburst, Kardelj's speech was also inspired by the Soviet secret memorandum which downgraded the importance of the Moscow Declaration.

It is not surprising that the Soviet press immediately lashed out at Kardelj. On 18 December 1956, *Pravda* published a two-page editorial entitled 'For Whose Benefit?' condemning Kardelj's speech. Both the length and the position of the column on the front page of this leading Soviet paper suggested that its criticism was in fact an official reply to the Yugoslavs. The international diplomatic corps in Moscow reported it as such. The Soviet reply rested on Lenin's principle that it is less important which state agency is in charge of activities and how the activities are being perceived. Instead it is more important to ask for whose benefit the activity is taking place. The *Pravda* article called Kardelj 'the self-assured Communist ideologist of heresy.' It compared his call for a purer form of worker's councils in Hungary to the demands of the Kronstad uprising when protesting Soviet sailors demanded that the workers' councils should be cleansed of Bolsheviks. The article concluded that Lenin had of course not accepted the sailors' demands, and therefore Kardelj was advocating a revisionism of Leninism. Even more scathingly, the article asked 'if Kardelj is denying the initial period of a Communist dictatorship as a form of rule, how is it then that in Yugoslavia, Djilas has been sentenced to prison? And why does the Yugoslav government maintain armed forces?'

The speeches by Tito and Kardelj were effective diplomatic tools to provide domestic and international explanations of Yugoslavia's role in the Hungarian events. Their criticism of Soviet actions guaranteed Western support for Yugoslavia, yet Tito's support of the new Kádár regime mollified the Soviets enough to prevent another schism. In Finland Tito's speech was publicized widely, as four out of the five most significant newspapers carried editorials about it.[128] The Finnish coverage concentrated on the first part criticizing the Soviet invasion. The Yugoslav Ambassador Slobodan Sardelić reported to Belgrade that the 'one organ of the [Kekkonen's] Agrarians' did not carry a story, which is understandable considering their caution against coming out on foreign policy questions which in this way or that way concern the Soviet Union.'[129] In opposition to the silence of the Agrarians' Party, Yugoslav Ambassador Sardelić rejoiced that the Conservative Party's press 'underlines the independence of our position, the decisiveness with which we fight, and firmly [states] that the speech in Pula represented support for Gomulka in his negotiations with the Russians.'[130] The Social Democratic Party similarly 'emphasized how after recent events in Eastern Europe it can only be said for Yugoslavia that it is leading its own independent road to socialism.'[131] Yet Sardelić also noted that the SDP unfortunately cautioned that 'the Yugoslav system is only in some measure a little more liberal system than those of the people's democracies, and that it is similarly ready to immediately close the mouth of those who are daring to think more freely, as for example Djilas.'[132]

In general, the Yugoslav Foreign Ministry's analysis accepted that the official Finnish leadership did not agree with Tito's evaluation of events in Hungary. For example, it was simply not true that Tito did not tacitly accept the Soviet incursion. The Finnish reading of Tito's and Kardelj's speeches questioned the necessity of Yugoslavia's returning to the Tito-Stalin split in its interpretations of the Hungarian events. The Finnish Foreign Ministry considered that the most plausible reason for the rhetorical tangent was 'Tito's political vanity—which forces the statesman to highlight the historical significance of his own role and the full equality of his position in comparison to his larger partner, which are the two points that are underlined in every part of Tito's speech.'[133] The Yugoslavs were however encouraged by the Finnish reactions which to them 'emphasized that Tito's thinking is always listened to with attention in Finland, that [it is important that] in the future Yugoslavia carried out with success its own politics of remaining out of blocs, which politics represents valuable experience for Finland.'[134]

Finnish diplomatic analysis concluded with reports from Moscow. Wuori told Helsinki with sarcasm that 'I have described this speech in my report mainly for the reason that it demonstrated that the "camaraderie" continues between the Muscovite and "Titoist" comrades.'[135] The Finnish analysis of the polemic between the Soviets and the Yugoslavs in December 1956 maintained that 'what is at the core here is that, for Yugoslavia to maintain its relations with the West, apparently in these [post-1956] circumstances she is forced to retreat further towards the West, more than in fact would be healthy for the sustenance of "Titoist Communism."[136]

The Independence of the Yugoslav Foreign Ministry: A Survivor of Hungary 1956

The Yugoslav Ministry had considered the best and worst possible outcomes of the events in Hungary for Yugoslav foreign policy. They concluded that Tito's involvement approving the Soviet intervention was only marginally detrimental to the future of Yugoslav foreign policy. As discussed earlier in this chapter, more damaging was Moscow's proclivity for ignoring the content of the Belgrade and Moscow Declarations, which spelled out the Yugoslav independent road to socialism.

The Yugoslav Foreign Ministry's analysis of Finland in 1956 testified to the way it wanted to apply Helsinki's example to relations with the Soviet Union. In December 1956 like in April 1953, the Foreign Ministry's 3rd Section requested more detailed and more extensive analysis from its Helsinki representation and generated a series of numbered questions from Belgrade to Helsinki.[137] Underlying the close Yugoslav interest in the Finnish Social Democratic Party in the mid-1950s was the fact that it was challenging the Agrarians' Party support for the Kekkonen-Paasikivi Line and its more careful attitude concerning Moscow. The pro-Western attitudes of the SDP and also the conservative NCP in Finland dealing with the Soviet Union were now preferred by the Yugoslav Foreign Ministry in the aftermath of the Soviet invasion of Hungary over any indication of increased Soviet influence.

Within its own documents from 1956, the ministry itself largely refrained from using ideological language as a tool of condemnation. Their language did not regularly identify foreign political parties as 'Cominformists' or 'Fascist elements,' which remained the tendency of public announcements originating from Tito's Presidential Office. These differences in tone with regard to ideological language clearly distinguish documents drafted by Tito and/or Kardelj for the Presidency, from those of the Yugoslav Foreign Ministry. The ministry documents did include the customary closing statement, 'Death to fascism, Freedom to the people,' at times to indicate the gravity or urgency of subject matter in cable correspondences between Belgrade and Helsinki, as when it was dissatisfied and demanded more detailed analysis from its Embassy in Helsinki.[138]

The Helsinki Embassy then took its own work very seriously by the mid-1950s. As the 3rd. Section of the Ministry in Belgrade made specific policy analysis requests to it, the Embassy itself also made suggestions to the Ministry. For example, the Embassy asked for personnel who could speak

Finnish (a language in the Finno-Ugric group and not widely taught), sarcastically adding 'at least passively,' so that the group could cover more newspapers, journals and other publications.[139] In December 1956 Sardelić wrote to Belgrade:

> These are facts, without hesitation: Comrade Bužek is a very fine official, disciplined, hardworking and has the best of qualities. [Upon arrival here] he quickly demonstrated his very limited experience and knowledge, yet once more confirming the thinking which was unanimously accepted by the Cadre's Commission: there is no need to send to a small embassy Comrades who do not have any kind of diplomatic experience abroad.[140]

The comrade in question had been sent to Helsinki as a favor to a high party member which is why Sardelić called him sarcastically 'comrade.' Above all, he and many Yugoslav ambassadors like him found it insulting if anyone was sent to the mission as the result of party favoritism rather than international experience. Such people would be better suited to embassies that contained larger staffs, suggesting that in such cases these employees would cause less harm to the important work of the mission.[141] Sardelić also requested:

> the Embassy be also given all records about the exchange of goods with Finland. The last time that the Secretariat delivered any records it was due to the intervention of the Embassy. I think there is no need to allow this kind of 'uninforming' of the Embassy. From the cable conversation of Comrade [Vladimir] Velebit with [Otso] Wartiovaara I can see that the Finns asked questions about corn. Please provide full information.[142]

Sardelić's serious and insistent attitude reflects those of others who felt motivated to make all efforts to develop a professional and effective Yugoslav mission abroad.[143]

In Belgrade, the Yugoslav Foreign Ministry tried to maintain the ties that were developed since 1948 (as discussed in Chapter 2) with the current Finnish Ambassador Otso Wartiovaara. Yet, after the departure of chargé d'affaires Ville Niskanen in February 1953, relations between the new Ambassador and the ministry had devolved into formal exchanges which provided little substance. In addition to Niskanen's departure, his trusted contact Ivan Vejvoda had moved on from his positions first as Section Head for Scandinavia in 1948 to become Ambassador of Yugoslavia to France. Niskanen's perhaps overly frank approach (later criticized internally by the Finnish Foreign Ministry) had interested Belgrade much more than formalistic Wartiovaara.

Wartiovaara was a highly accomplished civil servant within the Finnish Foreign Ministry. He had served as the Ministry's Chief of Staff in 1945, as Section Head for the Legal department in 1952 and was made into a full Minister in 1954. He had worked together with Kekkonen in 1944 on a commission dedicated to the safe placement of refugees from Karelia. From Belgrade onwards he would serve as an ambassador to Vienna and London before his retirement in 1974. His accomplishments and personal if not party-related connection to Kekkonen was the reason he was placed as Ambassador in Belgrade. Yet Wartiovaara, for example, approached Dobrivoj Vidić, the Yugoslav Deputy Foreign Minister, and ambassador to Hungary, on 17 December 1956 with a written list of six official questions concerning the Hungarian invasion.[144] Although discussions with Finland over reactions to the Hungarian events were sought after, the Yugoslavs deemed his approach neither sincere nor indicative of the interest of the Finnish government in Yugoslav relations but rather reflecting Wartiovaara's own desire to 'speak with us even briefly in a way that when the report will be submitted, it will at least state that there was a conversation with the President of the Government [Tito] and with the deputy Minister of Foreign Affairs.'[145] Wartiovaara presented Vidić with such vague questions as, 'What do [you] think should be the solution to the current situation in Hungary?' and 'Are the Russians actively in search of some acceptable solution in Hungary and do [you] deal with the Russians towards that direction?'[146] Vidić simply 'confirmed that [the Yugoslavs] do through normal diplomatic channels in general to deal with the Russians in that direction although it is not very easy.'[147] From his reply, it was completely unclear what 'that direction' meant. Vidić added to his report on the meeting that Wartiovaara seemed rushed and did not wish to bother him further.[148] The earlier connections between the Finnish Embassy in Belgrade and the Yugoslav Foreign Ministry were clearly absent by 1956. In any case Kekkonen had been sworn in as the Finnish President the same year. His control over the Finnish Foreign Ministry promised that more was to be gained by dealing directly with him, as the Yugoslav Ministry would indeed do in the subsequent years, as we shall see in Chapter 6.

The Yugoslav Foreign Ministry was still benefiting from previous ties in Helsinki. The Yugoslav representation there continued to consult Niskanen now resident in the Finnish capital. Having retired from the Foreign Ministry, Niskanen offered his opinions in 1956 as a private citizen on various issues, including the careers of various diplomats and the characteristics of new appointees to the Finnish Foreign Ministry.[149]

1956: Consequences

Khrushchev's foreign policy had at first displayed some impressive results in this period. Rapprochement with the Yugoslavs, and the endorsing of the Paasikivi-Kekkonen Line with Finland, helped to ratify the post-1945 Eastern borders for the Soviet Union. This was a real security and economic achievement for Khrushchev, and one realized before the détente with the West proceeded under Leonid Brezhnev in the 1970s. The fact that Social Democratic prime ministers led all Scandinavian governments except Iceland's in 1955 helped Khrushchev to find trade partners in Scandinavia. While Finland could not achieve complete parity with other Scandinavian states in Soviet foreign relations, in 1955 the Kremlin allowed Finland to join the UN and the Nordic Council. The Kremlin also returned Porkkala, concluding its lease of the island early. The most important aspect of Khrushchev's foreign policy, considered as a whole, was that he was able to constitute these crucial changes just in time: rapprochement with Tito less than five months before the Soviet invasion of Hungary, and solidifying the status quo Soviet bloc borders before the Social Democratic-Conservative party coalition was born in Finland. The SDP-NCP coalition rose partly as a consequence of the Soviet demonstration of military power in Hungary and was effective because of Kekkonen's silence on the events. Its effects were felt in 1958 when the Social Democrats and the Conservatives were able to briefly form a government that challenged Kekkonen's authority and the Paasikivi-Kekkonen Line.

Khrushchev's initial answers to the Stalinist dilemma of how to consolidate the Soviet bloc in Europe when the United States was unwilling to leave Western Europe, and when it proved to be impossible to integrate Finland in the north and Yugoslavia in the south to the bloc, were not easy to carry past the Hungarian uprising. Finnish analysis about the new direction of Khrushchev's foreign policy commented that post-1956 it faced the same difficulties as did the previous attempts to 'democratize' the system. Accepting Yugoslavia's independent road to socialism would make it seemingly necessary to offer this chance to Warsaw Pact countries as well and yet this was impossible from the point of view of Soviet security; 'in other words "speaking-over" the Soviet bloc [to Yugoslavia and Finland] is more difficult than using force.'[150] The Ministry argued that 'this Soviet flexibility concerning Tito cannot be explained as a show of weakness from Moscow. It should be remembered that military intervention in Hungary, and Bulganin's harsh warnings over the Suez events, demonstrate that the Kremlin trusts in the influence that their military and economic power represented within international affairs.'[151]

By the end of 1956, the Finnish analysis concluded that:

Although it is too early to begin to guess whether the relations between the Soviet Union and Yugoslavia will actually develop, it is clear that although Tito continues to identify himself as a Communist, and even seeks some kind of a leadership position—at least ideologically—'within the socialist world', certain priorities of the Yugoslav state—by this I mean Yugoslavia's relations with the West—direct the Yugoslav neutrality defined by him above all from the Soviet Union, which [Tito] attempted to assert in some ways in a bad-tempered tone, and not completely logical way, with his speech in Pula.[152]

The Belgrade and Moscow Declarations underlined this insoluble dilemma: at one and the same time, the Yugoslav state was supposed to occupy a position of independence from Moscow, while the Yugoslav party would remain linked to the Soviet party on important international questions, even if internally unconnected. The Yugoslav Foreign Ministry was only interested in pursuing bilateral relations outside the Soviet bloc. It was therefore interested in party politics only when they furthered that goal. The Yugoslav Foreign Ministry arrived at the conclusion that the Kremlin's suppression of the Moscow Declaration represented the biggest threat to Yugoslav policy of neutralism. Tito and Kardelj remained now similarly insulted at Moscow's unwillingness to admit to Yugoslavia's special position publicly in the Soviet press and privately in communications with its Eastern Bloc states following the Moscow Declaration. This led to Tito and Kardelj's outbursts criticizing Soviet actions in Hungary in 1956, despite the fact that Tito had personally previously sanctioned Soviet use of force. This dilemma predicted the continuation of public schisms between the Yugoslav and Soviet parties to be discussed in the next chapter.

Finnish analysis of what the Finnish Foreign Ministry in 1956 termed 'Tito's neutralism' hoped for a greater role for Soviet trade in the Yugoslav economy. This would have provided Finland with comparative information regarding its own trade with the Soviet Union, which remained a required element of the Paasikivi-Kekkonen Line. Moreover, Kekkonen's Ministry would have been glad to find a successful and comparative example to refer to in Soviet trade with another neutral country, as the SDP and NCP demanded more trade with the West and less trade with the Soviet Union. The Finnish Foreign Ministry was concerned over the role of Tito and his circle in discouraging the construction of these economic ties, which in fact never did strengthen significantly. Identifying more with the Yugoslav Foreign Ministry, the Finnish relationship with Yugoslavia continued despite the problems that the Hungarian events of 1956 had posed for both Finnish and Yugoslav policies of neutralism.

6

FREEZING OUT FINLAND AND YUGOSLAVIA: THE SOVIET RIFTS OF 1957–58

On 9 May 1958, *Pravda* printed an unsigned article as an official statement of the Central Committee of the Soviet Communist Party, asserting that the Yugoslavs had 'sold out their Communist ideology to the United States for a total of $164.3 million.'[1] Arguing that the Yugoslav leadership had recently adopted positions against the Soviet Union and the Soviet bloc similar to those of the American imperialists, the article went on to cite the public record of US economic aid to Yugoslavia and list the funds as paid to the Yugoslav Party for a series of actions undermining the bloc. For his speech in Pula in November 1956 (on the Soviet military intervention in Hungary), Tito had allegedly received the first $98.3 million, Kardelj's speech in December 1956 earning another modest $6 million, and the final $60.5 million provided for the Yugoslav refusal to sign the Soviet 12-Party Declaration in November 1957. An unspecified sum would also be forthcoming for the League of Communists' Seventh Party Congress Program in April 1953, which was characterized as hostile to the Soviet bloc.[2] The article even called the Yugoslav leadership 'falsifiers' and 'slanderers,' recalling Soviet rhetoric from the early years of the Tito-Stalin split.[3] While *Pravda* spoke of a Yugoslav government divided between anti-Soviet and pro-Soviet factions it condemned the entire party, including Tito, as opponents of the Soviet Union.[4]

This stark condemnation came less than two years after the signing of the Moscow Declaration. The Kremlin's censure of the Yugoslav party led to a diplomatic freeze between Yugoslavia and the USSR in 1958. The Kremlin instituted a similar rupture in their relations with Finland from

August 1958, in response to the new Social Democratic-Conservative government. As the previous chapters have shown, the Yugoslav and Finnish Foreign Ministries had been exchanging information and referencing each other's relations with the Soviet Union since 1948. The Foreign Ministries continued to do so again in 1958. Their attempts to maintain neutralism as a common policy toward the Soviet Union in the challenging circumstances of 1958 is the topic of this chapter.

The leadership of the League of Communists of Yugoslavia reacted immediately to the *Pravda* article by announcing the withdrawal of their Ambassador, Veljko Mićunović, from Moscow. Mićunović had enjoyed not only wide contacts within the international diplomatic corps in Moscow, but also an exceptional relationship with the Soviet leadership. As discussed in Chapters 3 and 4, Mićunović was more closely connected to the party and to Tito and Kardelj than to the Yugoslav Foreign Ministry. He was liked and respected by the Soviet foreign policy establishment as a party insider close to Tito, as opposed to the Yugoslav Foreign Ministry, which was more interested in pursuing a non-ideological relationship like that of Finland. As Chapter 4 indicated, Mićunović had, unlike Foreign Minister Koča Popović, been at the Brioni meeting of 2 November during which Khrushchev asked Tito to sanction Soviet military action in Hungary. Mićunović had been sent to Moscow as Yugoslav Ambassador in March 1956 to signal Yugoslav interest in improving relations after Khrushchev's secret speech on Stalin's mistakes. He had invested his own political capital in reconciliation between the two parties. The *Pravda* article made it clear that no permanent reconciliation between the parties was forthcoming. During his two-year stay, until the summer of 1958, Mićunović had never been refused a meeting with Khrushchev. His withdrawal and reassignment was perhaps the most personal rebuke Tito could make to Khrushchev. It also suggests Tito's acknowledgement that party reconciliation had not been a promising strategy, leaving the Foreign Ministry to reassume the leading role in Yugoslav-Soviet affairs that it had been taking prior to the Hungarian intervention.

Tito's and Kardelj's outbursts against Khrushchev's unwillingness to acknowledge the validity of Yugoslavia's own road to socialism since November 1956, as detailed in Chapter 4, had caused this new confrontation. Although it had been the analysis of the Foreign Ministry that originally identified the lack of recognition of the Moscow Declaration by the Soviets as the greatest threat to Yugoslav-Soviet relations, Popović and his Ministry did not support their leaders' provocative manner of lashing out against Khrushchev. Again, there was a Finnish connection in 1958. If Tito's and Kardelj's speeches at the Yugoslav Party Congress threatened Khrushchev's leadership within the Soviet bloc, the Finnish

Social Democratic-Conservative coalition threatened the Paasikivi-Kekkonen Line and therefore Khrushchev's regional Scandinavian policy that both coalition partners had opposed since the events of 1956.

The Soviet Union effected a de-facto suspension of economic trade with both Finland and Yugoslavia in the fall of 1958. The USSR refused to negotiate the 1959 trade agenda with Finland, simply delaying negotiations indefinitely. The Kremlin had already proposed changes to their trade agreements with Yugoslavia in January and August 1956. A Soviet credit for the proposed construction of an aluminum plant was delayed until 1962. All other trade and credits agreed upon in 1956 were also effectively cancelled.

While in 1956 Finnish and Yugoslav politics had supported the Soviet bloc by not criticizing Soviet response to the Hungarian Revolution, by 1958 the Yugoslav party's conflict with Khrushchev, and the Finnish political opposition to President Kekkonen, brought the tacit Yugoslav and Finnish acceptance of the Soviet bloc into question. This second Yugoslav-Soviet conflict made permanent reconciliation between the two Communist parties virtually impossible.

Khrushchev's Approach to Yugoslavia and Finland

In 1955, Khrushchev had been confident of Soviet technological, political and overall superiority in natural resources against the Western powers. He was enthusiastic about the future of his domestic political leadership. At that time, he was willing to permit a separate, autonomous Yugoslav road to socialism, as enumerated in the Belgrade and Moscow Declarations of 1955 and 1956. Renewed relations with Yugoslavia secured the Soviet bloc's border across Europe. These relations also helped to establish an internal critique of Stalinism within the Party, a critique that forged Khrushchev's own way forwards. Yet by the summer of 1958, Khrushchev's level of comfort with a divergent Yugoslavia had deteriorated. In November 1957, the Yugoslav Party had refused to sign the Soviet's 12-Party Declaration. This declaration of the 12 Communist parties in power was intended to establish the basic framework of an international Communist movement for building socialism, post-Cominform but under Soviet auspices with China included. Its signing coincided with festivities in Moscow for the Soviets' launch of the first earth satellite *Sputnik-1* and the 40th anniversary of the October Revolution. Tito was conspicuously absent.[5] The Declaration emphasized the leading role of the Communist Party, establishment of the dictatorship of the proletariat, public ownership of means of production, and various other necessities for a functioning Communist state. The declaration named 'Revisionism'—a Soviet term previously used to condemn the Yugoslav leadership—as the main threat to Communism.[6] The Yugoslav Seventh Party Congress followed in April 1958 with its own program. Once again condemning Stalin and Stalinism, the Yugoslav party demanded equality and autonomy between Communist parties.[7] Khrushchev took this as a Yugoslav rebuttal to the 12-Party Declaration. He demanded clarification of the draft program's statement that Yugoslav-Soviet trade relations were to be conducted on the basis of 'mutual' benefit. According to Khrushchev, the USSR was engaged primarily in giving economic aid to Yugoslavia.

These points of growing contention had been tempered when Khrushchev and Tito met in Romania in August 1957. Khrushchev then publicly recognized the continued legitimacy of the Belgrade and Moscow Declarations and the agreed principles of state sovereignty, party independence and non-interference in Yugoslav-Soviet relations. This apparent reconciliation in Romania was however deceptive. As early as 18 December 1956, *Pravda* commented, 'Kardelj at the session of the Yugoslav Federal People's Skupština, in a speech, devoted mainly to the Hungarian events attempted, to present some sort of "third line" but in its substance he only proved that there cannot be any such line.'[8] On 11 March 1957 *Pravda* had rebuffed the Yugoslav critique of Stalinism, calling it a 'monstrous and revolting sacrilege for any Communist even to compare those mistakes with the subversive activities of the imperialists.'[9] *Pravda*'s final enumeration on 9 May 1958 of the dollar amounts for which Yugoslav Communism had already sold out to the United States sent a clear message from the Kremlin: Tito was again a leader without credentials within the Soviet bloc. At the same time, the Kremlin was questioning Finland's credentials as a constructive if non-Communist neighbor to the USSR. Its parliamentary elections were to be held 6–7 July 1958. In those elections Kekkonen's Agrarians' Party won only 23 per cent of the popular vote, not enough to sustain the Paasikivi-Kekkonen Line on its own.

Khrushchev's initial willingness to first make peace with the Yugoslavs in 1955, his courting of Tito in connection with the Hungarian crisis in 1956, and his subsequent policy reversals in 1957 and 1958 have often been interpreted as evidence of the Soviet leader's inconsistency and generally contentious personality.[10] His persona thus embodied erratic decisions or, indecision, and a lack of diplomatic discretion and consistency. This line or argument, surfacing again in accounts of the Cuban Missile Crises in 1962, is often applied also to Khrushchev's rhetorical outbursts against Tito in 1957 and 1958. They come on the heels of a seemingly principled rapprochement with Yugoslavia and diplomatic re-engagement with the Scandinavian states in 1955.

Yet Khrushchev's anti-Tito outbursts also reflect his response to the challenges he faced in Soviet domestic politics. The so-called 'anti-Party group' of Vyacheslav Molotov, Lazar Kaganovich and Georgi Malenkov in the Presidium, together with Dimitrii Shepilov in the Central Committees Secretariat, had staged an attack against Khrushchev in June 1957. Khrushchev had survived, but during the power struggle these opponents brought forward his leniency towards Yugoslavia as a sign of weak political leadership. Khrushchev publicly contested these accusations, citing 'Comrade Molotov's erroneous stand on the Yugoslav question' as one of the reasons for his purging from the Presidium in July 1957.[11] Khrushchev's change of course in Yugoslav relations after 1956 can thus be interpreted as compensation for earlier softness.

Finnish analysis of Soviet foreign policy and its Yugoslav relations in 1958 further connected Khrushchev's policy reversal to Soviet nuclear politics. According to the Finnish Foreign Ministry, the main aim of Soviet foreign policy in 1958 was to attain a high-level meeting with the United States and to propose a bilateral agreement on the cessation of nuclear testing. President Dwight Eisenhower did exchange letters with Khrushchev on the subject of nuclear testing in April and May and frequently during the summer of 1958. The Soviets feared and opposed deployment of nuclear weapons in West Germany, which according to Soviet propaganda at the time, would require the reciprocal placement of nuclear weapons in Poland and the granting of nuclear capability to China.[12] The Soviet leadership similarly opposed US military flights over the North Pole. This path represented the shortest aerial distance between the United States and the Soviet Union, making the route strategically important given the development of intercontinental ballistic missiles.

The US government doubted the sincerity of Soviet intensions toward a so-called 'East-West' summit within the political context of 1958. It was possible that the Soviets merely sought to create a peace-seeking image for themselves by proposing a summit to which the US could not agree. After the launching of intercontinental *Sputnik* with the R-7 rocket, the Soviets possessed a short-term advantage in the capacity to deliver nuclear weapons. Khrushchev sought to make this advantage a permanent lead by seeking a freeze in the development of delivery systems. Because the US seemed unwilling to attend such a meeting, neither within a bilateral framework nor within the multilateral framework of NATO, the Soviet leadership had to be content with the British-American-Soviet moratorium on nuclear testing, signed in September 1958. Yet Khrushchev followed this limited agreement with provocations in divided Berlin in November. The Finnish Foreign Ministry concluded that Khrushchev was unable to accept any alternative to direct bilateral Soviet-American negotiations. The Ministry forecast that his stubbornness would create considerable difficulties for Finnish-Soviet and Yugoslav-Soviet relations. The Ministry concluded that:

> This inability to alter the adopted positions and strategy seems to be tightening the reigns within both camps. The situation will most probably become unpleasant for 'the neutrals', as for example the Soviet discussion of Yugoslav 'unorthodoxy' shows. If the relations [between the Soviet bloc and Western states] continue to worsen, it seems probable that the Nordic states will be placed in a 'headlining' position, as West German naval vessels—a NATO navy—will most likely appear as a significant force in the Gulf of Finland. There is no lack of indication towards these further moves.[13]

The ministry argued that hostile Soviet pronouncements against Yugoslavia were neither the product of Khrushchev's inconsistency as a leader, nor of Soviet domestic policy; their main concern was not even Yugoslav-Soviet relations. Their primary goal was to prevent or at least to stall the United States from overtaking the Soviet Union in nuclear and missile technology. Khrushchev's particular goal was to reduce the Cold War to an economic competition between the two super-powers, a competition that he believed the Soviet Union would win. The Finnish Ministry feared that against the threat of American nuclear superiority and access points via the North Pole by way of Finland or via Turkey and Italy by way of Yugoslavia, this Soviet security concern would challenge both Finnish and Yugoslav relations with the Soviet Union. Whether such fears were valid or not, a broader regional and geo-political perspective did not encourage the Kremlin to allow a Finnish government to be led by the anti-Communist Social Democratic Party, or be comfortable with a Yugoslav Communist party led by Tito and Kardelj. Their questionable loyalty called both of their roles as guarantors of the bloc's European border in to question.

An Independent Yugoslav Foreign Ministry and Soviet Relations, 1957–58

Veljko Mićunović's transfer from having primary responsibility for the Yugoslav Foreign Ministry into first a temporary and then a permanent high party position highlights the separate spheres which the Ministry and the party had come to occupy. With Partisan credentials from the Second World War, Mićunović became a Deputy Minister of the Interior in the Yugoslav government in 1945, only transferring to the Foreign Ministry to become a Deputy Minister in 1951. Immediately following Khrushchev's 'secret speech,' Mićunović was appointed as Yugoslav Ambassador to Moscow where he served from March 1956 to September 1958. However,

Mićunović was moving closer to the party than the Ministry, as can maybe be seen from his election while still Ambassador in January 1957 to the Yugoslav League of Communists Commission for the drafting of the controversial program of the Seventh Party Congress. In June 1958, after his recall from Moscow, he was appointed to the party's separate Commission for International Relations, effectively placing him within the top LCY hierarchy.

On his 20 June 1958 visit, Mićunović was asked by the Soviet Foreign Ministry whether he was to be identified (in the official Soviet transcript of their meeting) as an Ambassador, representing the Foreign Ministry, or a party official, representing the LCY.[14] Unwilling to choose between the party and Popović's Ministry, Mićunović replied that since 'we had talked about all sort of things and they could report it as they wished. I had no objections.'[15] The Soviets were less interested in diplomatic protocol than in confirming their own impressions that the party hierarchy must be more important than the Foreign Ministry. In 1958, the highest organ of the Yugoslav Party, its Secretariat of the Executive Committee, had only five members. They were Tito, Kardelj, Aleksandr Ranković, Svetozar Vukmanović-Tempo and Ivan Gošnjak. None were representatives of the Foreign Ministry, nor would there ever be a representative of the Foreign Ministry in the Secretariat.

By the summer of 1958, the Kremlin was clearly irritated by the Yugoslavs' ability to present themselves as Communists to Communist regimes, as neutrals to neutral states and as open-for-business partners to Western governments. Popović had been able by then to repair ties with the West by settling with Italy over Trieste, by not abandoning the Balkan Pact (despite the Kremlin's pressure), and by not allowing the party leadership to prevent him from bettering bilateral relations with party rhetoric over the recognition of East but not West Germany. When Tito had made public statements in support of the Soviet Union, it had been in the context of the Suez crisis in 1956 and not concerning relations with Western Europe or the United States. Even Mićunović adhered to the diplomatic protocol of neutralism when speaking as a representative of Yugoslavia to the international diplomatic corps in Moscow. He was perfectly capable of flying to Brioni on 2 November 1956 for a secret meeting on Hungary between Khrushchev and Tito, apparently endorsing the Soviet view and then criticizing Soviet actions there on his return to Moscow.

Mićunović's memoir *Moscow Diary* would later establish his international reputation, not as Tito's and the party's advocate who had challenged Popović for the seat of Foreign Minister already in 1953, and not as someone who retired to the party apparatus in 1958, but as a classic neutralist himself. Often-cited in English language scholarship on the Hungarian uprising, his memoir portrays Mićunović as simply a career diplomat keeping a diary during his tour as the Yugoslav Ambassador in Moscow. The chapters shift from general impressions of how 'Soviet disapproval in the field of party affairs will probably be carried over into other aspects of Yugoslav-Soviet relations' to personal opinions. 'I no longer had any doubt in my mind that the principal initiator of the current anti-Yugoslav moves by the Soviet Government was Khrushchev himself.'[16] Mićunović himself seeks to downplay the significance of his Party role in the memoir. For example in response to Enver Hoxha's emotional accusation that Deputy Foreign Minister Arso Milatović was 'a greater enemy of Albania than any of our previous ministers,' Mićunović writes that 'I expressed doubt about the charges against Milatović and rejected the assertion that he was an enemy of Albania...I rejected any suspicions that might be directed at Yugoslavia in this connection.'[17] Were it not for the book's introduction by translator David Floyd, which describes Mićunović as 'a fervent patriot, a sincere Marxist socialist...[who] did not hesitate in his loyalty to Tito,' one would likely not guess that Mićunović had established a close relationship to Tito on the strength of his Partisan credentials. In his own words, Mićunović tries to appear ideologically detached and engaged only in seeking practical benefit for the Yugoslav state through diplomatic correspondence.[18]

The contradiction posed by Mićunović's two roles became apparent in the first half of 1958; the Yugoslav party leadership was increasingly at odds with the Soviet leadership, while the Yugoslav Foreign Ministry hardly altered its correct formality with Soviet contacts. True, it was Foreign Minister Popović who in February 1957 expressed indirect criticism of the Soviet Union by stating the principles of Yugoslav neutralism policy in no uncertain terms:

> The heart of our dispute with the Soviets and satellites lies, in our opinion, in the differing viewpoints regarding our relations and standpoints towards the Socialist camp. We do not wish to enter the camp, as this would not be in accord with our established principles, the trend of our foreign policy, nor with the general interests of peace and socialism...to avoid a regression into Stalinism, which I am deeply convinced has been responsible in the post-war period for inflicting incomparably more harm on the cause of socialism than all the imperialist conspiracies together.[19]

Yet following the Seventh Yugoslav Party Congress in the spring of 1958, the strongest pronouncements against the Soviets in 1958 originated from the Yugoslav party leadership and not from the Foreign Ministry. In June 1958 Tito himself replied publicly to Soviet criticism of Yugoslav revisionism:

> The main reason for this [Soviet] campaign is that we refused to sign the Declaration of the 12 countries in Moscow last November and to join the so-called Socialist camp because, as is well known, we oppose the division of the world into camps...the United States started giving us aid in 1949, not so that Socialism would triumph in our country— they do not like Socialism and they do not conceal this; they state openly that they do not like it—but because we were threatened by famine and because Yugoslavia would in this way be able more easily to resist Stalin's pressure and strengthen its independence. Comrade Khrushchev says often that Socialism cannot be built on US wheat, but we think that those who can will do it, whilst those who do not know how will not be able to build it on their own wheat...After all, US wheat is no worse than the Soviet wheat we are not getting, and we are getting wheat from the United States.[20]

Rather than focus on the war of the words between the Yugoslav and Soviet parties, the Foreign Ministry still wanted to conduct relations as they had proceeded prior to the Seventh Party Congress. Even if there was no Soviet 'wheat' forthcoming, simply conducting normal diplomatic activities with the Soviet Union did not harm the Ministry's goals but could help to relieve the growing tensions between the two party leaderships. In September 1958, the Yugoslav Ministry issued visas to five members of the Soviet delegation of the trade union members for the chemical and petroleum industry, to five members of a separate delegation of Soviet trade unions of metallurgy and oil and to a 48-member 'team of the Soviet Circus' for a two-month stay in Yugoslavia.[21] Yugoslav and Soviet representatives visited each other's naval schools. In September, the Leningrad Admiralty Institute sent members to Rijeka, while a delegation from the Yugoslav ship *Djure Djakovic* visited 'the *Putilov*', a Soviet ship stationed in Leningrad.[22] Visits from delegations of Soviet press and university professors were planned for late September.

The Foreign Ministry was adhering to the principles of Yugoslav neutralism. Relations with the Soviets were established to assure the Soviet Union that their political border in Eastern Europe was guaranteed, while competing political and trade relations were also pursued with states outside the Soviet bloc. From this perspective of the Ministry, cessation of cultural or economic relations with the Soviet Union would damage these connections.

Mićunović himself was greatly upset with the Foreign Ministry's continuing issing of visas to Soviet persons, which he himself had to oversee. In his remarks to Belgrade, Mićunović commented, 'I heard only from the Russians that on 12 September a delegation of the Admiralty Institute of Leningrad leaves for Yugoslavia,' indicating his displeasure that he had not been informed of Belgrade's continuing collaboration.[23] Mićunović continued to express frustration, customarily citing his own views as the Moscow Embassy's: 'We were against these circus collaborations because it is harmful to us, and the Russians here have all advantages; the Russians forced us, and we fed them by our own hand.'[24] Mićunović complained that the Belgrade Circus arriving in Moscow was only half the size of the Soviet circus, would stay only a short time, and appear mainly in the minor Soviet cities.[25] In Mićunović's view, it was outrageous that a further '53 visas were issued for Soviet officials merely for the organization of a Soviet pavilion at the Zagreb International Fair and that another ten Soviet officials left for "temporary work" to Belgrade Fair.'[26] Mićunović strongly objected, calculating that by the end of September 'there will be close to 200 Soviet delegates, artists, specialists, foreign civil servants and others in Yugoslavia.'[27] Mićunović concluded:

> We think that this kind of situation is not normal considering the hostile politics that the Soviet government carries out against Yugoslavia. It is clear that the Russians are at the moment forcing different delegations on us at a time when they are intensifying their hostile campaign against the 'Yugoslav leadership'; while, for example, this spring when that campaign was more moderate and when they talked about preservation of normal relations, these kinds of delegations were postponed or refused by the Soviets themselves.[28]

Mićunović's *Moscow Diary* where he tries to portray himself as a diplomat adhering to the Yugoslav policy of neutralism makes no mention of these concerns or comments to Belgrade concerning Soviet-Yugoslav cultural cooperation or visa matters.

Beyond the unwillingness of the Yugoslav Foreign Ministry to cut back on activities with the Soviets, Mićunović raised several specific objections. Yugoslav delegations that arrived to the USSR in 1958 were isolated from the Soviet workers, while Soviet functionaries were unwilling to participate in even a minimal number of customary discussions, because in Mićunović's view, 'then they would have to say something about our relations and the politics of the USSR towards Yugoslavia.'[29] The Yugoslav delegations toured factories and city landmarks. Mićunović was incensed that 'the Soviets [we]re making toasts about the solidarity between workers and friendship between our nations while simultaneously the Soviet press writes the worst things against Yugoslavia and her leadership.'[30] These practices of the Soviet state were felt to be degrading. However, regular diplomatic exchanges, with no significant political commitment beyond the security guarantee for the Soviet bloc's border states, Hungary included, were precisely what the Yugoslav Foreign Ministry hoped to achieve.

In 1958, the Soviets did continue various cultural exchanges in place of trade and political relations. Trade union contacts were maintained separately, away from the quarrelling political parties. For Mićunović, this activity reduced Yugoslavia's status as an equal party and trade partner to a subordinate cultural one. Mićunović's goal in Moscow had been to elevate the status of the Yugoslav party, a task in which the *Pravda* article of May 1958 quoted at the beginning of this chapter made clear he had failed. Still, the cultural exchanges continued to serve their own propaganda value by demonstrating that Yugoslavia remained 'with' the Soviet Union. To counter this impression, Mićunović felt that Soviet visits should be closely supervised, and suggested that 'Belgrade suppl[y] a centralized program for this type of collaboration with the USSR. Without that, we can hardly maintain equilibrium with the Russians, who one-sidedly violate the agreed-upon program and are forcing collaboration which is in their interest and thus places us in the passive position of observers or participants in carrying out the Soviet propaganda scheme.'[31] Here Mićunović appealed for the reconnection of the special role of UDBa within the Foreign Ministry discussed in Chapter 4. Popović had however been able to contain the role of the security service and Aleksandr Ranković within the Foreign Ministry by 1958, after cutting off its access to the crucial Analytical Department as noted in Chapter 3. Removing UDBa's influence from the Foreign Ministry had made the latter's analysis more independent, and there was also less influence from the party leadership whom Ranković represented. This change did not help Mićunović in his efforts to maintain the controlling role of the party in Yugoslav foreign policy.

Yugoslav Foreign Ministry's Analysis of Soviet Foreign Policy in 1958

By 1958, Foreign Ministry analysis of the Soviet Union was less focused on the inter-party conflict than the existing historiography suggests. A ministry report from Moscow to Belgrade in March 1958 concludes:

> Our relations with the USSR have worsened because of the foreign political hardships [the USSR] has endured with the Western states, Socialist Europe and Asia in recent times. It is necessary not to lose

sight, because of the complex ideological disagreement, that our difficulties with the Russians are increasingly really the consequence of [the Soviet position] on West Germany, our refusal of American military aid, [Soviet] conflict with France, the anti-Yugoslav campaign of [European] socialists…³²

The Ministry's internal discussions demonstrate that the two most important elements of Soviet foreign policy from its perspective, similar to that of the Finnish Foreign Ministry, were Khrushchev's desire to attain 'a meeting at the highest level' with the United States and Soviet views on 'European integration.'³³

In a policy document produced in August 1958, titled 'Positions of FPRY and the USSR on international problems,' the Ministry comments only briefly on the conflict between the two parties:

> On a series of international problems our positions coincide with the Soviet position, but with those positions that are in agreement there remains fundamental difference…on the fundamental question of dividing the world into camps, the politics of the USSR as a great power and hegemony over their camp.³⁴

This policy document predicted that due to differing views on a number of international issues and declarations by the state-parties (specifically the 12-Party Declaration and the Yugoslav Seventh Party Congress program), agreement with Moscow in the future would be unattainable. Still, the ministry emphasized its own efforts to strengthen Yugoslav-Soviet relations by seeking collaboration within international organizations, noting that 'in contacts with Western diplomats, [the Ministry] worked to break distrust towards those Soviet foreign political acts,' but that the Soviets 'did not want to attribute political meaning to this kind of intermediary activity on our behalf, and therefore did not come to recognize our role within the camp.'³⁵ The conflict between the Soviet and Yugoslav Communist parties was considered permanent but also no reason to abandon a careful course in relations with the Soviet Union.

Instead, like the Finnish Foreign Ministry, the Yugoslav Ministry focused on the Soviet desire for a meeting between the Soviet Union and the United States. The Yugoslav ministry surmised that 'the initiative on this question was given by the USSR; prompted by the fact that on a certain number of very serious and acute problems, in the first place disarmament, [the Soviets] arrived at the conclusion that at a low level the solution cannot practically be reached.'³⁶ Yugoslav analysis predicted that, since all NATO states were involved, the Soviets would not achieve their desired ban on nuclear testing through multilateral negotiations. Neither did the Yugoslav Foreign Ministry see this as the goal of Soviet foreign policy. The ministry felt that by strongly attacking NATO throughout 1958, the Kremlin wished to weaken West European collaboration. The propaganda attacks might serve to relax tensions within the Soviet bloc. The Soviets were also discussing the creation of a demilitarized zone in Europe. Each of these Soviet initiatives, in the view of the Yugoslav Ministry, served Khrushchev's goal of keeping American missiles out of West Germany.

Even more than the Finnish Foreign Ministry, the Yugoslav Foreign Ministry was interested in European integration. The Yugoslavs believed that Soviet opposition to integration had not altered fundamentally since the end of the Second World War. According to the Yugoslav Ministry, Khrushchev's Scandinavian regionalism policy sought to stall West European integration. The aim of such bloc-politics was to promote the division of the world into two exclusive camps, and two world markets. According to the Yugoslav Ministry, 'there was generally not room for "issues" of European regional collaboration' in this world view.[37] Its analysis considered that, 'this kind of politics from the USSR had nonetheless the result of giving a powerful impulse for political integration of Western Europe and was one of the fundamental causes of its realization.'[38] The Soviet Union opposed West European economic collaboration and the Euro-Atom project, 'which will only facilitate the division of Europe more.'[39]

The Yugoslav Ministry noted the variation on this fundamental Soviet approach provided by Khrushchev's Scandinavian policy. It seemingly proposed to the countries of "the small Europe" a plan for organizing cooperation which would allow mutual trade and the Euro-Atom project.[40] And yet, the Yugoslav analysis continued the goal of Khrushchev's Scandinavian policy was to allow inter-Nordic cooperation as a way of 'weakening West European collaboration by striving to arouse opposition which exists between Western countries, which would divide them that much more and in that way weaken their collaboration from inside Western organizations, especially NATO.'[41] The Yugoslavs saw the new presidency of Charles de Gaulle in France as beneficial for these Soviet goals as pursued through Scandinavia.

The ministry emphasized that the Yugoslav relationship with wider West European organizations was more positive, concluding, 'Yugoslavia is of the opinion that the contemporary concrete forms of regional uniting, especially of West European politics and military organizations NATO, the European Council, the West European Union and others, carry in themselves no negative characteristics.'[42] This opinion reflected the Foreign Ministry's position but not necessarily that of the Yugoslav party. The LCY leadership viewed such organizations as instruments of the two-bloc competition, from which Yugoslavia should therefore abstain. But for the Foreign Ministry, Yugoslavia needed to take part in the 'positive' elements of West European integration, for example by working with the Organization for European Economic Collaboration (OEEC). This collaboration was preferable, as it was based on facilitating bilateral trade relations.

The conflict of interest between the Yugoslav Foreign Ministry and the Yugoslav party leadership concerning relations with the Soviet Union (between neutralism and Communist ideology) did not result in the permanent reassertion of control over foreign policy by the party leadership as the one-party structure of Yugoslavia would have implied. It might have been expected that Mićunović, through his elevated party position would have been able to prevail in his views on Soviet-Yugoslav relations over those of his superiors within the Foreign Ministry with little connections to Tito's inner circle. However, this was not the case. Instead, Mićunović was moved to a new position within the Party apparatus. The position guaranteed him higher leverage within the domestic Yugoslav hierarchy, but not a higher position with regard to determining Yugoslav foreign policy.

Among the key Yugoslav Ministries, the Foreign Ministry had by 1958 evolved into an institution that produced its own policy agenda independently from the Yugoslav party, as its analysis of the Soviet Union in 1958 shows. This is not to say that turbulent relations between the Yugoslav and the Soviet party leaderships did not surface again. Yugoslav revisionism was criticized by the 21st Soviet Party Congress in January–February 1959 and in October 1961, followed by repeated reconciliations between Tito and Leonid Brezhnev in October 1962. However, these rhetorical debates remained largely outside of the work of the Foreign Ministry.

For the Finnish Foreign Ministry, as discussed later in this chapter, Soviet pressure on the neutralist Paasikivi-Kekkonen Line worked without such problems of ministry and party coordination. Policy came from the office of the Finnish President to be implemented through a subservient foreign ministry. Soviet foreign policy towards Finland sought to head off any government, which was led by another party than that of President Kekkonen. This was done in order to prohibit the parliament from challenging the Paasikivi-Kekkonen Line. In the Yugoslav case however, the one-party Communist state left the parliament no independent role but tempted the Soviets to challenge the party itself.

Soviet-Finnish Relations in 1958: The Year of the 'Night Frost'

The largest concern for the USSR after the establishment of Finland's policy of neutralism was the prospect of a Social Democratic and Conservative coalition that would challenge the Paasikivi-Kekkonen Line and possibly shift Finnish foreign policy orientation towards the West. In the aftermath of the 1956 Hungarian Revolution both parties had gained support for their interest in expanding Western ties enough to form a government if they could agree on a coalition. In the July 1958 elections, the Social Democratic Party won 48 seats and the Conservative Party 29, making a proposed coalition of 77 in a total of 200 seats in the Finnish parliament. Despite the fact that the SDP had lost six seats and the NCP had only gained five, coalition was now possible because Kekkonen's Agrarians' Party had lost five seats. In the 1958 elections the AP won 48 seats against the 50 for the Finnish People's Democratic League, a coalition to which the Finnish Communist Party belonged. This made it very difficult for the AP to form a government as the remaining, minority parties were left with only 25 seats and three of them belonged to a party unlikely to unite with the AP. Unless it broke the general rule among all Finnish parties of excluding prominent Communists Party politicians from significant ministerial positions in any governing coalition, even with the 22 seats of the minorities' parties added, the Agrarians could muster only 70 seats, versus the 77 seats of the SDP and NCP. Kekkonen, fearing a Soviet reaction to a government which included both the West-leaning Social Democrats and the Conservatives but excluded the SKDL completely, demanded that his Agrarians simply not agree to participate in forming an SDP-NCP government.

Upon the announcement of election results, the Soviet press assumed the offensive, sounding-off warnings about the consequences of a Social Democratic-Conservative government for Finnish-Soviet relations. In the 13 August 1958 *Izvestia*, its Helsinki correspondent observed that 'the Agrarians' Party has in recent years played the most significant role in Finnish politics, it would therefore be difficult to understand now a withdrawal from those policies.'[43] The author blamed 'the faltering of some of the Agrarians' Party's political leaders who begun to consider the formation of a coalition government with the united bloc of rightwing Social Democrats and the Conservatives.'[44] The article sternly warned the Agrarians' Party against 'incredible forgetfulness' of the Social Democrats and Conservatives' 'real purpose especially in terms of foreign policy.' Soviet propaganda highlighted the Conservatives' goal of changing Finnish political orientation exclusively towards the West and of the danger of their co-opting the Social Democrats to pursue this goal. The obvious Soviet goal was to promote a majority government of Agrarians and Communists.

To emphasize the significance of the Soviet message in Moscow, the Deputy Foreign Minister Georgi Zarubin raised the article with the Finnish Ambassador Eero Wuori twice on the day of its publication, first at a luncheon concerning fishing rights and again at a Danish Embassy reception in the evening.[45] Referring to the Agrarians' Party's 'divided' position on forming a coalition government, Zarubin repeatedly warned 'how dangerous for Finland it would be if the political parties begin to divide internally.'[46] The matter of friendly political parties deviating from the Soviet line would prove to be a concern that stretched beyond Finland to Italy as well as to Yugoslavia.

Not limiting itself to grim warnings, the Soviet press also tried to counter the Social Democrats and the Conservatives by bolstering the profile of the Finnish Communist Party. On 30 August 1958 *Pravda* published an extensive article by the Finnish Communist Hertta Kuusinen together with a story about the 40th anniversary of the party distributed by the TASS news agency.[47]

Such Soviet scrutiny and pressure caused deep concern in the Finnish Foreign Ministry. The ministry expressed reservations over the 'very strict surveillance of the political situation in Finland over the summer' of 1958 which was 'not confined to the realm of the Soviet Foreign Ministry, which is very well aware of the situation in Finland, down to specific personal details, but also that of the rest of the Soviet apparatus.'[48] A most glaring example of this cryptic reference to the security apparatus was when the Finnish Military Attaché was made to answer questions about Finnish party politics upon his visit on military matters to the Moscow barracks 'pointing to the all around surveillance of Finland' even by the Soviet military.[49] By the end of August, Ambassador Wuori was exasperated. As he put it, 'recently I have had the distinct displeasure of not being able to avoid the question "is the Finnish governmental crisis over?" from any Soviet official anywhere…in the current context [of Soviet pressure] this intense interest does not confine itself exclusively to a compliment.'[50]

The Foreign Ministry was placed in the very difficult position of having to receive all of the Soviet pressure to stop the formation of a SDP-NCP government and yet having no influence in the negotiations over a new government. As noted in Chapter 1, the ministry had been obliged to carry out the politics of the Paasikivi-Kekkonen Line since 1948. By 1958, the ministry, not an autonomous institution like the Yugoslav one, was working under the direct guidance from Kekkonen as President and co-founder of 'the Line.' Ambassador Wuori carried on a detailed and frequent correspondence with Kekkonen himself, as noted in Kekkonen's private diary. In 1954, Kekkonen's closest collaborator within the Agrarians' Party, Johannes Virolainen, had replaced Kekkonen as Foreign Minister. Between

1957 and 1958 the ministry was lead by Paavo Johannes Hynninen who was without party affiliation and therefore easily co-opted by Kekkonen. This combination gave the ministry no direct line to the SDP or the NCP, but only one to Kekkonen. Wuori and Kekkonen shared concern over the Soviet reaction to a Social Democratic-Conservative government. But since Wuori's closest contact was the President, who proved to be unable to prevent his own party from joining an SDP-NCP-led government, Wuori found the ministry without leverage to raise its concerns over effects of the future government on Finnish-Soviet relations. Whereas in Yugoslavia in 1958, the ministry advised and led the party in foreign policy, in Finland the Foreign Ministry was lead by President Kekkonen until the Soviet reaction to the SDP-NCP government interrupted his ability to do so. On 25 August First Deputy Prime Minister Frol Kozlov approached Wuori, pointing out that 'concerning the question of the future parliament, from the Soviet perspective, it would be most important above all, that the relations would be able to continue to develop in friendly spirit.'[51] This led the customarily even-tempered Wuori to reply with considerable frustration 'as far as I know the importance of friendly relations is generally understood in Finland.'[52]

On 29 August a new government consisting of eight seats for the Social Democratic-Conservative coalition and seven for the Agrarians' Party and Minorities parties was formed under a Social Democratic Prime Minister, Karl-August Fagerholm.[53] The outcome left Soviet representatives dissatisfied. SKDL was left completely out of the government. The Kremlin further objected to the appointment of Social Democrats Väinö Leskinen as Social Minister and Olavi Lindholm as the Second Minister of Transport and General Works. They had fought in the Second World War against the Soviet Union and were known to have supported the Whites in the Finnish Civil War. For the first time in his political career Kekkonen was devastated. In his diary Kekkonen writes 'when I read the open letter of appointment [to the cabinet] I told them that "this is the worst speech which I as President have delivered, and it doesn't help much that it was written by others."'[54] Kekkonen privately added: 'now we must end the talk about a Paaskivi-Kekkonen Line...this is so ****** miserable. All the work I have done in domestic as well as foreign politics seems to be drifting into sand...' Someone in the Agrarians' Party's meeting had said, 'although it is risky we should try to see whether the ice breaks with a stick.'[55] Kekkonen was outraged that in return for ministerial seats the Agrarians' had decided to 'test' Finnish-Soviet relations. The next day Heikki Waris, the previous Social Minister 1957–58 from the Social Democratic Party, informed Kekkonen that he was traveling to Washington 'on confidential matters' to discuss loans from the World Bank and credits from the US government.[56]

This led Kekkonen in his own words to explode, 'I said do you ****** wood log-heads not understand that [acquiring increased US funding] is a completely impossible foreign political act after the formation of this new government?'⁵⁷ With the Social Democrats and Conservatives in power, Waris left, over Kekkonen's objections. On 1 September, Kekkonen wrote the Agrarians' Party's leadership a chilling personal letter which described his feeling of betrayal of those party leaders that had ignored his instructions not to join the government, and how he felt they had jeopardized the Paasikivi-Kekkonen Line:

> After the solution which the AP's central government and group made in the matter of forming the government, I must state that the work which I have performed since 1944 in domestic and in foreign policy is drifting out of my hands. I ask that the publications of *your* party will no longer refer to the Paasikivi-Kekkonen Line, because it no longer politically exists. It is similarly pointless to speak of a Paasikivi Line, it is best that *you* begin to speak of a NCP-[SDP] formula in 'entire nations' line. To quote the historian dedicated to the SDP 'Paasikivi was only a transitory politician.' Signed U.K.
>
> Ps. I will serve as President the remainder of my term, if that is alright with you, so that I will not cause harm to foreign political position of the country. I am following the actions of the AP with warm interest.⁵⁸

Kekkonen felt that not only had he been personally betrayed, so had his partner Paasikivi, recently deceased in 1956.

With no faith in the new government, Kekkonen told its new Foreign Minister Virolainen (at other times Kekkonen's closest confidant), that he objected to the visit of Waris to the US. 'You are like children at the "playground"', he said, 'if foreign policy was handled like this in the 1930s [referring to the last time NCP had been in government] it is no wonder that we ended up in a war.'⁵⁹ The same day, Kekkonen circumvented even the Foreign Ministry, which was under his own influence, to meet with 'Mr. G' who in fact was none other than Vladimir Zhenihov, the KGB's Helsinki Resident. Zhenihov would now pass on Kekkonen's communications to the Kremlin until December 1958. It is not possible to know if Zhenihov or the Committee of State Security (KGB) had played a previous role in Kekkonen's dealings with Moscow because his diary begins only in 1958. However, during what became known as the 'Night Frost' crisis, Kekkonen communicated with Zhenihov or another KGB contact weekly. Zhenihov confirmed to Kekkonen that 'the Soviet Union regards the new government very negatively and considers its purpose to change the foreign policy of Finland.'[60] While Kekkonen tried to 'convince [Zhenihov] that the foreign policy direction will not change, after all that depends on me,' Zhenihov replied that the Kremlin 'believes in that, but the Soviet Union considers this as the first post-war attempt to break Finland's foreign political line, and if this succeeds next time the attempts will go further.'[61] Kekkonen asked that the Kremlin not commence a 'newspaper war,' to which Zhenihov agreed. This however, was not a promise that the Kremlin kept.

In response to the new coalition, the Soviets froze all diplomatic exchanges with Finland and begun to publish intense attacks on the government. Khrushchev himself would later in January 1959 call his strategy the setting of a 'Night Frost' over Finnish-Soviet relations. Articles celebrating anniversaries of different events in the Second World War such as the 14th anniversary of the signing of the Finnish-Soviet armistice, covered by *Izvestija* in 19 September 1958, begun to appear.[62] The article underlined the benefits to Finland from the normalization of relations with the Soviet Union, adding that friendly relations are not supported by all Finnish politicians, 'those belonging to Leskinen's influence and the NCP members who stand behind them are Western reactionaries who calculate that they can fulfill their foreign political wishes.'[63] At the same time, the Soviet press attacked the Finnish media. On 23 September, *Literaturnaya Gazeta* published an article titled 'From the Point of View of the Retarded' which attributed anti-Soviet sentiment in the Finnish press to the fact that the alleged conservative Aatos Erkko owned the main Finnish newspaper *Helsingin Sanomat*; it was for this reason that the Social Democratic press had turned from the Paasikivi-Kekkonen Line. The article drew an unfavorable comparison between the 'retarded thinking of these publications' and the 'clear-headed thinking' of the Swedish-Finnish press that supported Kekkonen's Agrarians, commenting that many Finnish Swedes belonged to the landowning class but still held this view.

To Kekkonen, the Soviet press attacks were an extremely unwelcome development. He had already in the summer of 1957 remarked while viewing the Yugoslav-Soviet war of words in the press that 'newspaper polemics between Finland and the Soviet Union would be detrimental.'[64] Anticipating the onset of a rhetorical war in Finnish-Soviet relations in early September 1958 Kekkonen commented to himself in his diary that 'the Paasikivi-Kekkonen Line has been replaced by Sack-Line: you put a sack over your head and proceed running around in a circle.'[65] Yet, as with Yugoslavia, Kekkonen did not anticipate an actual military conflict between Finland and the Soviet Union. He considered that 'it is also difficult for the USSR to act against Finland because Finland is the display window for Soviet peaceful co-existence politics to the world.'[66] Kekkonen however believed that if the Kremlin thought that Finland had stepped too far away, and he himself was not able to contain the provocation in time, then a Soviet military reaction was also possible, explicitly as in Hungary in 1956.

The Soviet intellectual world played its own part in the censure and intimidation of the Finnish government. In November, the Military Club in Moscow hosted a lecture on the topic of 'current international political situation' in its lecture series 'For the Spread of Universal Knowledge.'[67] The first question put it bluntly: why had relations between Finland and Soviet Union grown colder in recent days? The lecturer replied that although the 'National Democrats' (referring to the SKDL) had won a considerable majority in the elections, 'reactionary forces' had still been able to form a government. 'The goal of these reactionary circles,' the lecturer asserted, 'is to push Finland closer to the West and America.'[68]

The USSR enlisted its satellites in more subtle rebukes. When the Finnish government hosted a reception to celebrate Finnish independence day 6 December 1958, the ambassadors of the Soviet bloc members protested by attending stag, leaving their wives at home.[69] High-level Soviet diplomats boycotted the event entirely. Though the head of the Scandinavian Department of the Soviet Foreign Ministry did in fact attend, Khrushchev himself stayed away, sending only his deputies from the Presidium, Kozlov and Aleksey Kosygin. The higher-level officials were replaced by representatives of the Soviet arts and sciences, which for the increasingly agitated Ambassador Wuori 'was actually a refreshing change' since the Soviets normally worked to censor both the arts and science.[70]

In these circumstances, instead of the Foreign Ministry restraining anti-Soviet expressions in Finland, Kekkonen did so directly. In October he personally prevented the publication of a confessional book titled 'A Communist as Minister of the Interior' by one of the leading Finnish members of the Communist Party which outlined how Yrjö Leino was trained by Moscow and how he had been able to advance his political career in the Finnish Parliament with the help of the Soviet Communist Party.[71] Kekkonen considered that in the future the Kremlin would make increasing demands for the SKDL to be included in any government, and considered SDP and Fagerholm to be behind attempts to publish it.[72] Including any Communist in a Finnish government would become even more implausible after the publications of such a book. Kekkonen personally stopped further publication of a Finnish cartoon imitating Ilya Repin's famous painting *Burlaks on the Volga* which portrays impoverished poor people pulling an expensive ship belonging to the nobility on to the shore in 1870s Russia. The Finnish cartoon by Kari Suomalainen had replaced the enslaved Burlaks with Soviet bloc states, and on board the ship, Khrushchev was shouting out 'be ashamed you imperialists.'[73] The cartoon (already having been displayed in London) was scheduled to be placed on a four-storey billboard facing the UN headquarters in New York. The subtext of the cartoon was that the Ukrainian Repin had actually retired to Kuokkala in Finland at the end of his career. Despite the many requests by the Soviet government for him to return to the USSR after Finnish independence in 1917, he had not done so. Moreover, Kuokkala had been lost to the Soviet Union in the post-war settlement. The cartoon was meant to remind the Finnish public of all of these embarrassing details.

On 27 October 1958 the Counsellor of the Yugoslav Embassy in Moscow Zoran Perišić met with the Finnish First Secretary Salomies at an event in the Iranian Embassy. The Yugoslav Foreign Ministry wished to know 'whether the recent strong articles criticizing the Government of Finland in the Soviet press meant that Finland and the Soviet Union had arrived at the point of "frozen relations" after the elections and the forming of the new government?'[74] Salomies confirmed that the relations had grown cold citing as its most significant proof that the Soviets 'did not begin the scheduled negotiations for the credit of 400–500 million rubles for the construction of a metallurgical plant at all, as was projected after Kekkonen's [May 1958] visit.'[75] Further, 'the negotiations over the use of the Saimaa Canal had been stopped completely' and 'the negotiations for the following trade agreement need to begin but the Russians do not show any desire for them and refuse to set the dates.'[76] The indefinite delay in the trade negotiations was a proven Soviet tactic against Finland and Yugoslavia in 1948 and in 1953 as discussed in Chapters 1–3. More importantly 'Soviet Ambassador [Vladimir] Lebedev was pulled from Helsinki a month ago [16 September], but a new one has not been named, and neither have the Soviets requested a protocol for a new one.'[77] In fact, Zhenihov had told Kekkonen privately already on 8 September:

> The position of Moscow [regarding trade relations] is negative, rational and final. The position will be one of passivity [towards Finland], except on some concrete questions, in which a negative stance can surface quickly…It would be best that those who wish to continue good Finnish relations with the Soviet Union seek maximum benefit [from the absence of trade]. The Soviet Union does not wish to conclude a trade agreement with Finland if this is bad for Finland, therefore it is better that the negotiations do not start at all.[78]

Zhenihov implied that economic difficulties might force the government to fall.

The Soviet policy of refusing to conduct normal diplomatic relations was confirmed to an interested Yugoslav Foreign Ministry on 5 November, when the Yugoslav Deputy Military Attaché Mutić met with the Finnish Deputy Military Attaché Raisinen over dinner to discuss Finnish-Soviet relations.[79] Raisinen confirmed that the Russians continued to stall on all trade negotiations:

> Regarding credits which the USSR needed still to approve for Finland from their side, Raisinen thinks that nothing will come of that. Based upon an earlier agreement these negotiations needed to begin at the latest by 20 October. The Finnish delegation had already waited, as he says, two months for an invitation to start negotiations, but still have not received one.[80]

Raisinen openly admitted that the reason for the Soviet approach was 'that the Russians are not satisfied with the composition of the current Finnish government, which they say has a "rightist character".' Raisinen told Perišić of the Finnish Foreign Ministry's concern over the growing strain in Finnish-Soviet relations. Raisinen 'pointed out how Finland has altogether four million people and the USSR close to 200 million and they have in every matter to carry out friendly politics with the USSR' based on this calculation alone.

Finnish Analysis of Soviet-Yugoslav Relations, 1957–58

The Finnish Foreign Ministry recognized that Soviet disapproval of the political change in Finland was compounded by the situation in Yugoslavia. There were strong parallels between the Soviet pressure on the Finns and their excoriation of Yugoslav party leadership in November of 1958. In their analysis of the continued Soviet denunciations of the Yugoslav leadership, the Finnish Ministry noted a strong polemical article in the November 1958 issue of the journal *Communist* B.N. Ponomarjev:

> Leaders of rightwing Social Democratic parties have renewed their visits to Yugoslavia attempting to transmit to the Yugoslavs their experiences of serving the imperialists and the betrayal of both socialism and the working class. Folk wisdom says 'state the name of your friends, and I will tell you who you are.' Facts point out that the leadership of the Yugoslav Communist Party, after having stepped on to the shaky road of 'national Communism' are sinking deeper and deeper into the swamp of opportunism, and further away from socialist ideals.[81]

The Foreign Ministry considered that one of the purposes of the article was to prevent closer cooperation between the Finnish Social Democrats now in charge of the government and Yugoslavia. Despite the Soviet pressure, in November the SDP-NCP government continued to hope that Khrushchev would sustain his 'realist politics' he had pursued since 1955 and would come to accept the government eventually. The ministry however, found it increasingly worrisome that Ponomarjev found absolutely no redeeming qualities in the Yugoslav political situation. The article 'does not refer to anything positive in Soviet relations with the Yugoslav state [outside the Party], but condemns with ferocity the neutral position adopted by Yugoslavia.'[82] Ambassador Wuori consulted his 'trusted Yugoslav source' in Moscow in November 1958 but both concluded that 'it is necessary to wait and see what will be the final orientation of the Soviet leadership towards the Yugoslav state.'[83]

As Wuori told Kekkonen on 14 October:

> I am worried about the fact that there was complete 'rest' between the USSR and Finland, as between USSR and Yugoslavia. Nothing is happening. Only one Finnish businessman is in Moscow. Rauma-Repola [company] has made an offer to renew the machinery in four paper factories in the Soviet Union, but now Swedish industrialists have visited those same factories. No one will talk to Finns.[84]

Overall, Finnish analysis for 1958 concluded that Soviet foreign relations had become more anxious, especially in pressing for high-level negotiations with the United States. The Finns noted with special concern 'the continued Soviet desire to demonstrate their critical attitude towards the Yugoslav Communist Party by refusing to attend its [7th] Party Congress and in that way effecting also the refusal to attend of all Soviet 'bloc' states.'[85] These actions were interpreted as steps toward 'strengthening the Soviet bloc' through a hostile campaign against a 'neutral bordering state.' Finnish analysts became increasingly concerned when the Soviet critique was accompanied by Khrushchev's visits to Hungary and Voroshilov's to Poland.[86] The Finnish Foreign Ministry interpreted these visits as direct criticism of Yugoslavia: first, they noted that Hungary was, in contrast to Yugoslavia, a bloc state par excellence; second, they pointed out that Voroshilov had been originally scheduled to visit Yugoslavia in May of 1958, only to cancel his state visit on the morning of his scheduled arrival. This put the Yugoslavs in the embarrassing position of having to first erect, then hurriedly disassemble banners of welcome for him in Belgrade.[87] Mićunović, still in Moscow in early May, guessed that Voroshilov would not in fact leave for Belgrade, but because he was made unable to reach any Soviet official to verify the cancellation of the visit in time, the banners had to be raised.

A Finnish report titled 'Yugoslavia—aka Socialist Bloc's challenger' closely connected the emerging discussion of ideological questions within the Soviet press in April and May 1958 with the Soviet discrediting of the Yugoslav party leadership.[88] The Soviets trotted out examples of former leaders who had 'acted against the Soviet Communist Party', categorically labeling Malenkov, Molotov and others 'dogmatists', 'servants of dead letters' and 'those detached from life.'[89] In addition to these domestic offenders, the Soviet press called the Party Program of the Austrian Social Democratic Party 'revisionist.' In the Finnish Foreign Ministry's view, the actual goal of this press campaign was to discredit the Yugoslav party leadership, a campaign that became worrisome for Finland as well when the Social Democratic-Conservative government was formed in the fall of 1958. On Yugoslav ratification of the program for its 7th Party Congress in May, the Soviet press printed 'more or less official condemnations of the Yugoslavs by the Communist Parties of other states', including China's, as wider evidence of Yugoslav deviation.[90] These denunciations were followed by a plethora of additional propaganda, culminating in the aforementioned *Pravda* article of 9 May, dividing up US aid to Yugoslavia as sales for specific anti-Soviet speeches and acts. The article appeared following a full session of the Central Committee on the issue of Yugoslavia and was read in its entirety on *Radio Moscow* the same day.[91]

To the Finnish Foreign Ministry, the *Pravda* attack against the Yugoslav party and the previous months' criticism of domestic and European revisionists were clearly linked. In the ministry's view, the Yugoslav refusal to sign the 12-Party Declaration 'called the authority of the Soviet Union into question as "the first and most experienced socialist country" for the second time...The Yugoslavs charge the Soviet Union and its leadership with seeking hegemony over and suppression of other socialist states under their command.'[92] The Finnish analysis understood that 'the Yugoslav [Party] leadership fears being placed under the increasing control of the Soviets.'[93]

The Finnish Foreign Ministry, like Kekkonen, found this rhetorical battle unhelpful to European security and security-oriented neutralism in Europe. For Finland, the Soviet charge that US economic aid was a pay-off raised the question of whether Finnish-Western trade might also be labeled bribery in the future. As the *Pravda* article put it, 'The Imperialists do not give anything to anyone for free.'[94] Finnish reports noted with caution, 'Finland is also a state which has received credits "from both sides," and from both sides these credits obtained from the opposition are being followed with increasing suspicion.'[95]

The Finnish analysis found differences in state interests of the Soviet Union and of Yugoslavia to be 'as alive now without Stalin as they were while Stalin was pursuing them...Tito continues to say, "Stalin did this and Stalin did that." These claims cannot conceal the fact that there are factual conflicts of interest between his state and that of Stalin's successors.'[96] Beyond the ideological framework, the coherence of the Soviet bloc held primary and practical importance for the Soviets at this time. Finnish analysts noted that after the launch of Sputnik and the subsequent American initiative for a space program, Yugoslavia's absence from the Warsaw Pact and enrolment in the Balkan Pact with Turkey and Greece acquired a larger significance for the Soviet Union, even if the main significance of the Balkan Pact to Yugoslavia was as a 'security guarantee.'[97]

In this context, the occasional unwillingness of the Yugoslav delegation to the United Nations (led by Foreign Minister Popović) to abstain from voting against Soviet initiatives and several votes for the US position, as on the question of recognition of Taiwan, in the Finnish judgment constituted, a further challenge to the Soviet Union.[98] Kekkonen wanted to make sure that the Finnish delegation would not do the same. Such actions reduced the collective strength of the Soviet bloc directly and the Yugoslav 'fronting' of their political status outside the Soviet camp constituted an obstacle to the Soviet foreign policy effort to ratify a 'European status quo.'[99] Finnish conclusions mirrored those of the Yugoslav Foreign Ministry. Both considered the Yugoslav-Soviet party conflict detrimental in that it reflected no specific political goal on the part of the Yugoslavs. The Finnish Foreign Ministry concluded 'from the Yugoslav perspective, it would seem beneficial if Soviet-Yugoslav relations remained approximately the same' without further interruptions from the party.[100]

Two Roads to Repairing Soviet Relations

In the course of October 1958, Kekkonen grew increasingly worried about a further Soviet reaction to the SDP-NCP government. On 23 October, Boris Pasternak received the Nobel price for literature, and although Pasternak refused to accept it, he was ousted from the Union of Soviet Writers. Kekkonen thought that this indicated 'a world-political hardening in the Soviet Union, since the Soviets were not afraid of the criticism of the West to which this act would undoubtedly lead.'[101] Simultaneously, the SDP continued to consider it possible for Finland to survive without a trade agreement with the Soviet Union until spring 1959, and therefore wanted to pursue 'a hard-line' until then.[102] A prominent economist and representative of the Swedish People's Party, Nils Meinander, commented that 'the scare concerning Finnish-Soviet relations and their worsening has been exacerbated. It has been invented by Kekkonen in order to strengthen his own position.'[103] On 6 November, Kekkonen demanded that the AP's Virolainen resign from the post of Foreign Minister. He told Virolainen that the only solution to Finnish-Soviet relations was the formation of a new government. Virolainen did not agree, instead he argued that Khrushchev would come to accept the SDP-NCP government. Virolainen referred directly to Yugoslavia as evidence for his position: 'after all Yugoslavia has received loans from the USSR. Therefore Soviet-Yugoslav relations should be an example to us!'[104] This Kekkonen found incredible. For him, his Kekkonen-Paasikivi Line was the example for Yugoslavia in relations with the Soviets, not the example of party disputes between Tito and Khrushchev.

On 12 November, the Finnish Secret Police reported to Kekkonen that the Finnish Communist Party had instructed its publications to print rumors that 'Finland is no longer capable of fulfilling its 1948 agreement with the Soviet Union.'[105] His aforementioned KGB contact informed Kekkonen that the Kremlin would not change its position before the end of December, but that Kekkonen should act by that time.[106] On 25 November Virolainen agreed to resign. The following day Kekkonen told parliamentary groups' representatives that simple substitutions in the existing government would not do and demanded that a new one be formed. Kekkonen then met with Zhenihov who promised Kekkonen that 'as soon as there is a new government a Soviet trade agreement would be made and an Ambassador would be sent to Helsinki.'[107] Wishing to speak with Khrushchev privately, Kekkonen proposed that immediately after the forming of a new government he would travel on a private trip with his wife to Leningrad. In December Zhenihov informed Kekkonen that the Kremlin 'does not want official Social Democrats in the government, but some Conservative experts and two unknown Communists' and none of the former Ministers.[108] To this Kekkonen replied simply 'No.' The Kremlin further threatened to then send either Molotov or Marshal Zhukov as the next Ambassador to Helsinki.[109] On 4 December Virolainen's resignation was made official and later that day Fagerholm handed in the resignation of his government to Kekkonen who had demanded it. On 13 January 1959 a Conservative minority government consisting only of Kekkonen's Agrarians' Party and the Swedish People's Party was formed. It contained 15 ministers entirely from the AP.[110] Two of the positions, Foreign Minister and Minister for Trade and Industry, were filled by members of the minority by the Swedish People's Party who served for less than a half term each. Kekkonen included no Communists or anyone else from the SKDL. Finnish-Soviet relations were thereby repaired.

Now when party pressure towards Tito and Kardelj no longer worked in late 1958, the Yugoslav Ministry was left to manage relations with no more opportunities for the Kremlin to manipulate Yugoslav domestic politics.

The ministry was from here on able to be the primary originator of foreign policy for Yugoslavia. This it did from the basis of the recommendations of its analytical department and Foreign Minister Popović. As Khrushchev's ability to consume Tito's and Kardelj's ideological statements was cut off, so was Soviet influence from domestic Yugoslav affairs. In Finland however, Soviet policy succeeded in seeing power taken from the Social Democrats, who had won enough seats in the Parliament to lead a coalition government for the first time since the establishment of the Paasikivi-Kekkonen Line in 1948. The Paasikivi-Kekkonen Line had indeed been jeopardized by the formation of the Social Democratic-Conservative government in August 1958. However, by January 1959, Kekkonen was a President who commanded the Foreign Ministry and was supported by a government in which only ministers from his party served until the end of their term, 14 July 1961. In 1958, the Finnish foreign policy of neutralism was thereby preserved, but the parliament that had been influential under Paasikivi no longer played any role in foreign policy. Finland was not a one-party state, but its foreign policy was directed by a leader of one party, Kekkonen. Simultaneously the Foreign Ministry of a one-party Yugoslavia directed its foreign policy based on the institution's collective analysis. In sum, the pursuit of neutralism in Finnish and Yugoslav policies toward the Soviet Union in 1958 was a compromise by which none of the three state's political goals were completely fulfilled or totally frustrated.

7

CONCLUSION AND AFTERWORD: FROM NEUTRALISM TO NON-ALIGNMENT

The smaller European countries displayed a particular eagerness for contact with us after the split, for example Scandinavia, Belgium etc…and although the volume of trade with them did not increase much, their political influence proved useful.

Edvard Kardelj in *Edvard Kardelj Reminisces.*[1]

The Tito-Stalin split of 1948 had one neglected but important consequence for Yugoslavia. The Yugoslav Foreign Ministry received crucial resources for fighting Soviet propaganda attacks against Yugoslavia and went on to build up an independent role as well as an international network for representation. This meant operating separately, sometimes independently from the daily direction of Josip Broz 'Tito,' his inner party circle and his presidential Secretariat. Nevertheless, it was Tito himself who enabled the Foreign Ministry to assume this relative independence. As noted in Chapter 1, Tito had appointed Edvard Kardelj, the second-ranking member of the Communist leadership, as the Ministry's head immediately after Yugoslavia's expulsion from the Cominform in June 1948. Tito then appointed Koča Popović to succeed Kardelj as Foreign Minister in 1953. While never a member of Tito's inner party circle, Popović remained in the position until 1966 and expanded the international reach and reputation of Yugoslav diplomacy. As noted in Chapter 5, when Tito withdrew his close party associate Veljko Mićunović from the post of Yugoslav Ambassador to Moscow in 1958, he indirectly acknowledged that even Yugoslav relations with the Soviet Union were better directed through the Yugoslav Foreign Ministry than through the League of Communists of Yugoslavia.

The Finnish example was already becoming important during Stalin's last years. On the day that his death was announced in March 1953, the Yugoslav Foreign Ministry wanted first to know the Finnish reaction. From that time forward, as detailed in Chapter 3, the Yugoslav Foreign Ministry regularly compared notes with Finnish analysis of the Soviet Union. In addition, Finland's policy of neutralism, as outlined in the post-war Paasikivi-Kekkonen Line, had been an important example for the Yugoslav Foreign Ministry as early as 1948. Finland had drafted a foreign policy program as seen in Chapter 2, that relied on diplomatic relations to avoid confrontation and promote trade, thereby staving off the Soviet imposition of military and political obligations. The Paasikivi-Kekkonen Line gave up West European political integration in return for state sovereignty and a political process outside the Soviet bloc. A Finnish Communist Party, loyal to Moscow, continued to exist, but none of its leading members were ever included in a post-war government. Simultaneously with the Yugoslav-Soviet split, Finland concluded an Agreement on Friendship, Cooperation and Mutual Assistance with the Soviet Union. Unlike Yugoslavia, Finland henceforth maintained a closely managed relationship with the Kremlin. Between 1948 and 1953, the Finnish example showed the Yugoslav Foreign Ministry that a political position outside the Soviet bloc was possible for a bordering state. Yugoslav-Finnish political contacts and cultural exchanges expanded between 1953 and 1956. The Yugoslav Foreign Ministry believed that similarly managed relations with the Soviet Union would greatly help to end the Soviet military and economic threat to Yugoslavia.

Repeated outbursts from Tito and Kardelj against first Stalin, and then Nikita Khrushchev and the Soviet leadership, asserted the independence of Yugoslavia's Communist party and its policies, but interrupted the Foreign Ministry's pursuit of Finnish-style relations with the USSR. The Ministry, led by the Sorbonne-educated Popović and the Ministry's university-educated officials saw the Tito-Stalin split reborn, to Yugoslav disadvantage, as an ideological argument between the two party leaderships that challenged the Belgrade and Moscow agreements with the Kremlin in 1955 and 1956. These arguments not only impeded the pursuit of broader diplomatic and trade relations but also threatened to divert policy priorities and resources away from the Foreign Ministry. Popović had already used his position to facilitate the signing of the Balkan Pact (1953–54), the resolution of the Trieste question (1954) and the expanding of Yugoslav relations with the Western governments. Beyond economic and political cooperation, he even discussed a military connection with NATO. Significantly, as noted in Chapter 3, he eliminated the de facto influence of the Yugoslav Security Service UDBa. Nothing came of the NATO talk, but from 1953, Popović asked his Foreign Ministry to pursue a course balanced between good relations with the Soviet Union and the freedom to explore other non-military relations. The model for this kind of foreign policy was found in Finland.

By 1958 however, it had become clear to the Foreign Ministry that if Yugoslavia, like Finland, wished to remain outside the Soviet bloc, its relations could not focus entirely on Europe. In 1956, Tito and Kardelj had promised Khrushchev that they would side with the Soviet Union in support of East Germany and its claim to West Berlin. Tito, Kardelj and Mićunović (independently of Popović and the Foreign Ministry) had sanctioned Soviet military action in Hungary in November of that year, as explained in Chapter 4, in order to preserve one-party Communist rule there. Yugoslavia's involvement in the suppression of the Hungarian uprising quickly became public. The abortive revolution's Communist leader Imre Nagy had taken refuge in the Yugoslav embassy, where the Yugoslav Ambassador—loyal to the Ministry— had welcomed him.[2] Tito and the rest of the party leadership subsequently insisted upon turning him over to Hungarian (read Soviet) officials, which lead to Nagy's long detention and execution in 1958. But Tito and the Yugoslav party's support of the Soviet's maintenance of control over bloc members was not enough for the Kremlin. The renewal of ties between the Yugoslav and Soviet parties in 1956 soon led Khrushchev, as we saw in Chapter 5, to push Tito to sign the 12-Party Agreement recognizing the hegemony of the Soviet party over other Communist parties in 1957. The Yugoslav Foreign Ministry joined Tito and Kardelj in arguing that this would make Yugoslavia a de facto part of the Soviet bloc. The Yugoslav 'no' to the 12-Party Agreement led to another escalating war of words between Tito and Kardelj on one side, Khrushchev and the Soviet party on the other.

The Yugoslav Foreign Ministry saw Finland facing a similar rupture in relations with the Soviets in 1958, as also noted in Chapter 5. The successful post-war assertion of the Paasikivi-Kekkonen Line, had exempted Finland from pressure to join the bloc after 1948. The Yugoslav Ministry had since 1953 recognized the success and usefulness of the Paasikivi-Kekkonen Line and sought to follow its practice in maintaining a working relationship with Moscow while building bilateral political and trade ties with the West. But by early 1959, the Ministry had come to the conclusion that such a policy that focused on the European balance of power would not be sufficient to safeguard Yugoslav independence. Despite Tito's approval of the Soviet military action in Hungary, it became clear that the Yugoslav security guarantee for the Soviet bloc border, now like Finland's, was not enough for Soviet leadership. At least it was not enough if Tito and Kardelj kept challenging the Soviet Union with polemics presented in the international press. To pursue peaceful relations with the Soviets, the Yugoslav party would have to demonstrate submission to or at least silence towards the Soviet party. Khrushchev, had traveled to Belgrade in 1955 to apologize for Stalin's refusal to accept Yugoslavia's independent Communist path; now in 1957 he was asking Yugoslavia to acknowledge the inferior position of its party and ideology.

The Paasikivi-Kekkonen Line demanded the pursuit of stable, cordial and extensive trade and diplomatic ties. This was impossible for Yugoslavia as long the Soviets periodically challenged Tito and Kardelj to a duel; a duel that they were generally all too eager to join. As for the Finnish example, the Yugoslav Ministry watched the Kremlin bring down a pro-Western Social-Democrat-Conservative government in 1958 by suspending diplomatic relations, interrupting trade and attacking the government in the press. In bringing it down, the Soviet Union dealt directly with President Kekkonen, a model for relations which the Yugoslav Ministry had no desire to replicate. In the Yugoslav Ministry's view, the Soviets had practically dictated the form of the government that followed. Although Kekkonen had been able to exclude all Communists and even socialists from the government that would last from 1959 to 1961, it had still required the Kremlin's approval. This rendered the Paasikivi-Kekkonen Line far less appealing to the Yugoslav Foreign Ministry in 1959 than it had been in 1948 or 1953. Moreover, the so-called 'Night Frost Crisis' was not resolved to the benefit of an independent Finnish Foreign Ministry. The Ministry remained under Kekkonen's effective control. The Yugoslav Ministry concluded that all this meant a Soviet reassertion of control over Helsinki.

Between 1959 and 1961, Yugoslavia's Foreign Ministry began to seek out connections beyond Europe, turning away from Finland in the process. The Ministry felt that in order to avoid the Finnish predicament and to increase its own independence, the Yugoslav version of neutralism should focus on non-Communist states beyond the Soviets' immediate purview. Foreign Minister Kardelj's 1949 speech, delivered at the United Nation's General Assembly, had already expressed Yugoslav interest in the less-developed, non-European members. As he turned to the Tito-Stalin split Kardelj stated that 'the attitude of the USSR towards Yugoslavia is enough to show that the Soviet government cannot always be seen as the interpreter of contemporary aspirations for peace and democracy.'[3] Kardelj linked Yugoslavia's economically disadvantaged position not only to the Soviet conflict but to the problems of less developed countries in general, 'This is precisely why the offering of economic help as a means of developing and strengthening the independence of the less developed countries is an open question in the world today. There is no doubt that this is a problematic aspect of the work of the UN; nevertheless, its resolution should be among our most urgent tasks.'[4] In 1949 Kardelj was appealing to the United Nations for more United Nations Relief and Rehabilitation Aid (UNRRA).[5]

A decade later, his comments came in handy for the Yugoslav Foreign Ministry as they searched for a precedent in forming ties with newly independent African and Asian states. Their number had increased significantly since Yugoslavia had begun what was then a search for wider bilateral relations, outside the Soviet orbit, with embassies opened in New Delhi and Rangoon in 1950.[6] In the decade after the Tito-Stalin split the number of Yugoslav embassies nearly doubled, from 53 embassies in 1948 to 91 in 1958. In 1948 Yugoslavia had diplomatic relations with 64 countries.[7] By the end of that year Kardelj had created embassies in most of these states, as evidenced by the number 53. Popović actively sought diplomatic relations with additional states and increased the number of embassies accordingly. The number of Yugoslav embassies in the 1950s is particularly impressive when compared to the First Yugoslavia, which in 1939 had only 31 embassies.[8] Tito, always fond of international travel, now toured this longer list of non-European states extensively. In 1958 and 1959 he visited Indonesia, Burma, India, Ceylon, Ethiopia, Sudan and Egypt. In 1961 he went to Ghana, Togo, Liberia, Guinea, Mali, Morocco, Tunisia and Egypt. By this time, Yugoslavia was ready to be more than the observer of the Asian stirrings of the mid-1950s that would now become the Non-Aligned Movement. Tito's brief meetings with India's Nehru and Egypt's Nasser in 1956, as acknowledged in the introduction, now served as building blocks to connect to these stirrings.

Between 1959 and 1961 the Yugoslav Foreign Ministry begun to promote cooperation with African and Asian states based on these previous contacts. Popović remained uninterested in an ideological approach to these new partners. He ordered the Ministry to examine practical arrangements, such as Yugoslav arms sales to Rangoon. Already in 1958 Tito had agreed to the withdrawal of his close associate Mićunović from Moscow, a clear sign that he was willing to let Popović guide the Ministry and Yugoslav foreign policy. Between 1959 and 1961, the Ministry discussed furthering bilateral relations with Asia and Africa, ties that would now lead to association with the emergence of a formal Non-Aligned Movement. The Yugoslav turn began only after 1958, after the Finnish-Soviet 'Night Frost Crisis' and the renewed freeze in Yugoslav-Soviet relations. Only the Yugoslav interest after 1958 led to the Belgrade conference of 1961 when 32 heads of state, mostly from Asia and Africa, met to launch the Movement. The non-aligned framework presented Yugoslavia with a new extra-European opportunity. The Ministry could easily bring Tito on board as the presidential representative of Yugoslav foreign policy. The Asian and African context also offered Tito's public persona room to breathe outside of Yugoslav-Soviet relations.

To Popović's displeasure, the Yugoslav policy of non-alignment did come to be known for its ideological position. The influence of the previous Yugoslav policy of accepting Soviet security interests could still be seen in the Non-Aligned Movement's siding with Soviets on the questions of West Berlin and East Germany. These were positions that supported Soviet policy in Europe, which could hardly have been a priority to any of the other African and Asian states more concerned with anti-colonialism than the significance of a divided Germany. This non-alignment, not fully in place until 1961, would distinguish Yugoslav and Finnish foreign policy from one another from 1961 onwards. The Yugoslav Ministry would nonetheless continue its close attention to Finnish relations with the Soviet Union and unite with Kekkonen's interest in launching the Conference on Security and Cooperation in Europe in 1975.

Neutralism as Political Strategy

In this book I have juxtaposed the development, content and purpose of two parallel but separate political strategies of neutralism. Neutralism is a concept not often defined or examined in detail. It is often understood as an ideology. Historians of Yugoslavia such as Duncan Wilson have referred to it as 'some such policy.'[9] As an ideological construct, neutralism is supposed to imply non-adherence to predominant power structures, such as the Soviet and Western blocs in the Cold War. Understood as an ideology, neutralism is purported to have a superior political quality in that it is expected to oppose militarism and preclude military conflict. This comes from the legal concept of neutrality, according to which the legal status of abstention from participation in a war between other states and the maintenance of an attitude of impartiality towards the belligerents can be claimed.[10]

What do the two separate Finnish and Yugoslavia examples comparatively tell us about neutralism? Two political leaders, Juho Kusti Paasikivi and Urho Kekkonen, at the end of the Second World War conceptualized the Finnish policy of neutralism. Both had intimate knowledge of Russia and the Soviet Union, as we saw in Chapter 2. Paasikivi worked as State Treasurer at the turn of the twentieth-century when Finland was an autonomous Grand Duchy of Tsarist Russia. Kekkonen began his career within the Finnish police force and worked to build up the Secret Police (SUPO). Its main purpose was surveillance of Soviet representatives or their Finnish contacts. Both men participated in negotiations with the Soviet Union in the closing days of the Second World

War. For them, neutralism was not based on an ideological commitment to any form of non-militarism. Instead it was a political strategy designed to get Finland out of facing renewed military intervention from the Soviet Union. Its purpose was to prevent another unwinnable confrontation with the Red Army and to keep Finland from becoming part of what became the emerging Soviet bloc. Paasikivi and Kekkonen did not choose neutralism because they thought it was the best possible foreign policy. Securing independence militarily and then pursuing ties with the West was a better option in their view. Since this was impossible, especially when the Soviet Union became a post-war superpower, the Finnish policy of neutralism accepted the payment of heavy war reparations, the permanent loss of Karelia, and the temporary loss of the Porkkala naval base in 1948. It thereby admitted Finland's war guilt but did not forfeit state sovereignty. With the drafting and signing in 1948 of the Finnish-Soviet Agreement on Friendship, Cooperation and Mutual Assistance, this Finnish policy of neutralism sought to guarantee to the Soviet Union that Finland would not join a military alliance with the West. Finnish neutralism promised to limit cooperation with the West to trade which it also would carry out with the Soviet Union. Finnish neutralism was a political and economic bargain with the Soviet Union that allowed Finland to remain outside the Soviet bloc.

The Yugoslav policy of neutralism, as shaped by its Foreign Ministry, was similarly a political strategy and not an ideological commitment. It followed the Finnish example and was a reaction to the Tito-Stalin split. Similarly to Finland, Yugoslavia needed to avoid a military conflict with the Soviet Union. The Yugoslav Ministry saw its best strategy to achieve an independent position outside the Soviet bloc as the building up of formal diplomatic and trade relations with the Soviet Union. Yugoslavia could use them to demonstrate that it would not challenge the Soviet Union or the borders of the Soviet bloc in Eastern Europe. This, the Ministry hoped, would leave Yugoslavia free to pursue bilateral trade and political relations outside the Soviet orbit. Yet Tito and Kardelj insisted that ideological distinction in the aftermath of the Tito-Stalin split was needed if Yugoslavia were to assert its independence from the Soviet Union. The two party leaders demanded that their presumed ideological superiority not only justified the split but now defined the states' political independence as well. The Cold War was a competition between two ideological systems of government, and Tito and Kardelj as ardent Marxists argued that the Yugoslav conflict with the Soviet Union could also be won on ideological grounds. In 1956 and 1957, their affirming outbursts against the Soviet Union competed with Yugoslav Foreign Ministry's policy of neutralism. Yet in the face of this renewed conflict with Khrushchev's Kremlin, the Ministry won back priority in foreign relations by 1958.

Yugoslav and Finnish relations with the Soviet Union between 1948 and 1958 tell us that neutralism is at best a successful political strategy of smaller states against states with larger political and/or military power. This is its only connection to formerly colonial states. In itself, neutralism does not suggest nor guarantee anti-militarism. Neither Paasikivi, Kekkonen, nor Popović were pacifists. They were also not ideologues. Neutralism was only applied as a second best strategy when confrontation was not a tenable option. Nor does neutralism imply moral impunity for its practitioners. Finnish non-reaction to and Yugoslav sanctioning of Soviet military action against the Hungarian revolution displays such a failing. But when Walter Laqueur raised the undesirable 'Specter of Finlandization' in his 1977 essay, cited in the introduction, his concern that Finnish accommodation with the Soviet Union had extended beyond the necessities of its geopolitical situation prompted a wider worry. The other European states might turn to this sort of neutralism in the optimistic 1970s atmosphere of détente that obscured the clear and present danger still posed, for Laqueur and many others, by the Soviet Union. In identifying the sort of 'domestic adjustment' he feared from the Finnish model for 'behaving responsibly', he pointed only to self-censorship and Kekkonen's long tenure as President.[11] For Laqueur, its policy of neutralism had made Finland a client state of the Soviet Union. To him the Finnish policy presented 'a slow almost imperceptible retreat from independence – not just in foreign affairs but also on the domestic front.'[12] In terms of foreign policy he fairly points to Finnish abstention from voting at the United Nations in favor of demanding that Soviet troops leave Hungary in 1956 and the general silence over the Hungarian revolution by the Finnish political leadership, as discussed here in Chapter 4.[13] But on the domestic front, as we have seen, the Finnish policy of neutralism did not lead to such an internal accommodation until 1958. Then, as we saw in Chapter 5, Kekkonen's direct consultation with the KGB in Helsinki in the fall of 1958 to broker Finnish-Soviet relations and his subsequent bringing down of the government of his political opponents in order to rescue the Finnish policy of neutralism does indeed support Laqueur's critique. But changing the course by 1961, Kekkonen's Agrarians' Party government would be forced out by new elections. In 1961, Kekkonen signed off on Finland's accession to the European Free Trade Association as an associate member, marking a clear step away from its Soviet neighbor.

In conclusion, as the Finnish and the Yugoslav examples from the 1950s show, a policy of neutralism can help a state gain or maintain state sovereignty. It can lead to successful economic policies and trade ties. Through its very visible successes neutralism can provide its promoters, in the Finnish case President Kekkonen and in the Yugoslav case the Foreign

Ministry, more political autonomy than would be expected, more time to pursue political goals than would be otherwise be admitted. For the three years of his constructed government, Kekkonen did abuse that autonomy in the name of neutralism. As for Yugoslavia's Foreign Ministry it would unfortunately not be joined by other strong and relatively independent federal ministries needed for Yugoslavia to have a chance to survive after Tito. Neutralism, unlike its mythic ideology is not a policy of moral right or wrong.[14] It is however a political strategy of compromise. In the Finnish and the Yugoslav cases, it was a foreign policy of post-war compromise acted out at a time of continuing political uncertainty. We may conclude that neutralism as a political strategy served the purpose of getting Finland and Yugoslavia out of some very difficult situations from 1948 forward for another decade.

NOTES

Archive material quoted below retains its original date pattern.

Chapter 1
1 For example, William H. McNeill, *America, Britain and Russia: Their Cooperation and Conflict* (Oxford: Oxford University Press, 1953).
2 For example, William Appleman Williams, *The Tragedy of American Diplomacy*, 3rd edition (New York: W. Norton & Company, 1972).
3 See for example, John Lewis Gaddis, *Strategies of Containment: A Critical Appraisal of Postwar American National Security Policy* (New York: Oxford University Press, 1982). John Lewis Gaddis, 'The Emerging Post-Revisionist Synthesis on the Origins of the Cold War,' *Diplomatic History* 7 (3) (1983): 171. Melvyn Leffler, *The Specter of Communism: The United States and the Origins of the Cold War, 1917–1953* (New York: Harper Collins, 1995).
4 Communist Information Bureau (Cominform).
5 Dennison Rusinow, *The Yugoslav Experiment 1948–1974* (Berkeley: Published for the Royal Institute of International Affairs, London, by the University of California Press, 1977).
6 Neutralism here is defined as a political strategy appropriate to the circumstances of the Cold War. The policy of neutralism in the Finnish case according to the formulation by Presidents J.K. Paasikivi and Urho Kekkonen meant that Finland established bilateral relations with the Soviet Union and remained outside of NATO as well as abstaining from other defensive international alignments.
7 Juho Paasikivi President 1946–56; Urho Kekkonen President 1956–81.
8 David Holloway, *Stalin and the Bomb: The Soviet Union and Atomic Energy 1939–1954* (New Haven, Conn: Yale University Press, 1994).
9 Notable exceptions include Melvyn P. Leffler and David S. Painter eds. *Origins of the Cold War: An International History*, 2nd edition. (New York: Routledge, 2005). This volume unlike the majority of the international histories of the Cold War also focuses on Europe. Its approach to Europe also encompasses more than Eastern Europe. Also please see, David Reynolds ed. *The Origins of the Cold War in Europe: International Perspectives* (New Haven, Conn.: Yale University Press, 1994). For the most recent perspectives on the Cold War please see Melvyn P. Leffler, 'The Cold

War: What Do "We Now Know"?' *The American Historical Review*, 104 (2) (1999), 501.

[10] Finland became an Associate Member in 1961 and a full member in 1986, and gave up membership in 1995 when joining the European Union.

[11] Adam Ulam, *Titoism and the Cominform*, (Cambridge, Mass.: Harvard University Press, 1952), 70.

[12] Jeronim Perović, 'The Tito-Stalin Split: A Reassessment in Light of New Evidence' *Journal of Cold War Studies* 9 (2) (2007): 34. Although published in English this study draws mostly on Soviet and Yugoslav sources.

[13] Vladislav Zubok and Constantine Pleshakov, *Inside the Kremlin's Cold War* (Cambridge, Mass.: Harvard University Press, 1996), 34–35, 54. Silvio Pons and Francesca Gori (eds.): *The Soviet Union and Europe 1943–1953* (New York: St. Martin's Press, 1996).

[14] Vladimir Dedijer, *The Battle Stalin Lost: Memoirs of Yugoslavia 1948–1953* (New York: Viking Press, 1971). In Serbo-Croatian Vladimir Dedijer, *Izgubljena bitka J. V. Staljina* (Belgrade: Prosveta, 1969); other works include Vladimir Dedijer, *Josip Broz Tito: Prilozi za biografiju* (Zagreb: Kultura, 1953).

[15] Čedomir Štrbac, *Jugoslavija i Odnosi Izmedju Socijalističkih Zemalja: Sukob KPJ I Informbiroa.* (Belgrade: Instituta za Medjunarodnu Politiku I Privredu, 1975).

[16] Ranko Petković, *1948: Jugoslavija i Kominform – pedeset godina kasnije.* (Belgrade: Medjunarodna Politika, 1998).

[17] Also see Leo Mates, *Medjunarodni odnosi socijalističke Jugoslavije.* (Belgrade: Nolit, 1976).

[18] Tvrtko Jakovina, *Američki komunistički saveznik; Hrvati, Titova Jugoslavija i Sjedinjene Američke Države 1945–1955* (Zagreb: Srednja Europa, 2003).

[19] Dragan Bogetić, *Nova strategija spoljne politike Jugoslavije 1956–1961* (Belgrade: Institut a Savremenu Istoriju, 2006). See also the edited work Slobodan Selinić et.al. *Spoljna politika Jugoslavije 1950–1961* (Belgrade: Institut a Savremenu Istoriju, 2008).

[20] Ulam, *Titoism and the Cominform…*; Milovan Djilas, *Conversations with Stalin* (New York, Harcourt, Brace & World, 1962); Ivo Banac, *With Stalin against Tito: Cominformist Splits in Yugoslav Communism.* (Ithaca: Cornell University Press, 1988); The edited volume by Wayne S. Vucinich discusses this literature as well. Please see Wayne S. Vucinich ed. *At the Brink of War and Peace: The Tito-Stalin Split in a Historic Perspective* (New York: Social Science Monographs, 1982).

[21] Perović, 'The Tito-Stalin Split…,' 32.

[22] Alvin Rubinstein, *Yugoslavia and the Nonaligned World* (Princeton, New Jersey: Princeton University Press, 1970).

[23] Edvard Kardelj, *Sećanja. Borba za priznanje I nezavisnost nove Jugoslavije, 1944-1957.* (Ljubljana and Belgrade: Državna založba Slovenije—Radnicka štampa, 1980).

[24] Perović's account discusses also the role of ideological differences prior to the split; he seeks to demonstrate they were not the main cause. Perović 'The Tito-Stalin Split…,' 35.

[25] Adam Ulam's best known works on Soviet foreign policy include Adam Ulam, *The New Face of Soviet Totalitarianism* (Cambridge, Mass., 1963); Adam Ulam, *Understanding the Cold War: A Historians Personal Reflections*, 2nd ed. (New Brunswick,

N.J. , 2002). For more on the significance of Ulam's contribution to the study of Soviet foreign policy please see David Engermann, *Know Your Enemy: The Rise and Fall of America's Soviet Experts*. Oxford: Oxford University Press, 2009.

[26] Vladimir Dedijer, *Dnevnik 1–3* (Belgrade: Drzavni izdavacki zavod Jugoslavije, 1945-1950). Later accounts echoing Dedijer's account: Milovan Djilas, *Conversations With Stalin*. (New York: Harcourt, Bruce & World, 1962); Edvard Kardelj, *Reminiscences: the Struggle for Recognition and Independence: the New Yugoslavia, 1944–1957*. (London: Blond & Briggs in association with Summerfield Press, 1982).

[27] Ulam, *Titoism and the Cominform…*, 189; Djilas, *Conversations with Stalin*.

[28] Ibid. 70.

[29] Ann Lane and Howard Temperley (eds.): *The Rise and Fall of the Grand Alliance, 1941–1945* (Basingstoke: Macmillan, 1995).

[30] Rusinow, *The Yugoslav Experiment…*, 23.

[31] Banac, *With Stalin against Tito…*, 4–6.

[32] Ibid. 26.

[33] Ibid. 35.

[34] Rubinstein, *Yugoslavia and the Nonaligned World…*

[35] Norman Naimark, 'Cold War Studies and New Archival Materials on Stalin' *The Russian Review* 61 (January 2002); Norman Naimark, 'Post-Soviet Russian Historiography on the Emergence of the Soviet Bloc' *Kritika* 5(3) (Summer 2004) also see Sheila Fitzpatrick: 'Politics as Practice: Thoughts on a New Soviet Political History' *Kritika* 5(1) (Winter 2004). In his exhaustive article in footnote no. 6 Jeronim Perović details the early discussion of the Tito-Stalin split and the released documents since 1988. Jeronim Perović, 'The Tito-Stalin Split: A Reassessment in Light of New Evidence' *Journal of Cold War Studies* 9 (2) (2007): 32.

[36] T.V. Volokitina et. al., *Sovietskiĭ factor v Vostochnoi Evrope 1944-1953: dokumenty* and *Moskva i Vostochnaia Evropa: Stanovlenie politicheskikh rezhimov sovetskogo tipa, 1949–1953* (Moscow : ROSSPEN, 1999–2002) 53.

[37] Recent article in English on this topic is Perović, 'The Tito-Stalin Split…,' Perović also agrees with this conclusion on the basis of the Soviet documents that it was Tito's expansionist foreign policy agenda specifically in relation to his actions in Albania that primarily caused the split in late 1948. Similar views of the importance of Yugoslav provocations in Albania in 1948 and longer term ambitions since 1943 have been developed through the extensive work of the Russian historian most frequently engaged with the topic, Leonid Gibianskii. See for example, Leonid Gibianskii, 'The Soviet-Yugoslav Split and the Cominform' in Norman Naimark and Leonid Gibianskii, *The Establishment of Communist Regimes in Eastern Europe, 1944–1949*. (Boulder, Co.: Westview Press, 1997). Leonid Gibianskii, 'Ideya balkanskogo ob'edineniya I plany ee osushchestyleniya y 40-e gody XX Veka' *Voprosy istorii*, 11 (2001), 43.

[38] Ibid. 501.

[39] Ibid. 17.

[40] Leonid Gibianskii, 'Sovetskii Soiuz i novaia Yugoslaviia, 1941–1947 gg.,' in *otvetstvennyi redaktor* in V.K. Volkov. (Moscow: Nauka, 1987) And Leonid Gibianskii ed. *U istokov 'sotsialisticheskogo sodruzhestv': SSSR i vostochnoevropeiskie strany v 1944–1949*

(Moscow: Nauka, 1995). Gibianskii's numeous works on the period also include: Leonid Gibianskii 'Balkanskii uzel' in *Moskva Vtoraya mirovaya voina: Aktualnye problemy*, ed. in O.A. Rzheshevskii. (Moskva: 1995); Leonid Gibianskii, 'Problemy mezhdunarodno-politicheskogo strukturirovaniya Vostochnoi Yevropy v period formirovaniya sovet·skogo bloka v 1940-ye gody' in *Holodnaya voina: novye podhody, novye dokumenty*. Ed. M.M. Narinskii (Moskva: 1995).

[41] Ibid. 26.
[42] Ibid. 31.
[43] Arkhiv Vneshnei Politiki Rossiiskoi Federatsii (AVP RF) (Archive of Foreign Policy of the Russian Federation), f. 07, op. 21, por. 471, p. 31; f. 07, op. 11, por. 503, p. 30; f. 06, op. 9, por. 1285, p. 82; f. 06, op. 10, por. 1106, p. 70; f. 06, op. 8, por. 943, p. 56; f. 0144, op. 31, por. 16, p. 123.
[44] Ibid. and AVPRF, f. 0144. op.31, p. 124.
[45] A.I. Mikoian, *Tak bylo: Razmyshleniia o minuvshem*, (Moscow: Vagrius, 1999). L.M. Kaganovich, *Pamiatnye zapiski rabochego kommunista-bol'shevika, profsouznogo,partiinogo i sovetsko-gosudartsvennogo rabotnika* (Moscow: Vagrius, 1996).
[46] A.S. Anikeev, *Kak Tito ot Stalin Ushel: iugoslaviia, sssr I ssha v nachal'nyi period kholodnoi voiny 1945–1957*, (Moscow, Russia: In-t. slavianovedeniia RAN, 2002).
[47] Alter Litvin and John Keep, *Stalinism: Russian and Western Views at the Turn of the Millennium* (London: Routledge, 2006) 82.
[48] Duncan Wilson, *Tito's Yugoslavia* (Cambridge: Cambridge University Press, 1979), 123.
[49] Ibid.124.
[50] Rubinstein, *Yugoslavia and the Nonaligned...*, 40, 114, 62.
[51] Ibid. 33.
[52] Ibid. 63.
[53] Ibid. 64.
[54] Peter Willetts, *The Non-Aligned Movement: The Origins of a Third World Alliance*. (London: Frances Pinter Ltd., 1978).
[55] Fred Singleton, *Twentieth Century Yugoslavia* (New York: Columbia University Press, 1976), 178.
[56] Sabrina Ramet, *The Three Yugoslavias: State-Building and Legitimation, 1918–2004* (Bloomington, Ind.: Indiana University Press, 2007), 186.
[57] John R. Lampe, *Yugoslavia as History: Twice There was a Country*, 2nd ed. (Cambridge: Cambridge University Press, 2000), 272.
[58] Wilson, *Tito's Yugoslavia...*, 124.
[59] Ibid. 123.
[60] Ibid. 124.
[61] Anikeev, *Kak Tito ot Stalin Ushel...*,
[62] Dragan Bogetić, *Nova Strategija Spoljne Politike Jugoslavije 1956–1961*. (Belgrade: Institut za Savremenu Istoriju, 2007). Radovan Radonić, *Izgubljena Orijentacija*. (Belgrade: Radnička Štampa, 1985).
[63] Edvard Kardelj, *Istorijski koreni nesvrstavanja*. (Belgrade: Komunist, 1975).
[64] Duncan Wilson, *Tito's Yugoslavia*, 1.
[65] Kardelj, *Reminiscences*, 126–30.

66 Ibid.
67 Fred Singleton, *Twentieth Century Yugoslavia*…, 177.
68 'The Brioni Communiqué.' *New York Times*, 21 July 1956.
69 Ibid.
70 Walter Laqueur, *The Political Psychology of Appeasement: Finlandization and Other Unpopular Essays* (New Brunswick, N.J. : Transaction Books, 1980), 7.
71 Ibid.
72 Ibid.
73 Ibid. 8.
74 Jukka Nevakivi, 'Finland and the Cold War,' *Scandinavian Journal of History*, Vol.10 (3) (1985): 43.
75 Ibid.
76 Max Jakobson, *Finland: Myth and Reality* (Helsinki: Otava, 1987).
77 Roy Allison, *Finland's Relations with the Soviet Union 1944–84* (London: Macmillan, 1985).
78 Juhani Suomi as a civil servant of the Foreign Ministry also had early access to documents concerning Urho Kekkonen within the Foreign Ministry archive.
79 Juhani Suomi, *Urho Kekkonen 1972–1976: Liennytyksen akanvirrassa* (Helsinki: Otava, 1998).
80 Timo Vihavainen, *Kansakunta Rähmällään: Suomettumisen lyhyt historia* (Helsinki: Otava, 1991).
81 Petković, *Subjektivna Istorija Jugoslovenske*…
82 Mita Miljković, *Burne Diplomatske Godine iz Sofijskog Dnevnika 1953–1956* (Belgrade: Službeni list SRJ, 1995); Arso Milatović, *Pet Diplomatskih Misija: Bukurešt – Varšava*. (Ljubljana and Zagreb: Cankareva Založba, 1986).
83 Jukka Nevakivi, *Ulkoasiainhallinnon historia. 1: 1918–1956* (Helsinki: Ulkoaisiainministerio, 1988).

Chapter 2

1 Stephen Clissold (ed.), *Yugoslavia and the Soviet Union 1939–1973: A documentary survey* (Oxford: Oxford University Press, 1975), 202. See also Perović, 'The Tito-Stalin Split…,' 32. And Giuliano Procacci et al, (eds.), *The Cominform: Minutes of the Three Conferences 1947/1948/1949* (Milan: Feltrinelli, 1994).
2 Ibid.
3 Clissold (ed.), *Yugoslavia and the Soviet Union 1939–1973*…, 204.
4 Nada Kisić Kolanović, *Andrija Hebrang: iluzije i otrežnjenja*. (Zagreb: Institut za Suvremneu Povijest, 1996). Considered by Tito not to be loyal to his authority, Hebrang was relieved of his duties as Federal Planning Commissioner on 8 January 1948 and placed under house arrest in April. On 7 May, he was arrested and subsequently tried on a series of fabricated charges such as collaboration with the Ustaša, working as a long time Soviet agent, and advocating a chauvinist policy against the Serbs.
5 Dedijer, *The Battle Stalin Lost*…, 129; Vladimir Dedijer, *Tito* (New York: Simon and Schuster, 1953), 361; Banac, *With Stalin Against Tito*…, 124.

6 James Frusetta, *'Bulgaria's Macedonia: nation-building and state-building, centralization and autonomy in Pirin Macedonia, 1903–1952'* Unpublished Ph.D. Thesis, (College Park: University of Maryland, 2006), 304. Peter J. Stavrakis, *Moscow and Greek communism, 1944–1949* (New York: Cornell University Press, 1989).
7 Vladimir Dedijer, *Josip Broz Tito: Prelozi za biografiju.* (Belgrade: Kultura, 1953), 345.
8 Logistically, the Soviet war effort in 1941 and early 1942 could hardly spare resources for outside aid. Nazi Germany invaded the Soviet Union in June 1941. The Soviet Union was unprepared for the attack; Stalin had sought to uphold the Nazi-Soviet Pact to the very last minute. On the western front only Britain remained at war with Nazi Germany, her resources concentrated on the defence of the British Isles and the Mediterranean lifeline to India. Soviet defence efforts suffered heavy losses in 1941, and some in the Ukraine welcomed the Nazi soldiers as liberators. In November 1941 Nazi troops reached the outskirts of Leningrad. The first successful Soviet counteroffensive was launched in December 1941. 1942 was characterized by two German advances in the summer—to Stalingrad in the Volga region—and Russian winter recoveries. Under these circumstances it seemed impossible for Stalin to grant Tito much assistance until early 1943. This did not satisfy Tito, who saw the strategy as an illegitimate excuse.
9 Dedijer, *Josip Broz Tito…*, 354 and 369.
10 Moša Pijade, *Priča o Sovjetskoj Pomoći za Diranje Ustanka u Jugoslaviji* (Belgrade: Borba, 1950), 11.
11 Ibid. 12.
12 Dedijer, *Josip Broz Tito,* 332.
13 Winston Churchill, *The Second World War: Closing the Ring* (Boston: Houghton Mifflin, 1951), 414. Other accounts disagree that there were serious strains in Soviet-Yugoslav relations. For example see Perović, 'The Tito-Stalin Split…,' 36 and Nikola Popović, *Jugoslavensko-sovjetski odnosi u drugom svetskom ratu (1941–1945)* (Belgrade: Institute za savremenu Istoriju, 1988).
14 Clissold, *Yugoslavia and the Soviet Union 1939–1973…*, 159.
15 In late 1944, Djilas for example told the CPY Central Committee that he 'considered the English officers, from a moral standpoint, superior to Soviet officers' in the Second World War, referring to the looting and destructive behavior of the Red Army as it passed through parts of Yugoslavia. While the Soviets did not deny that 'a few incidences and offenses were committed by individual officers and soldiers of the Red Army in Yugoslavia' in early 1945, the Central Committee of the CPSU still protested against the CPY's 'slander' of the Red Army in their correspondence. Savez Komunista Jugoslavije. Centralni Komitet: Pisma C.K.K.P.J.Belgrade: Jugoslovenska Knjiga, 1948.
16 Albert Reiss, 'The Churchill-Stalin Secret "Percentages" Agreement on the Balkans, Moscow, October 1944,' *American Historical Review*, 83 (1978): 368.
17 Other interpretations have argued that Yugoslavia was looking to gain territory in Northern Greece and/or that engagement in the Greek Civil War served as a pretext to strengthen the Yugoslav presence (for example bilateral trade) in neighboring Albania. See Perović, 'The Tito-Stalin Split…,' 45. Here I argue instead

that the Tito leadership fundamentally supported the Communist and Partisan cause in Greece.

[18] The First Round was the failed 1943 effort of Communist-led EAM/ELAS to wipe out its rival EDES resistance group. John Iatrides, *Revolt in Athens: The Greek Communist 'Second Round' 1944–1945* (New Jersey: Princeton University Press, 1972).

[19] Richard Clogg ed., *Greece 1940–1949: Occupation, Resistance, Civil War: A Documentary History* (London: Palgrave Macmillan, 2002), 19–20.

[20] C. M. Woodhouse, *The Struggle for Greece 1940–1949* (New York: Beekman-Esanu Press, 1976), 250–54, 262–65, 272–76, 284–85.

[21] Nicholas Pappas, 'The Soviet-Yugoslav Conflict and the Greek Civil War' in *At the Brink of War and Peace: The Tito-Stalin Split in a Historic Perspective,* ed. Wayne S. Vucinich (New York: Columbia University Press, East European Monographs, 1982), 222.

[22] Zubok and Pleshakov, *Inside the Kremlin's Cold War…*, 127.

[23] Ibid. 128, Rossiiskii Tsentr Khraneniia i Izucheniia Dokumentov Noveishei Istorii (RTsKhIDNI) (Russian Centre for the Preservation and Study of Documents of Modern History), f.17, op.128, d.1068, l.107.

[24] Vesselin Dimitrov, *Stalin's Cold War: Soviet Foreign Policy, Democracy and Communism in Bulgaria, 1941–1948* (Doctoral Thesis, London School of Economics and Political Science, 2006), 235.

[25] Ibid. Also see Silvio Pons, 'The Twilight of the Cominform' in Giuliano Procacci et al. *The Cominform: Minutes of the Three Conferences 1947/1948/1949* (Milan: Feltrinelli, 1994).

[26] Ibid. 237.

[27] Ivo Banac, (ed.) *The Diary of Georgi Dimitrov 1933-1949* (New Haven, Connecticut: Yale University Press, 2003), 343 (Entry 23 November 1944).

[28] Edvard Kardelj, *Reminiscences: The struggle for recognition and independence: the new Yugoslavia, 1944–1957* (London: Blond & Briggs Press, 1982), 95.

[29] Dimitrov, *Stalin's Cold War…*, 238.

[30] Banac (ed.) *The Diary of Georgi Dimitrov…*, 422 (Entry 12 August 1947).

[31] Leonid Gibianskii, 'The Soviet-Yugoslav Conflict and the Soviet Bloc' in Gori, Francesca and Silvio Pons (eds.): *The Soviet Union and Europe in the Cold War, 1943–53* (New York: St. Martin's Press, 1996), 231. RTsKhIDNI, f 575, op. 1, d. 41, 1. 20–1

[32] Ibid. 229. Norman Naimark, 'Post-Soviet Russian Historiography on the Emergence of the Soviet Bloc' *Kritika* 5(3) (Summer 2004), 577.

[33] Rossiiskii gosudarstvennyi arkhiv sotsial'no-politicheskoi istorii (RGASPI) (Russian State Archive of Socio-Political History), F.17, Op.128, d.1161, l.9–24 T.V. Volokitina, et al. *Moskva i Vostochnaia Evropa : stanovlenie politicheskikh rezhimov sovetskogo tipa : 1949–1953* (Moscow: Rosspen, 2002), 787. Also cited in Jeronim Perović, 'The Tito-Stalin Split…,' 41.

[34] RGASPI, F.17, Op.128, d.1161, l.9–24. This extensive report lists five chapters on the following descriptive topics: 'Contempt for Marxist Theory'; 'Disregard for the Soviet Union as Deciding Power in the Camp for Democracy and Socialism'; 'Reevaluation of Achievements in the Development of Yugoslavia on the Path to Socialism'; 'Underestimation of the Class Struggle in the Countryside and the Threat

of the Kulak'; 'Opportunism and Liquidation on the Question of the Role and Place of the Communist party in the System of Social-Democratic Government.'
35 Ibid.
36 T.V. Volokitina, et al. *Moskva i Vostochnaia Evropa* 53. Perović, 'The Tito-Stalin Split…,' 41 has argued that these reports point towards an equal measure of criticism being directed towards Poland, Czechoslovakia and Yugoslavia.
37 'Dimitrov Foresees Federation in East: Even Greece is on list of nations for joint action "when time is ripe,"' *The New York Times*, 18 January 1948, 9. Other accounts have quoted Dimitrov in a slightly different translation than the *Times* as saying 'When the time is ripe [for federation or confederation] – and it is turning ripe now – our people, the people of the people's democracies, that is Romania, Bulgaria, Yugoslavia, Albania, Czechoslovakia, Poland, Hungary and Greece (please not, Greece as well!), will solve this question.' This quote has Dimitrov citing Greece also as a 'people's democracy' while the *Times* quote refers to 'popular democracies.' Cited in Jeronim Perović, 'The Tito-Stalin Split…,' 51 and Leonid Gibianskii, 'U nachala konfikta – Balkanskii uzel: Otkrytyi arkhiv – K istorii sovetskoyugoslavskogo konflikta 1948–1953' *Rabochii klass i sovremennyi mir* 2 (1990), 173.
38 Ibid.
39 Ibid.
40 'Russia Striving to Create Balkan Federation' *The New York Times*, 11 January 1948, E5.
41 Ibid.
42 Ibid.
43 Ibid.
44 Milovan Djilas, *Rise and Fall* (New York, New York: Hardcourt, Brace and Jovanovic, 1983), 167.
45 Banac, (ed.) *The Diary of Georgi Dimitrov…*, 435 (Entry 24 August 1948).
46 'Pravda Rules Out An Eastern Union, Rebukes Dimitrov' *The New York Times*, 29 January 1948, 1.
47 Other accounts have attributed the summons to the Kremlin and the wording 'serious differences exists between us with regards to questions of foreign policy' to refer to the Yugoslav decision to deploy troops into Albania in the near future. See Jeronim Perović, 'The Tito-Stalin Split…,' 50.
48 Djilas, *Rise and Fall…*, 168–9. Dimitrov, *Stalin's Cold War…*, 240. See also for example, Leonid Gibianskii, 'Report of Milovan Djilas about a Secret Soviet-Bulgarian –Yugoslav Meeting 10 February 1948,' *Cold War International History Project Bulletin*, 10 (March 1998), 128.
49 Djilas, *Rise and Fall…*, 165.
50 Volokitina et al. *Moskva i Vostochnaia Evropa…*, 496.
51 Dimitrov, *Stalin's Cold War…*, 240.
52 John R. Lampe, *Yugoslavia as History: Twice there was a country*, 2nd Edition (Cambridge: Cambridge University Press, 2000), 240; Bogdan C. Novak, *Trieste 1941–1954: The Ethnic, Political and Ideological Struggle* (Chicago: Chicago University Press, 1970), 161. For an account based on Soviet sources see Leonid Gibianskii,

'Tretskii vopros v kontse vtoroi mirovoi voiny (1944–1945),' *Slavanovedenie* 4 (2001), 3.
53 Ibid. 199.
54 Lampe, *Yugoslavia as History*..., 241.
55 Novak, *Trieste 1941–1954*..., 257.
56 Ibid. 281.
57 Lampe, *Yugoslavia as History*..., 258.
58 Volokitina, *Vostochnaia Evropa v dokumentakh rossiiskikh arkhivov: 1944–1953: Tom I 1944–1948* (Moscow: Novosibirsk : Sibirskii khronograf, 1997–1998), 889.
AVP RF, F. 0138, Op. 29. p. 147. d. 10. l. 143–145.
59 Arhiv Predsednika Republike (APR) (Archive of the Office of the President Josip Broz 'Tito'): KMJ I-3-b/666, 10.1. -31.8.1949, N.1440.
60 Petković, *Subjektivna istorija Jugoslovenske*..., 31. Not many significant works on Kardelj have been published outside of his own biography and his published speeches. For example: Edvard Kardelj, *Nations and Socialism* (Belgrade: STP, 1981). For the most comprehensive description and discussion of his later role as the ideologue of the Yugoslav state and the role of workers' self-management please see Dejan Jović, *Yugoslavia: A State that Withered Away* (West Lafayette, Indiana: Purdue University Press, 2009).
61 Petković, *Subjektivna istorija Jugoslovenske diplomatije*...
62 Ibid.
63 Banac, (ed.) *The Diary of Georgi Dimitrov*..., 362 (Entry 12 March 1945).
64 APR, KMJ I – 3 – b/663, I – 3 1949, 'Informacije o pisanju štampe socijalističkih i kapitalističkih zemalja, vestima radio stanica i pisanju naše štampe, I- III 1949.'
65 Ibid.
66 Ibid.
67 APR, KMJ I – 3 – b/663, I – 3 1949, 'Informacije o pisanju štampe socijalističkih i kapitalističkih zemalja, vestima radio stanica i pisanju naše štampe, I- III 1949.'
68 Petković, *Subjektivna istorija Jugoslovenske diplomatije*..., 31.
69 Ulam, *Titoism and the Cominform*..., Milovan Djilas, *Conversations with Stalin* (New York, New York: Harcourt, Bruce & World, 1962).
70 Milovan Djilas, 'Tito and Stalin,' *Survey* v.23, no.3: 75.
71 APR, KMJ I-3-b/655: 13.4.1948, p.41–134.
72 APR, KMJ I-3-b/655: 20.3.1948; APR: KMJ I-3-b/655: 27.3.1948; APR: KMJ I-3-b/655: 13.4.1948; APR, KMJ I-3-b/655: 4.5.1948; APR, KMJ I-3-b/655: 17.5.1948; APR, KMJ I-3-b/655: 22.5.1948.
73 The letters were published without the hand-written side notes and corrections but in their sent form in Royal Institute of International Affairs, *The Soviet-Yugoslav Dispute: Text of the Published Correspondence* (London: RIIA, 1948); Leonid Gibianskii, 'Sekretnaya sovetsko-yugoslavskaya perepiska 1948 (I)' *Voprosy istorii* 4–5 (1992), 119.; Leonid Gibianskii, 'Sekretnaya sovetsko-yugoslavskaya perepiska 1948 (II)' *Voprosy istorii* 6–7 (1992), 158.; Leonid Gibianskii, 'Sekretnaya sovetsko-yugoslavskaya perepiska 1948 (III)' *Voprosy istorii* 10 (1992), 141.
74 APR, KMJ I-3-b/655: 13.4.1948, p.41–134
75 Ibid.

76 The article of Jeronim Perović interprets these same letters differently to indicate only a prelude to the split in June, and to demonstrate that the Soviets attacked the Yugoslav system and its leaders for going their own way in terms of Communist ideology, and the Yugoslavs insisted that they were not deviating from the Marxist-Leninist line. Jeronim Perović, 'The Tito-Stalin Split...,' 35.
77 Djilas, *Rise and Fall*, 149.
78 Ibid. 148.
79 Ibid.
80 APR, KMJ.I.3.b.653.33: 4.2-3.4.1948.
81 Ibid.
82 Ibid.
83 See for example, APR, KMJ I.3.b.653. 33. 4.2-3.4.1948: 12.2.1948.
84 APR, KMJ I.3.b.653. 33. 4.2-3.4.1948: 22.2.1948.
85 Jozo Tomasevic, 'Immediate Effects of the Cominform Resolution of the Yugoslav Economy,' in *At the Brink of War and Peace: The Tito-Stalin Split in a Historic Perspective*, ed. Wayne S. Vucinich (New York: Columbia University Press, East European Monographs, 1982), 89.
86 APR, KMJ.I.3.b.653.33: 4.2-3.4.1948.
87 Ibid.
88 Ibid.
89 Dedijer, *The Battle Stalin Lost...*, 73.
90 Edvard Kardelj, Edvard Kardelj, *Reminiscences: the Struggle for Recognition and Independence: the New Yugoslavia, 1944–1957*. (London: Blond & Briggs in association with Summerfield Press, 1982), 75.
91 Ibid, 77.
92 Djilas, *The Rise and Fall...*, 163.
93 APR, KMJ I.3.b.653. 33. 4.2-3.4.1948: 22.2.1948
94 Ibid.
95 Ibid.
96 APR, KMJ I.3.b.652/46170: 10.3.1948.
97 Ibid.
98 APR, KMJ I.3.b.655: 20.3.1948, 16-24.
99 Ibid.
100 Perović, 'The Tito-Stalin Split...,' 57.
101 Ulam, *Titoism and the Cominform*, 70.
102 APR, KMJ.I.3.b.653.33: 4.2-3.4.1948.
103 APR, KMJ I.3.b.655: 20.3.1948, 16-24.
104 Ibid.
105 APR, KMJ I.3.b.655: 24-25.3.1948, 25-28.
106 Ibid.
107 Ibid.
108 APR, KMJ I.3.b.655: 27.3.1948, 29-40.
109 Ibid.
110 Ibid.
111 Ibid.

112 APR, KMJ I-3-b/655: 13.4.1948.
113 Ibid.
114 Gibianskii, 'The Soviet-Yugoslav Conflict…,' 231.
115 T.V Volokitina, *Kholodnaia voina i sotsial-demokratiia Vostochnoi Evropy, 1944–1948 gg.: ocherki istorii* (Moskva : Rossiiskaia akademiia nauk, In-t slavianovedeniia, 1998), 69.
116 APR, KMJ I.3.b.655: 13.4.1948, 29-40.
117 Ibid.
118 Ibid.
119 Ibid.
120 Ibid.
121 Ibid.
122 Ibid.
123 Ibid.

Chapter 3

1 The Soviet-Hungarian Agreement on Friendship, Cooperation and Assistance was signed in Moscow on 18 February 1948; The Soviet-Romanian Agreement on Friendship, Cooperation and Assistance was signed in Moscow on 4 February 1948. Ulkoministeriön arkisto (UM) (Archive of the Foreign Ministry of Finland), 12 L, 29: Neuvostoliitto – YYA – Sopimus 6.4.1948: SNT-Liiton Ministerineuvoston Puheenjohtaja, Moskova, Kremlin, 22.2.1948.
2 Ibid.
3 'Finland-Soviet Union Armistice, 19 September 1944,' *The American Journal of International Law* 39 (2) (1945): 85.
4 Ibid.
5 'The Treaty of Peace with Finland 1947,' *The American Journal of International Law* 42 (3) (1948): 203.
6 John H. Wuorinen. 'The Finnish Treaty,' *Annals of the American Academy of Political and Social Science.* 257 (1948): 87.
7 'The Treaty of Peace with Finland 1947,' *The American Journal of International Law* 42 (3) (1948): 203.
8 During the Second World War Zhdanov had been in charge of the territorial defence of Leningrad. UM, 12 L, 29: Neuvostoliitto – YYA – Sopimus 6.4.1948: Muistiinpanoja Valtioneuvoston Neuvottelukokouksesta Tasavallan Presidentin luona, 1.4.1948.
9 Ibid.
10 Carl Gustaf Emil Mannerheim, elected President of Finland by the Parliament 4 August 1944 to 8 March 1946. Zubok and Pleshakov, *Inside the Kremlin's Cold War…*, 118.
11 Dmitri Volkogonov, *Stalin: Triumph and Tragedy.* Edited and translated by Harold Shukman (New York, New York: Grove Weidenfeld, 1991), 554; RTsKhIDNI f.77, op.3, d.54, l.1-4.

[12] Zubok and Pleshakov, *Inside the Kremlin's Cold War*..., 118. Please also see Alfred J. Rieber, *Zhdanov in Finland* (Pittsburgh, Pennsylvania: Center for Russian and East European Studies, University of Pittsburgh, 1995).
[13] UM, 12 L, 29: Neuvostoliitto – YYA – Sopimus 6.4.1948: Muistiinpanoja Valtioneuvoston Neuvottelukokouksesta Tasavallan Presidentin luona, 1.4.1948.
[14] Ibid.
[15] Ibid.
[16] Zubok and Pleshakov, *Inside the Kremlin's Cold War*..., 118.
[17] UM, 12 L, 29: Neuvostoliitto – YYA – Sopimus 6.4.1948: Muistiinpanoja Valtioneuvoston Neuvottelukokouksesta Tasavallan Presidentin luona, 1.4.1948.
[18] See for example, Robert Paxton, *Europe in the Twentieth Century*. Fourth edition (Forth Worth, Texas: Harcourt College Publishing, 2002), 484.
[19] Zubok and Pleshakov, *Inside the Kremlin's Cold War*..., 117.
[20] UM, 12 L, 29: Neuvostoliitto – YYA – Sopimus 6.4.1948: Esittely Tasavallan Presidentille Valtioneuvostossa, 13.8.1948.
[21] UM, 1918-81: YYA-Sopimus 1948, Pravda (TASS), 14.3.1948.
[22] UM, 1918-81: YYA-Sopimus 1948, Neuvotteluvaltuuskunan Pöytäkirja. 25.3.1948.
[23] UM, 12 L Venäjä 31/366 Sala D 46 18.6.1947.
[24] UM, 1918-81:YYA-Sopimus 1948, Neuvotteluvaltuuskunan Pöytäkirja. 29.3.1948.
[25] UM, 12 L Venäjä 6/2 Sala D 47 5.2.1948.
[26] UM, 12 L Venäjä 48/371Sala D 48 5.2.1948.
[27] Original in Swedish: 'Svenskar äro vi icke längre, ryssar vilja vi icke bli, låt oss alltså bli finnar.'
[28] For information on Kardelj's background see p.35–39 in Chapter 1. Josip Broz 'Tito,' served in the Austro-Hungarian army in the First World War and was captured as a prisoner of war by the Russians. After 1917 he served as a Red Guard in Omsk. Tito returned to Yugoslavia in 1920 and became a member of the Communist Party of Yugoslavia in Croatia. In 1934 he became a member of the KPJ Politburo in Vienna, representing the KPJ in the Comintern from 1935 to 1936.
[29] Matti Simola and Tuula Sirviö, *Isänmaan puolesta - Suojelupoliisi 50 vuotta.* (Helsinki: Gummerus, 1999), 20.
[30] Jukka Seppinen, *Urho Kekkonen—Suomen Johtaja: Poliittinen elämänkerta* (Jyväskylä: Gummerus, 2004,) 16.
[31] Ibid.18. Soviet intelligence was interested in Finnish politics, the evaluation of Finnish military preparedness, the furthering of Communism in Finland, support for the political actions of Soviet emigrants in Finland and analyzing public opinion.
[32] In 1925, 1931, 1937, 1950, 1956, 1962, 1968, 1978, 1982 and 1988 the Finnish President was elected indirectly by an Electoral College for which members were chosen by popular vote. In 1919 and 1946 Parliament elected the President.
[33] UM, 12 L, 29: Neuvostoliitto – YYA – Sopimus 6.4.1948: Valtioneuvoston Yleinen Istunto, 27.3.1948.
[34] UM, 1918-81: YYA-Sopimus 1948, Neuvotteluvaltuuskunan arkisto. 29.3.1948.
[35] Ibid.

36 UM, 12 L, 29: Neuvostoliitto – YYA – Sopimus 6.4.1948: Valtioneuvoston Yleinen Istunto, 27.3.1948.
37 UM, 1918-81: YYA-Sopimus 1948, Neuvotteluvaltuuskunan Pöytäkirja. 30.3.1948.
38 UM, 12 L, 29: Neuvostoliitto – YYA – Sopimus 6.4.1948: Valtioneuvoston Yleinen Istunto, 27.3.1948.
39 UM, 1918-81: YYA-Sopimus 1948, Neuvotteluvaltuuskunan Pöytäkirja. 30.3.1948.
40 UM, 1918-81: YYA-Sopimus 1948, Neuvotteluvaltuuskunan arkisto. 25.3.1948.
41 UM, 1918-81: YYA-Sopimus 1948, Luonnos 24.3.1948.
42 UM, 1918-81: YYA-Sopimus 1948, Neuvotteluvaltuuskunan Pöytäkirja. 29.3.1948.
43 UM, 1918-81: YYA-Sopimus 1948, Salasähke. 25.3.1948.
44 UM, 12 L, 29: Neuvostoliitto – YYA – Sopimus 6.4.1948: Esittely Tasavallan Presidentille Valtioneuvostossa, 13.8.1948.
45 UM, 12 L, 29: Neuvostoliitto – YYA – Sopimus 6.4.1948: Valtioneuvoston Yleinen Istunto, 27.3.1948.
46 UM, 12 L, 29: Neuvostoliitto – YYA – Sopimus 6.4.1948: Esittely Tasavallan Presidentille Valtioneuvostossa, 13.8.1948.
47 Ibid.
48 UM, 12 L, 29: Neuvostoliitto – YYA – Sopimus 6.4.1948: Valtioneuvoston Yleinen Istunto, 31.3.1948.
49 UM, 1918-1981: YYA-Sopimus 1948, Neuvotteluvaltuuskunan Pöytäkirja. 25.3.1948.
50 UM, R-Sarja, Moskova, 1948-1949: Raportti No. 12, 19.2.1948.
51 UM, 12 L, 29: Neuvostoliitto – YYA – Sopimus 6.4.1948: Puhelinsanoma No.80, Moskovasta 5.3.1948, 10:30; *Izvestija* 3 March 1948.
52 UM, 12 L, 29: Neuvostoliitto – YYA – Sopimus 6.4.1948: Esittely Tasavallan Presidentille Valtioneuvostossa, 13.8.1948.
53 UM, 1918-81: YYA-Sopimus 1948, Neuvotteluvaltuuskunan arkisto. Neuvotteluvaltuuskunnan Pöytäkirja 29.3.1948.
54 Ibid.
55 Ibid.
56 UM, 12 L, 29: Neuvostoliitto – YYA – Sopimus 6.4.1948: Esittely Tasavallan Presidentille Valtioneuvostossa, 13.8.1948.
57 Ibid.
58 Ibid.
59 Ibid.
60 UM, 1918-81: YYA-Sopimus 1948, Kenr. Heinrichs ja Kenr. Lausunto 31.3.1948.
61 UM, 1918-81: YYA-Sopimus 1948, Neuvotteluvaltuuskunan arkisto. Neuvotteluvaltuuskunnan Pöytäkirja 29.3.1948.
62 Ibid.
63 Ibid.
64 Ibid.
65 UM, 1918-81: YYA-Sopimus 1948, Salasähke 'Vain Presidentille'. 29.3.1948.
66 UM, 1918-81: YYA-Sopimus 1948, Neuvotteluvaltuuskunan Pöytäkirja. 1.4.1948.
67 UM, 1918-81: YYA-Sopimus 1948, Neuvotteluvaltuuskunan Pöytäkirja. 25.3.1948.
68 UM, 1918-81: YYA-Sopimus 1948, Neuvotteluvaltuuskunan arkisto.

Neuvotteluvaltuuskunnan Pöytäkirja 29.3.1948.
[69] UM, 1918-81: YYA-Sopimus 1948, Neuvotteluvaltuuskunan Pöytäkirja. 30.3.1948.
[70] UM, 1918-81: YYA-Sopimus 1948, Neuvotteluvaltuuskunan Pöytäkirja. 25.3.1948.
[71] UM, 1918-81: YYA-Sopimus 1948, Neuvotteluvaltuuskunan Pöytäkirja. 1.4.1948.
[72] UM, 12 L, 29: Neuvostoliitto – YYA – Sopimus 6.4.1948: Valtioneuvoston Yleinen Istunto, 27.3.1948
[73] Ibid.
[74] Ibid.
[75] Ibid.
[76] Ibid.
[77] UM, 1918-81: YYA-Sopimus 1948, Neuvotteluvaltuuskunan Pöytäkirja. 1.4.1948. Leino had been part of a left-wing organization during the inter-war period. In 1935 he was found guilty of treason and crimes against the state after having been under investigation for a prolonged period of time by the EK.
[78] Ibid.
[79] UM, 1918-81: YYA-Sopimus 1948, Neuvotteluvaltuuskunan arkisto. Neuvotteluvaltuuskunnan Pöytäkirja 30.3.1948.
[80] UM, 1918-81: YYA-Sopimus 1948, Neuvotteluvaltuuskunan Pöytäkirja. 1.4.1948.
[81] UM, 12 L, 29: Neuvostoliitto – YYA – Sopimus 6.4.1948: Valtioneuvoston Yleinen Istunto, 31.3.1948.
[82] Ibid.
[83] UM, 1918-81: YYA-Sopimus 1948, Neuvotteluvaltuuskunan Pöytäkirja. 7.4.1948.
[84] Ibid.
[85] Ibid.
[86] Ibid.
[87] Ibid.
[88] Ibid.
[89] Ibid.
[90] Ibid.
[91] Ibid.
[92] Ibid.
[93] UM, R-Sarja, Moskova, 1948–49: Raportti No. 9: 'Suomen ja Neuvostoliiton Taloudelliset Suhteet', 25.2.1949.
[94] Ibid.
[95] UM, R-Sarja, Moskova, 1948–49: Raportti No. 7, 24.2.1949.
[96] UM, R-Sarja, Moskova, 1948–49: Raportti No. 9 : 'Suomen ja Neuvostoliiton Taloudelliset Suhteet', 25.2.1949.
[97] Ibid. By comparison the Soviets had initially had proposed a shipment protocol according to which Yugoslav exports would amount to $57.5 million in value and Soviet imports to $58.6 million (APR, KMJ.I.3.b.653.33: 4.2-3.4.1948).
[98] *Dirty Hands* was first performed in Paris in April 1948. The play is set in a fictional state named Illyria between 1943 and 1945. This state is presumably Yugoslavia. The story of the play focuses around the assassination of a leading politician. The main character, a young Communist figure, is ordered to conduct talks with non-Communist political parties, including fascists and a liberal nationalist resistance

group, in order to establish a joint anti-Nazi front. The instruction for collaboration with non-Communist groups originates from Moscow. The Communist party leadership makes plans to enter government with other political parties and then place blame on them for post-war hardships, and through discontentment become the leading political group. Expectations of the Red Army arrival and the detrimental effects of its ensuing occupation are also discussed in the play. UM, 12 L Venäjä 6/586 Sala D 48 5.12.1948.
[99] Ibid.
[100] UM, 12 L Venäjä 6/586 Sala D 48 10.12.1948. 35742.
[101] Ibid.
[102] Ibid.
[103] UM, 12 L Venäjä 6/586 Sala D 48 20.12.1948. 28188.
[104] Ibid. An altercation occured in November 1948 between Soviet Vice-Counsellor Pavel Matjević Tarsavo, Finnish doorman Viljo Viinanen and two Finnish police officers, Matti Laine and Markku Nieminen, during an event of the Children's Day winter circus in Helsinki. Tarasov and Aeroflot representative, Georgi Darsjki, left the event tent to smoke cigarettes outside only to find themselves unable to return. Tarasov and Darsjki confronted the Finnish police in Russian. Tarasov and Darsjki were handcuffed and brought to Töölö police station. Tarasov claimed he was hit in the eye by Finnish police. The police claimed that Tarasov and Darsjki were drunk and walked into a door at the circus instead. Tarasov was detained without representation for almost one hour. Criminal Police carried out an investigation - the police officers testified that they did not know the two were Soviet officials or even Russian. However, this is completely unlikely in a post-war circumstance. The High Prosecutor's Office found 'no ill-meaning actions on the behalf of the police,' but the Finnish Foreign Ministry kept exchanging notes with the Soviet Foreign Ministry over protests that continued until 1952. UM, 12-L Venäjä, 'Helsingin Kaupungin Poliisilaitos: Rikospoliisiosasto: SP 2340.'
[105] UM, 12 L Venäjä 6/586 Sala D 48 10.12.1948. 15055/P.
[106] UM, 12 L Venäjä 6/586 Sala D 48 10.12.1948. 35742.
[107] Ibid.
[108] 'One by One,' *New York Times*, 1 March 1948, 22.
[109] Ibid.
[110] UM, 12 L Venäjä 6/586 Sala D 19 5.11.1947.
[111] UM, 12 L Venäjä 14/363 Sala D 46 27.4.1946.
[112] UM, 12 L, 29: Neuvostoliitto – YYA – Sopimus 6.4.1948: 12 L Venäjä 31/3-48 Sala D 48, 30.3.1948.
[113] Ibid.
[114] Ibid.
[115] UM, 12 L, 29: Neuvostoliitto – YYA – Sopimus 6.4.1948: 12 L Venäjä 19/323 Sala D 46, 16.3.1948.
[116] UM, 12 L, 29: Neuvostoliitto – YYA – Sopimus 6.4.1948: 12 L Venäjä 25/324 Sala D 46, 9.4.1948.

Chapter 4

[1] Diplomatski arhiv Saveznog ministarstva za inostrane poslove (DASMIP) (Archive of the Yugoslav Foreign Ministry), F-26, 'Finska,' 33, 11.4.1953. 45830.

[2] DASMIP, F-84, 'SSSR,' 5.3.53. 43026. One recent work disagrees with the Finnish and the Yugoslav reports of the immediate consequences of Stalin's death that highlight growing international fears. Zubok and Pleshakov, *Inside the Kremlin's Cold War:...*, 139, write that 'Most Western analysts felt that the Kremlin's initiatives after Stalin's death were either new, improved Soviet tactics in waging the Cold War or the implementation of a policy designed to reduce international tensions gradually.' But they were not privy to the questions asked by the Finnish or the Yugoslav representatives or the answers they received from other diplomats in Moscow.

[3] DASMIP, F-84, 'SSSR,' 5.3.53. 43026.

[4] DASMIP, F-26, 'Finska,' 20.4.1953. 45671.

[5] DASMIP, F-26, 'Finska,' 33, 11.4.1953. 45830.

[6] DASMIP, F-25, 'Finska,' 11.3.1953, 43640.

[7] Ibid.

[8] Khrushchev became the First Secretary of the Soviet Communist Party in 1953, then Chairman of the Council of Ministers in 1958.

[9] *Pravda*, 17 June 1953.

[10] Zubok and Pleshakov, *Inside the Kremlin's Cold War...*, 139.

[11] Ibid.188.

[12] Molotov was placed in charge of the Soviet war effort against Finland in 1939-1940. During the Winter War, the Finnish Army coined the phrase 'Molotov cocktail' for the hand-thrown bomb. Finnish army adapted the bomb used during the Spanish Civil War. The Finnish version consisted of ethanol, tar and gasoline mixed in glass bottles that were ignited with matches when the bottles broke. The weapon proved inexpensive and effective against Soviet tanks, so the Finnish state alcohol monopoly ALKO continued to mass-produce Molotov Cocktails during the Continuation War in 1944. Molotov's orchestration of the Soviet war effort against Finland became well known and popularized through ALKO's efforts. The Finnish war efforts were popularized in everyday language as 'against Molotov.' Molotov's public broadcasts concerning the Soviet-Finnish war, which the Finnish public could hear broadcast from Leningrad or Tallinn, further amplified Molotov's reputation as a leading enemy. DASMIP, F-84, 'Finska,' 6.3.1953. 43103.

[13] DASMIP, F-26, 'Finska,' 33, 11.4.1953. 45830.

[14] Ibid.

[15] DASMIP, F-26, 'Finska,' 34, 13.4.1953. 45302.

[16] Of the 44 billion Finnish marks of exports (from Finland) agreed to in the Finnish-Soviet trade agreement of 1953, just 6.7 billion went to Soviet satellites. DASMIP, F-26, 'Finska,' 17.4.1953. 417763.

[17] Ibid.

[18] DASMIP F-26, 'Finska,' 38, 20.4.1953. 45671.

[19] Zubok and Pleshakov in *Inside the Kremlin's Cold War...*, 139; Peter Grose *Gentleman Spy: A life of Allen Dulles* (Boston: Houghton Mifflin, 1994), 350.

[20] DASMIP F-26, 'Finska,' 38, 20.4.1953. 45671.

21 Molotov was Soviet Minister for Foreign Affairs 1939–1949, 1953–1956.
22 DASMIP f-26, 'Finska,' 626, 19.12.1953. 417491.
23 Ibid.
24 DASMIP. F-26, 'Finska,' 32, 10.4.1953. 44999. DASMIP, F-26, 'Finska,' 33, 11.4.1953. 45830.
25 DASMIP, F-85, 'SSSR,' 8.4.1953. 44624.
26 DASMIP, F-86, 'SSSR,' 7.4.1953. 46634.
27 DASMIP, F-45, 'Jugoslavija,' 6.5.1953. 45924.
28 Ibid.
29 Ibid.
30 DASMIP, F-87 'SSSR,' 8.4.1953. 44624; DASMIP, F-45, 'Jugoslavija,' 106, 6.5.1953. 45924; DASMIP, F-26, 'Finska' 32, 10.4.1953. 44999; DASMIP, F-87, 'SSSR,' 180, 21.4.1953. 46006.
31 DASMIP F-86 'SSSR,' 7.4.1953. 46634.
32 Ibid.
33 Second Division of the Yugoslav Foreign Ministry for Information and Circulation.
34 DASMIP, F-84, 'SSSR,' 6.4. 1953. 45309.
35 Ibid.
36 DASMIP, F-84 'SSSR,' 7.4.1953. 45648.
37 DASMIP, F-84 'SSSR,' 6.4.1953. 45309.
38 Ibid.
39 Fred Singleton, 'Yugoslavia's Defense and Foreign Policy in the Context of Non-Alignment' in Marko Milivojević, John B. Allcock and Pierre Maurer eds. *Yugoslavia's Security Dilemmas: Armed forces, national defense and foreign policy* (Oxford: Berg Press, 1988), 175.
40 DASMIP, F-84, 'SSSR,' 6.4.53. 45309.
41 Ibid.
42 Ibid.
43 *Pravda*, 17 June 1953.
44 DASMIP, F-26, 'Finska' 32, 10.4.1953. 44999.
45 Petković, *Subjektivna Istorija Jugoslovenske Diplomatije...*, 39.
46 Open Society Archives (OSA) 76-4-179, Radio Free Europe Report: Communist Area: Yugoslavia: Government 14 July 1966; Vladimir Dedijer, *Tito Speaks: His self portrait and struggle with Stalin* (London: Weidenfeld and Nicolson, 1953), 387.
47 Petković, *Subjektivna Istorija Jugoslovenske Diplomatije...*, 40.
48 Ibid. 41.
49 OSA: 76-4-179, Radio Free Europe Report: Communist Area: Yugoslavia: Government, 14 July 1966.
50 Wilson, *Tito's Yugoslavia...*; Fred Singleton, *Twentieth Century Yugoslavia...*
51 From July 1948 Vejvoda had established regular contacts with Finnish chargé d' Affaires Ville Niskanen in Belgrade. In 1949 Vejvoda served as Head of the Economic Section of the Foreign Ministry and from 1950 onwards as one of the seven deputy ministers of foreign affairs. In January 1950 Vejvoda was appointed as Deputy Minister to handle problems of reorientation of Yugoslav foreign policy.

Other Deputy Foreign Ministers were Yugoslav Ambassador to Moscow Vladimir Popović, Leo Mates who served on the Danubian Commission, Joze Vilfan former Yugoslav representative to the United Nations, Srdjan Prica former Head of the Western Department of the Foreign Ministry, Joze Brilej, former Head of the Political Section of the Foreign Ministry and Rados Jovanovitch, Ambassador to Bucharest.

[52] Petković, *Subjektivna Istorija Jugoslovenske Diplomatije*, 42.
[53] Lampe, *Yugoslavia as History...*, 252.
[54] Banac, *With Stalin Against Tito...*, 145–220.
[55] Petković, *Subjektivna Istorija Jugoslovenske Diplomatije...*, 43.
[56] OSA: 76-4-179, Radio Free Europe Report: Communist Area: Yugoslavia: Government 14 July 1966.
[57] Wilson, *Tito's Yugoslavia...*, 90.
[58] Rubinstein, *Yugoslavia and the Nonaligned World...*
[59] Petković, *Subjektivna Istorija Jugoslovenske Diplomatije...*, 44.
[60] Ibid.
[61] OSA: 76-4-179, Radio Free Europe Report: Communist Area: Yugoslavia: Government 14 July 1966.
[62] DASMIP, F-26, 'Finska,' S-4. 16.12.1953. 417494.
[63] DASMIP, F-26, 'Finska,' 626, 19.12.1953. 417491.
[64] Ibid.
[65] DASMIP, F-26, 'Finska,' S-4. 16.12.1953. 417494.
[66] Ibid.
[67] DASMIP, F-26, 'Finska,' 50. 19.5.1953. 46914.
[68] Ibid.
[69] DASMIP, F-26, 'Finska,' S-4. 16.12.1953. 417494.
[70] DASMIP, F-26, 'Finska,' 33, 11.4.1953. 45830.
[71] DASMIP, F-26, 'Finska,' 626, 19.12.1953. 417491.
[72] Ibid.
[73] DASMIP, F-26, 'Finska,' 16.12.1953. 417494.
[74] Ibid.
[75] Ibid.
[76] Ibid.
[77] Ibid.
[78] Ibid.
[79] Ibid.
[80] DASMIP, F-47, 'Jugoslavija,' 121, 2.12.53. 416479.
[81] DASMIP, F-26, 'Finska,' 626, 19.12.1953. 417491.
[82] Ibid.
[83] DASMIP, F-86, 'SSSR,' 7.5.1953. 46587.
[84] DASMIP, F-26, 'Finska,' 25.2.1953. 44652.
[85] DASMIP, F-86, 'SSSR,' 7.5.1953. 46587.
[86] DASMIP, F-84, 'SSSR,' 6.4.53. 45309.
[87] Ibid.
[88] UM, 12L, 1954, Neuvostoliitto, 1, 21.1.1954.

89 Ibid. For example, Mikko Mäkinen had left Finland in 1939 enthusiastically to fight on the Soviet side only to discover that it was impossible for him to withdraw from the Red Army, or attain an exit visa after the war.
90 DASMIP, F-44, 'Jugoslavija,' 1953. 415074.
91 DASMIP, F-84, 'USSR,' 6.4.53. 45309.
92 DASMIP, F-86, 'USSR,' 2.9.1953. 417992.
93 Ibid.
94 Ibid.
95 UM, 12-L, 'Jugoslaavia,' 20, 20.6.1953.
96 Clissold (Ed.), *Yugoslavia and the Soviet Union 1939-1973*…, 248.
97 DASMIP, F-44, 'Jugoslavija,' 1953. 415074.
98 DASMIP, F-86, 'USSR,' 43. 12.9.1953. 412827.
99 UM, 12-L, 'Jugoslavia,' 20, 20.6.1953.
100 DASMIP, F-86, 'SSSR,' 49, 14.10.1953. 416101.
101 Ibid.
102 DASMIP, F-86, 'SSSR,' 627, 1.12.1953. 416096.
103 Ibid.
104 DASMIP, F-86, 'USSR,' 2.9.1953. 417992.
105 Ibid.
106 Wilson, *Tito's Yugoslavia*…, 92.
107 DASMIP, F-86, 'SSSR,' 627, 1.12.1953. 416096.
108 Ibid.
109 DASMIP, F-26, 'Finska,' 626, 19.12.1953. 417491.

Chapter 5

1 Charles Gati, *Failed Illusions: Moscow, Washington, Budapest, and the 1956 Hungarian Revolt* (Stanford, California: Stanford University Press, 2006), 14, 143.
2 Ibid.17.
3 G.A Krivosheev, (ed.), *Grif sekretnosti snyat: Poteri vooruzhenykh sil SSSR v voinakh, boevykh deistviyakh I voennykh konfliktakh: Statisticheskoe issledovanie*. (Moskva: Voenizdat, 1993), 397.
4 Gati, *Failed Illusions*…, 17.
5 Krivosheev (ed.) *Grif sekretnosti snyat*…, 397.
6 Gati, *Failed Illusions*…, 4, 188, 190.
7 DASMIP, F-23 'Finska,' 13.12.1956, 422224.
8 Gati, *Failed Illusions*, 4, 129.
9 Richard Sakwa, *The Rise and Fall of the Soviet Union 1917–1991* (London: Routledge, 1999), 316.
10 Clissold (ed.), *Yugoslavia and the Soviet Union 1939–1973*…, 67.
11 For example in September 1949 the number of newspaper columns and cartoons against Yugoslavia in the Hungarian *Szabad Nep* totaled 106, while the next most numerous anti-Yugoslav effort that month in the Soviet Union's *Pravda* totaled only 53. DASMIP, F-49, 'Jugoslavija,' 43421. 15.12.1949. For Rákosi's statements see *Bela Knjiga: Agresivnim postupcima vlada SSSR, Polske, Čekoslovačke, Madjarske, Rumunije,*

Bugarske I Albanije prema Jugoslaviji (Belgrad: Ministarstvo Inostranih Poslova Federativne Narodne Republike Jugoslavije, 1951), 52.

12 The Royal Institute of International Affairs, *Documents on International Affairs 1956* (Oxford: Oxford University Press, 1959), 67.

13 *Helsingin Sanomat*, 23 November 1956.

14 DASMIP, F-23, 'Finska,' 10.12.1956, 418672.

15 Ibid.

16 Mark Kramer, '"The Malin Notes" on the Crises in Hungary and Poland, 1956.' *Bulletin of the Cold War International History Project*, issues 8–9 (Winter 1996–97): 393.

17 Dmitri Volgokonov, *The Rise and Fall of the Soviet Empire: Political leaders from Lenin to Gorbachev* (London: HarperCollins, 1991), 212.

18 Robert Service, *A History of Modern Russia: From Nicholas II to Vladimir Putin* (Cambridge, Mass.: Harvard University Press, 2005), 356–360.

19 RTsKhIDNI f.82, Op.2, d.1382, l.124.

20 Arhiv Srbije Crne Gore (ASCG)(Archive of Serbia and Montenegro), AJ-03f, 16/10459.

21 Ibid.

22 APR, KPR I-3-a/SSSR, 3. 27.5.1955.

23 Ibid.

24 APR, KPR I-3-a/SSSR, 3, 3.6.1955.

25 UM, Kc6, Suomen ja Neuvostoliiton Väliset Suhteet 1947–1957, 27.6.1956, Raportti 41.

26 Ibid.

27 Ibid.

28 Ibid. After Khrushchev's secret speech Molotov came increasingly to represent the 'old guard'. He had also challenged Khrushchev in the Stalin's succession battle. Therefore there were several reasons for his ousting only one of which was his key role in the Tito-Stalin split. However, his forced resignation while Tito was in Moscow was intended as a concession to the Yugoslav leadership.

29 Ibid.

30 AVP RF, F.144. Op. 17, P.38, D.12, L.24-25.

31 Ibid.

32 Ibid.

33 DASMIP, F-89, 'SSSR,' 1955, 423548.

34 DASMIP, F-89, 'SSSR,' 1955, 423182.

35 DASMIP, F-89, 'SSSR,' 1955, 423548.

36 Ibid.

37 Ibid.

38 Ibid.

39 Ibid.

40 Hans Christian Hansen in Denmark; Tage Erlander in Sweden, Einar Gerhardsen in Norway and Karl-August Fagerholm in Finland.

41 Denmark, Iceland and Norway were members of NATO since its founding in 1949.

42 DASMIP, F-89, 'SSSR,' 15.6.1956, 49143.

43 Volkogonov, *The Rise and Fall*, 202.
44 DASMIP, F-33, 'Jugoslavija,' 24.6.1955. 48437.
45 Veljko Mićunović, *Moscow Diary*. (London: Chatto and Windus, 1980), 135.
46 Vladimir Dedijer, *History of Yugoslavia* (New York: McGraw-Hill, 1974).
47 Ranko Petković, *Subjektivna Istorija Jugoslovenske Diplomatije 1943–1991* (Belgrade: Službeni List, 1991), 43.
48 Edvard Kardelj, *Reminiscences: the Struggle for Recognition and Independence: the New Yugoslavia,1944–1957*. (London: Blond & Briggs in association with Summerfield Press, 1982), 133.
49 Ibid. 149.
50 Ibid. 400.
51 DASMIP, F-33, 'SSSR,' 1956, 4-0471.
52 DASMIP, F-23, 'Finska,' 1956, 49143.
53 DASMIP, F-89, 'SSSR,' 1956, 423548.
54 Ibid.
55 Ibid.
56 Ibid.
57 Ibid.
58 Ibid.
59 Ibid.
60 DASMIP, F-89 'SSSR,' 15.2.1956.
61 DASMIP, F-89, 'SSSR,' 1956, 423548.
62 Ibid.
63 Ibid.
64 Ibid.
65 Ibid.
66 Ibid.
67 Ibid.
68 DASMIP, F-89, 'SSSR,' 1956, 423548.
69 DASMIP, F-87 'SSSR,' 16.11.1956. 419582.
70 Ibid.
71 Ibid.
72 DASMIP, F-89 'SSSR,' 1956, 423548.
73 Ibid.
74 Ibid.
75 Ibid.
76 Ibid.
77 DASMIP, F-23 'Finska,' 1956, 15.6.1956, 49143; DASMIP, F-88, 'USSR', 1956, 423045; DASMIP, F-88, 'USSR,' 1956, 424000.
78 DASMIP, F-23, 'Finska,' 6.1.1956. 4303.
79 Ibid.
80 DASMIP, F-23, 'Finska,' 10.12.1956, 418672.
81 DASMIP, F-23, 'Finska,' 6.1.1956, 4303.
82 Ibid.
83 DASMIP, F-23, 'Finska,' 15.12.1956, 452, 418672.

84 Ibid.
85 Ibid.
86 Ibid.
87 Ibid.
88 Ibid.
89 Ibid.
90 DASMIP, F-23, 'Finska,' 10.12.1956, 418672.
91 Ibid.
92 Ibid.
93 Ibid.
94 Ibid.
95 Ibid. DASMIP, F-23, 'Finska' 1956, *Odnosi Finska –SSSR,* 'Territotijalne Pitanje – Karelija' (Relations between Finland and the USSR: The territorial question of Karelia); DASMIP, F-23:422224, 13.12.1956
96 DASMIP, F-23:418672, 10.12.1956; DASMIP, F-23, 'Finska' 1956, *Odnosi Finska –SSSR,* 'Territotijalne Pitanje – Karelija' (Relations between Finland and the USSR: The territorial question of Karelia). DASMIP, F-23, 'Finska', 13.12.1956, 422224.
97 Ibid.
98 Ibid.
99 UM, Kc6, Suomen ja Neuvostoliiton Väliset Suhteet 1947–57, 27.6.1956, Raportti 41.
100 John R. Lampe, Russell O. Prickett and Ljubiša S. Adamović, *Yugoslav-American Economic Relations Since World War II* (Durham: Duke University Press, 1990), 70–71.
101 UM, Kc6, Suomen ja Neuvostoliiton Väliset Suhteet 1947–57, 27.6.1956, Raportti 41.
102 Ibid.
103 Ibid.
104 Ibid.
105 Ibid
106 Ibid.
107 Text of Khrushchev's speech issued by the United States Department of State 4 June 1956. United States Information Service and British United Press, quoted in Richard Sakwa, *The Rise and Fall of the Soviet Union 1917–1991.* (New York: Routledge, 1999) 1.
108 UM, Kc6, Suomen ja Neuvostoliiton Väliset Suhteet 1947–57, 27.6.1956, Raportti 41.
109 Ibid.
110 Ibid.
111 UM, Kc6, Suomen ja Neuvostoliiton Väliset Suhteet 1947–57, 6.11.1956, Raportti 47.
112 Ibid.
113 Ibid.
114 Ibid.
115 Ibid.

116 UM, Kc6, Suomen ja Neuvostoliiton Väliset Suhteet 1947–57, 13.11.1956, Raportti 49.
117 Ibid.
118 Ibid.
119 UM, Kc6, Suomen ja Neuvostoliiton Väliset Suhteet 1947–57, 13.11.1956, Raportti 49.
120 Ibid.
121 Ibid.
122 Ibid.
123 UM, Kc6, Suomen ja Neuvostoliiton Väliset Suhteet 1947–57, 7.12.1956, Raportti 54.
124 *Pravda*, 23 November 1956.
125 The Royal Institute of International Affairs, *Documents on International Affairs 1956* (Oxford: Oxford University Press, 1959), 69.
126 Ibid.
127 *Pravda*, 18 December 1956.
128 DASMIP, F-23, 'Finska,' 13.12.1956, 422224.
129 Ibid.
130 Ibid.
131 Ibid.
132 Ibid.
133 UM, Kc6, Suomen ja Neuvostoliiton Väliset Suhteet 1947–57, 7.12.1956, Raportti 54.
134 DASMIP, F-23, 'Finska,' 13.12.1956, 422224.
135 UM, Kc6, Suomen ja Neuvostoliiton Väliset Suhteet 1947–57, 20.12.1956, Raportti 57.
136 Ibid.
137 DASMIP, F-23, 'Finska,' 10.12.1956, 418672.
138 Ibid. DASMIP, F-23, 'Finska,' 15.12.1956, 452, 418672.
139 Ibid.
140 Ibid.
141 Ibid.
142 Ibid.
143 See for example, Mita Miljković, *Burne Diplomatske Godine: iz sofijskog dnevnika 1953–1956* (Belgrade: Službeni List, 1995).
144 APR, KPR I-3-a/26-2, 9 – 11.12.1956.
145 DASMIP, F-23, 'Finska', 17.12.1956, 418672.
146 Ibid.
147 Ibid.
148 Ibid.
149 DASMIP, F-23, 'Finska,' 18.5.1956, 49717.
150 UM, Kc6, Suomen ja Neuvostoliiton Väliset Suhteet 1947–57, 27.6.1956, Raportti 41.
151 Ibid.

152 UM, Kc6, Suomen ja Neuvostoliiton Väliset Suhteet 1947–57, 7.12.1956, Raportti 54.

Chapter 6

[1] 'Constant Unity of the Marxist-Leninist parties is the guarantee of further victories by the Socialist World,' *Pravda* 9 May 1958.
[2] Ibid.
[3] Veljko Mićunović, *Moscow Diary*, translated by David Floyd. (New York, Garden City: Doubleday and Company, 1980), 376.
[4] An article in *Pravda* of 13 February already reflected the post-Stalin position that 'within Yugoslavia there are still manifestations of ill will and even direct attacks against the USSR and some of the peoples democracies by certain elements.'
[5] Tito claimed he had a debilitating illness. This was nonetheless considered a major insult by the Soviet leadership. The Soviet Ambassador Juri Bjernov told the Joze Bačić Councilor in the Yugoslav Warsaw Embassy in September 1958 that 'had Tito been present on the occasion of the celebration of the 40th anniversary of the October Revolution in Moscow, then the position of Yugoslavia now would very be different.' As Bačić tried to defend the Yugoslav position that alternative representation had been sent, Bjernov commented, 'Tito is something else from Kardelj and Ranković.' The Soviets were not pacified by the Yugoslav signing of only the concurrent Soviet sponsored 'Peace Manifesto.' DASMIP, F-177, 1958 USSR, 77158, 27.9.1958
[6] DASMIP, F-116, 1958 Jugoslavija, 'Reakcija U SSSR-u Na Naše Nepotpisivanje Deklaracije Pretstavnika Komunističkih Partija 12 Socijalističkih Zemalja u Moskvi' (Our Nonsigning of the Declaration of the Representatives of the Communist Parties of the 12 Socialist Countries in Moscow), 31031.
[7] DASMIP, F-116 1958 Jugoslavija, 'Politika SSSR-a Prema FNRJ Posle Deklaracije' (Politics of the USSR towards the SFRY after the Declaration), 31080.
[8] *Pravda*, 18 December 1956. 'Third line' here can also be translated as 'third way,' however, line from the original is consistent with the wording of the term 'Paasikivi-Kekkonen Line.'
[9] *Pravda*, 11 March 1957.
[10] For example, William Taubmann, *Khrushchev, The Man of his Era* (New York, New York: W.W. Norton, 2003), 408. Robert Service, *A History of Modern Russia: From Nicholas II to Vladimir Putin* (Cambridge, Mass.: Harvard University Press, 2005), 347–249, Volgokonov, *The Rise and Fall of the Soviet Empire…*, 210.
[11] *Pravda*, 4 July 1957.
[12] UM, R-Sarja, Moskova 1958, 13.5.1958, 'Ydinasekokeilut, huippukonferenssi, napalennot, Y.K:n luonne' (Report 26, Nuclear testing, high-level conference, flights over the north pole, U.N's character). Raportti 26.
[13] Ibid.
[14] Mićunović, *Moscow Diary…*, 399.
[15] Ibid.
[16] Ibid. 369, 381
[17] Ibid. 231

18 Ibid. xxi.
19 *Borba*, 27 February 1957.
20 Josip Broz 'Tito' *Govori i članci*, Vol Xiii (Zagreb: Naprijed, 1959), 250.
21 DASMIP: F-117, 'SSSR,' 646, 8.9.1958. 421467.
22 Ibid.
23 Ibid.
24 Ibid.
25 Ibid.
26 Ibid.
27 Ibid.
28 Ibid.
29 Ibid.
30 Ibid.
31 Ibid.
32 DASMIP: F-117, 'USSR,' 1958, 12.3.1958. 45938.
33 DASMIP: F-117, 'USSR,' 1958, 'Stavovi FNRJ i SSSR-a Po Medjunarodnim Problemima' (Positions of FPRY and USSR on International Problems), 32419.
34 Ibid.
35 Ibid.
36 Ibid.
37 Ibid.
38 Ibid.
39 Ibid.
40 Ibid.
41 Ibid.
42 Ibid.
43 UM, R-Sarja Moskova 1958, 14.8.1958, 'Moskova Seuraa Tilanteen Kehitystä Suomessa' (Moscow Follows Developments in Finland) No. 32.
44 Ibid.
45 Ibid.
46 Ibid.
47 UM, R-Sarja Moskova 1958, 246, 9.1958, 'Suomi Neuvostolehdistössä' (Finland in the Soviet Press), No.46.
48 UM, R-Sarja Moskova 1958, 14.8.1958, 'Moskova Seuraa Tilanteen Kehitystä Suomessa' (Moscow Follows Developments in Finland) No. 32.
49 Ibid.
50 UM, R-Sarja Moskova 1958, 26.8.1958, 'Suomi Coctail-Keskusteluissa' (Finland as a topic of conversation at cocktail-parties), No. 37.
51 UM, R-Sarja Moskova 1958, 26.8.1958, 'Suomi Coctail-Keskusteluissa' (Finland as a topic of conversation at cocktail-parties), No. 37.
52 Ibid.
53 Prime Minister: Karl-August Fagerhold (SDP), Foreign Minister (29.8.1958–4.12.1958): Johannes Virolainen (AP), Foreign Minister (4.12.1958–13.1.1959): Karl-August Kagerholm (SDP), Minister of Justice: Sven Högström (Swedish People's Party), Minister of the Interior: Atte Pakkanen (AP), Minister of Defence Toivo

Wiherheimo (NCP), Minister of Finance: Päiviö Hetemäki (NCP), Second Minister of Finance: Mauno Jussila (AP), Minister of Education: Kaarlo Kajatsalo (Finnish Peoples' Party), Minister of Agriculture (29.8.1958–14.11.1958): Martti Miettunen, Minister of Agriculture (14.11.1958–13.1.1959): Urho Köhönen (AP), Second Minister of Agriculture: Niilo Kosola (AP), Minister of Transport and General Works: Kustaa Eskola (AP), Second Minister of Transport and General Works: Olavi Lindblom (SDP), Minister of Trade and Industry: Onni Hiltunen (SDP), Second Minister of Trade and Industry: Toivo Wiherheimo (NCP), Social Minister: Väinö Leskinen (SDP), Second Social Minister: Rafael Paasio (SDP).

[54] Urho Kaleva Kekkonen, *Urho Kekkosen Päiväkirjat I* (Juhani Suomi: Helsinki: Otava, 2001), 29.8.1958, 110.
[55] Ibid.
[56] Waris returned from Washington with a promise for a $40 million loan for the cellulose and paper industry.
[57] Kekkonen, *Urho Kekkosen Päiväkirjat*. 30.8.1958, 111.
[58] Ibid. 1.9.1958, 111.
[59] Ibid. 3.9.1958, 112.
[60] Ibid.
[61] Ibid.
[62] *Izvestija*, 19 September 1958.
[63] Ibid.
[64] Kekkonen, *Urho Kekkosen Päiväkirjat*, 31.8.1958, 111.
[65] Ibid. 12.9.1958, 115.
[66] Ibid.
[67] UM, R-Sarja Moskova 1958, 26.11.1958, 'Kysymys Suomesta' (Question about Finland), Raportti No.69.
[68] Ibid.
[69] UM, R-Sarja Moskova 1958, 10.12.1958, 'Itsenäisyyspäivän Vietto' (Independence Day Reception), Raportti No.72.
[70] Ibid.
[71] Kekkonen, *Urho Kekkosen Päiväkirjat* 17.10.1958, 127.
[72] Ibid. 20.10.1958, 129.
[73] Ibid. 18.10.1958, 127.
[74] DASMIP F-117, 1958, 'SSSR,' 27.10.1958. 853.
[75] Ibid.
[76] Ibid. Kekkonen, *Urho Kekkosen Päiväkirjat*. 8.9.1958, 117.
[77] DASMIP F-117, 1958, 'SSSR,' 27.10.1958. 853.
[78] Kekkonen, *Urho Kekkosen Päiväkirjat*. 8.9.1958, 117.
[79] DASMIP F-117, 1958, 'SSSR,' 5.11.1958. 427485.
[80] Ibid.
[81] UM, R-Sarja Moskova 1958, 20.11.1958, 'Nliiton ja Jugoslavian Suhteista' (About Soviet-Yugoslav Relations), Raportti No.66.
[82] Ibid.
[83] Ibid.
[84] Kekkonen, *Urho Kekkosen Päiväkirjat*, 14.10.1958, 126.

85 UM, R-Sarja Moskova 1958, 3.5.1958, 'Nliiton Ulkopoliittiselta Rintamalta' (From the Soviet Union's Foreign Policy Front), Raportti No.23.
86 Ibid.
87 UM, R-Sarja Moskova 1958, 14.5.1958, 'Jugoslavia – aka "Sosialistisen Leirin Kyljessä"' (Yugoslavia – aka Bordering the Socialist Bloc), Raportti No. 27.
88 Ibid.
89 Ibid.
90 Ibid.
91 Ibid.
92 Ibid.
93 Ibid.
94 'Constant Unity of the Marxist-Leninist parties is the guarantee of further victories by the Socialist World', *Pravda*, 9 May 1958, pp.3–4
95 UM, R-Sarja Moskova 1958, 14.5.1958, 'Jugoslavia – aka "Sosialistisen Leirin Kyljessä"' (Yugoslavia – aka Bordering the Socialist Bloc), Raportti No. 27.
96 Ibid.
97 Ibid.
98 Ibid.
99 Ibid.
100 Ibid.
101 Kekkonen, *Urho Kekkosen Päiväkirjat*, 30.10.1958, 133.
102 Ibid. 5.11.1958, 135.
103 Meinander's opinions on the ability of Finland to survive without Soviet trade were taken seriously in 1958 because of his long career in finance. He had work in the Inter-Scandinavian Central Bank from 1929 to 1934, and as the chief of State Information Agency of Finland during the war years from 1939 to 1944.
Kekkonen, *Urho Kekkosen Päiväkirjat*, 6.11.1958, 135.
104 Ibid.
105 Ibid. 13.11.1958, 139.
106 Ibid. 14.11.1958, 140.
107 Ibid. 26.11.1958, 146
108 Ibid. 2.12.1958, 149.
109 After Molotov and the 'Anti-Party Group' were defeated by Khrushchev in the summer of 1957, Molotov was sent in to exile as the Soviet Ambassador to Mongolia. Zubok and Pleshakov in *Inside the Kremlin's Cold War…*, 81, argue that 'later Khrushchev saw [Molotov's] proximity to Mao's China as a risk. There were plans to transfer Molotov to Helsinki, but the Finns objected strongly and Khrushchev decided against it.' However, Kekkonen's private diary shows that Molotov's proposed dispatch to Helsinki served as a threat from the Kremlin to Kekkonen in order to urge him to bring down the SDP-NCP government. This threat was communicated to Kekkonen through his KGB contact.
110 Prime Minister: V.J. Sukselainen (AP), Foreign Minister (13.1.1959–16.5.1961): Ralf Törngren (SPP), Foreign Minister (16.5.1961–19.6.1961): V.J. Sukselainen (AP), Foreign Minister (19.6.1961–14.7.1961): Ahti Karjalainen (AP), Second Foreign Minister: Ahti Karjalainen (AP), Minister of Justice (13.1.1959–14.4.1961): Antti

Hannikainen (AP), Minister of Justice (14.4.1961–14.7.1961): Pauli Lehtosalo (AP), Minister of the Interior (13.1.1959–4.2.1960): Eino Palovesi (AP), Minister of the Interior (4.2.1960–14.7.1961): Eemil Vihtori Luukka (AP), Minister of Defence: Leo Häppölä (AP), Minister of the Economy: Vihtori Sarjala (AP), Second Minister of the Economy (13.1.1959–14.4.1961): Pauli Lehtosalo (AP), Second Minister of the Economy (14.4.1961–14.7.1961): Juho Niemi (AP), Minister of Education: Heikki Hosia (AP), Minister of Agriculture (AP): Juho Jaakkola (AP), Second Minister of Agriculture: Toivo Antila (AP), Minister of Transport and Public Works: Kauno Klemola (AP), Second Minister of Transport and Public Work: Arvo Korsimo (AP), Minister of Trade and Industry (13.1.1959–19.6.1961): Ahti Karjalainen (AP), Minister of Trade and Industry (19.6.1961–14.7.1961): Björn Westerlund (SPP), Second Minister of Trade and Industry: Pauli Lehtosalo (AP), Social Minister: Vieno Simonen (AP), Second Social Minister: Eeli Erkkilä.

Chapter 7

[1] Edvard Kardelj, *Reminiscences: The struggle for Recognition and Independence: The New Yugoslavia, 1944–1957* (London: Blond & Briggs, Summerfield Press, 1982,) 128.

[2] Kardelj, *Reminiscences...*, 133.

[3] Ibid. 261.

[4] Ibid. 260.

[5] Yugoslavia received a total of $415 million in UNRRA aid.

[6] Cambodia (1955), Morocco, Tunisia, Sudan (1956), Ghana (1957), Guinea (1958), Mali, Cyprus, Somalia, the Belgian Congo (1960), Algeria (1962).

[7] Number of embassies calculated in person from the separate files in the Archive of the Ministry for Foreign Affairs, Belgrade, Serbia in March 2008.

[8] Ibid. By comparison, in the period when the Finnish Foreign Ministry specifically instituted an expansion program for its embassies between 1952 and 1954, Finland upgraded only 10 of its representations to embassies. Between 1948 and 1953 Yugoslavia built 19 new embassies but Finland only upgraded 10 already existing representations.

[9] Wilson, *Tito's Yugoslavia...*, 123.

[10] The legal concept replies on the following precedents: The Declaration of Paris of 1856, The Hague Convention V, 1907, the Hague Convention XIII, 1907.

[11] Laqueur, *The Political Psychology of Appeasement...*, 3.

[12] Ibid. 4.

[13] Ibid. 9.

[14] For a definition of the myth of Yugoslav non-alignment see the Introduction pages 11–17; for a definition of the Finnish myth of neutralism see the Introduction pages 17–20.

BIBLIOGRAPHY

Primary Sources

Arhiv Srbije Crne Gore (Archive of Serbia and Montenegro)
Fond 78 Propaganda Abroad 1948–58
Fond 79 Inquiries and Circulars 1948–58
Fond 83 War Crimes 1948–58
Fond 57 Personal Letters and Circulars 1948–58
Fond 63 Fish Culture 1948–58

Arhiv Predsednika Republike (Archive of the Office of the President Josip Broz 'Tito')
Bulgaria 1948–Bulgaria 1961
Finland 1948–Finland 1961
Hungary 1948–Hungary 1961
Poland 1948–Poland 1961
Romania 1948–Romania 1961
USSR 1948–USSR 1961
Letters and Correspondence 1948–Letters and Correspondence 1961
State Visits 1956: USSR
State Visits 1957: Romania

Arkhiv Vneshnei Politiki Rossiskoy Federatsii (Archive of Foreign Policy of the Russian Federation)
Fond 0140 (Sweden Department Moscow 1930–62)
       Op.38 Years 1947–61
              D.43, p.153: Nordic cooperation
              D.46, p.146: Soviet documents on Finnish-Swedish and Nordic cooperation
       Op.39 d
              D.1, p.154: Nordic cooperation
              D.47, p.163: Nordic cooperation 1950
              D.48, p.163: Nordic cooperation with NATO
       Op.44 v
              D.1, p.175: Nordic states and European Coal and Steel Union Nordic cooperation 1953

Op.45 D.13, p.181: Nordic cooperation 1954
Op.46 D.14, p.185: Nordic cooperation and European cooperation 1955
Op.47 D.18, p.190: Nordic cooperation and European cooperation 1956
Op.48 D.9, p.193: Nordic cooperation 1957
Op.50 D.11, p.198: Nordic cooperation 1959
Op.52 D.3, p.203: 'Contacts between Scandinavian foreign ministries concerning Nordic cooperation' 1961

Diplomatski arhiv Saveznog ministarstva za inostrane poslove (Archive of the Yugoslav Foreign Ministry)
PA 1948: 45-Finland
PA 1948:78-Yugoslavia
PA 1948:132-USSR
PA 1948:133-USSR
PA 1949:33-Finland
PA 1949:57-Yugoslavia
PA 1949:63-Yugoslavia
PA 1949:99-USSR
PA 1949:100-USSR
PA 1950:26-Finland
PA 1950:47-Yugoslavia
PA 1950:48-Yugoslavia
PA 1950:85-USSR
PA 1951:24-Finland
PA 1951:45-Yugoslavia
PA 1951:80-USSR
PA 1952:24-Finland
PA 1952:44-Yugoslavia
PA 1952:45-Yugoslavia
PA 1952:80-USSR
PA 1952:81-USSR
PA 1952:46-Yugoslavia
PA 1953:26-Finland
PA 1953:44-Yugoslavia
PA 1953:45-Yugoslavia
PA 1953:46-Yugoslavia
PA 1953:47-Yugoslavia
PA 1953:84-USSR
PA 1953:85-USSR
PA 1953:86-USSR
PA 1954:21-Finland
PA 1954:45-Yugoslavia
PA 1954:46-Yugoslavia
PA 1954:47-Yugoslavia
PA 1954:85-USSR

PA	1954:87-USSR
PA	1954:88-USSR
PA	1955:17-Finland
PA	1955:32-Yugoslavia
PA	1955:33-Yugoslavia
PA	1955:62-USSR
PA	1955:63-USSR
PA	1956:23-Finland
PA	1956:87-USSR
PA	1956:88-USSR
PA	1956:89-USSR
PA	1956:90-USSR
PA	1956:91-USSR
PA	1956:92-USSR
PA	1957:30-Finland
PA	1957:48-Yugoslavia
PA	1957:49-Yugoslavia
PA	1957:50-Yugoslavia
PA	1957:51-Yugoslavia
PA	1957:96-USSR
PA	1957:97-USSR
PA	1957:98-USSR
PA	1958:28-Finland
PA	1958:55-Yugoslavia
PA	1958:56-Yugoslavia
PA	1958:58-Yugoslavia
PA	1958:59-Yugoslavia
PA	1958:60-Yugoslavia
PA	1958:64-Yugoslavia
PA	1958:115-USSR
PA	1958:116-USSR
PA	1958:117-USSR
PA	1958:118-USSR
PA	1959:29-Finland
PA	1959:58-Yugoslavia
PA	1959:59-Yugoslavia
PA	1959:65-Yugoslavia
PA	1959:67-Yugoslavia
PA	1959:117-USSR
PA	1959:188-USSR
PA	1959:119-USSR
PA	1959:120-USSR
PA	1959:122-USSR
PA	1960:28-Finland
PA	1960:54-Yugoslavia
PA	1960:57-Yugoslavia

PA   1960:123-USSR
PA   1960:124-USSR
PA   1960:125-USSR
PA   1960:126-USSR
PA   1960:128-USSR
PA   1961:26-Finland
PA   1961:52-Yugoslavia
PA   1961:53-Yugoslavia
PA   1961:55-Yugoslavia
PA   1961:131-USSR
PA   1961:132-USSR
PA   1961:133-USSR

Rossiiskii gosudarstvennyi arkhiv sotsial'no-politicheskoi istorii (Russian State Archive of Socio-Political History)
Fond 17 Central Committee of the Communist Party of the Soviet Union 1903–1965)
    Op.128 (Department of International Information 1944–1950)

Fond 575 Information Bureau of Communist and Workers Parties Abroad (1947–1956)

Suojelupoliisi (Finnish Protection Police)
'Bulajic, Kristo'
'Djikic, Julijana'
'Djinkic, Zivorad'
'Grujovic, Jelena'
'Maletic, Basiljka'
'Werikov, Arkadi'
'Radojcic, Ilja'
'Scuric, Stjepan'
'Zdravrovski, Petar'
'Zore, Slavko'
'Bace, Vanda'
'Bace, Marko'
'Bozic, Mladen'
'Buzek, Radmila'
'Buzek, Vilin'
'Grulovic, Nikola'
'Kapicic, Jova'
'Lebedev, Viktor'
'Sardelic, Mirko'
'Sardelic, Ksenija'
'Vlahovic, Miodrag'
'Vujovic, Petar'
'Vukmanovic, Svetozar'

Ulkoministeriön arkisto (Archive of the Foreign Ministry of Finland)
Yugoslavia 1948 R-12
Yugoslavia 1948; R-5
Yugoslavia 1949; R-5
Yugoslavia 1950; R-5
Yugoslavia 1948–50; R-100
Yugoslavia 1951–53; R-12
Yugoslavia 1955–59; R-12
Yugoslavia 1952–59; R-100
Yugoslavia 1960–69; R-100
Soviet Union 1945–48; Fb 12-28-12L
Soviet Union 1949–50; Fb 12-30-12L
Russia 1949–50; I-12L
Agreement on Friendship and Cooperation 1948; Negotiations' Delegations Archive; UM 1918–81
Soviet Union: Agreement on Friendship and Cooperation 6.4.1948; Fb 12-12L
Moscow 1948–49; R
Moscow 1950; R
Moscow 1951–52; R
Moscow 1953–55; R
Moscow 1956; R
Moscow 1957; R
Moscow 1958; R
Moscow 1959; R
Moscow 1961; R
Top Secret Memorandums 1947–72; Kc 1
Moscow, Group 5, Section B, Sunstrom; 1945–53
Finnish-Soviet Relations 1947–57; Kc 6
Finnish-Soviet Relations 1958–72; Kc 6
Top Secret Memorandums 1959–61; Kc6
Finnish Foreign Relations: Soviet Union; UM 1951–81; 12L:37
UM 1951–1981; 12L: 41 SSMM; Soviet Union Note Crises

Urho Kekkosen Arkisto (Presidential Archive of Urho Kekkonen)
Diary of Urho Kekkonen 1958–62
1-P-a: Politics: Foreign Policy: East Europe, National Democracies 1948–57
1-P-a: Politics: Foreign Policy: East Europe, National Democracies 1960–67
1-P-a: Politics: Foreign Policy: Nordic cooperation 1959–68
Yugoslavia 1954–56
State Visits: Yugoslavia 1963
State Visits: Yugoslavia 1964

Newspapers

The New York Times (New York 1948–58)
Izvestii'a (Moscow 1948–58)
Pravda (Moscow 1948–58)

Secondary Sources

Allison, Roy. *Finland's Relations with the Soviet Union 1944–84*. London: Macmillan, 1985.
Anikeev, A.S. *Kak Tito ot Stalin Ushel: iugoslaviia, sssr I ssha v nachal'nyi period kholodnoi voiny 1945–1957*. Moscow, Russia: In-t. slavianovedeniia RAN, 2002.
Banac, Ivo. *With Stalin against Tito: Cominformist Splits in Yugoslav Communism*. Ithaca: Cornell University Press, 1988.
Banac, Ivo (ed.) *The Diary of Georgi Dimitrov 1933–1949*. New Haven: Yale University Press, 2003.
Bela Knjiga: Agresivnim postupcima vlada SSSR, Polske, Čekoslovačke, Madjarske, Rumunije, Bugarske I Albanije prema Jugoslaviji. Belgrad: Ministarstvo Inostranih Poslova Federativne Narodne Republike Jugoslavije, 1951.
Bogetić, Dragan. *Nova Strategija Spoljne Politike Jugoslavije 1956–1961*. Belgrade: Institut za Savremenu Istoriju, 2007.
Broz, Josip 'Tito'. *Govori i članci* Vol Xiii. Zagreb: Naprijed, 1959.
Churchill, Winston. *The Second World War: Closing the Ring*. Boston: Houghton Mifflin, 1951.
Clissold, Stephen (ed.) *Yugoslavia and the Soviet Union 1939–1973: A documentary Survey*. Oxford: Oxford University Press, 1975.
Clogg, Richard (ed.) *Greece 1940–1949: Occupation, Resistance, Civil War: A Documentary History*. London: Palgrave Macmillan, 2002.
Dedijer, Vladimir. *Dnevnik 1–3*. Belgrade: Drzavni izdavački zavod Jugoslavije, 1945–1950.
Dedijer, Vladimir. *Josip Broz Tito: Prelozi za biografiju*. Belgrade: Kultura, 1953.
Dedijer, Vladimir. *Izgubljena bitka J. V. Staljina*. Belgrade: Prosveta, 1969.
Dedijer, Vladimir. *The Battle Stalin Lost: Memoirs of Yugoslavia 1948–1953*. New York: Viking Press, 1971.
Dedijer, Vladimir. *History of Yugoslavia*. New York: McGraw-Hill, 1974.
Dimitrov, Vesselin. *Stalin's Cold War: Soviet Foreign Policy, Democracy and Communism in Bulgaria, 1941–1948*. Doctoral thesis. London School of Economics and Political Science 2006.
Djilas, Milovan. *Conversations with Stalin*. New York: Harcourt, Bruce & World, 1962.
Djilas, Milovan. 'Tito and Stalin.' *Survey*, 23:3: 75.
Engermann, David. *Know Your Enemy: The Rise and Fall of America's Soviet Experts*. Oxford: Oxford University Press, 2009.
Frusetta, James Walter. 'Bulgaria's Macedonia: Nation-Building and State-Building, Centralization and Autonomy in Pirin Macedonia, 1903–1952.' PhD Thesis. University of Maryland College Park, 2006.
Gaddis, John Lewis. *Strategies of Containment: A Critical Appraisal of Postwar American National Security Policy*. New York: Oxford University Press, 1982.

Gaddis, John Lewis. 'The Emerging Post-Revisionist Synthesis on the Origins of the Cold War', *Diplomatic History* 7 (3) (1983): 171.
Gaddis, John Lewis. *What We Now Know: Rethinking Cold War History*. Oxford: Oxford University Press, 1997.
Gati, Charles. *Failed Illusions: Moscow, Washington, Budapest, and the 1956 Hungarian Revolt*. Stanford: Stanford University Press, 2006.
Gibianskii, Leonid. 'Sovetskii Soiuz i novaia Yugoslaviia, 1941–1947 gg.,' in *otvetstvennyi redactor* in V.K. Volkov, Moscow: Nauka, 1987.
Gibianskii, Leonid. 'U nachala konflikta — Balkanskii uzel: Otkrytyi arkhiv — K istorii sovetskoyugoslavskogo konflikta 1948–1953' *Rabochii klass i sovremennyi mir* 2 (1990), 173.
Gibianskii, Leonid. 'Sekretnaya sovetsko-yugoslavskaya perepiska 1948 (I)' *Voprosy istorii* 4–5 (1992), 119.
Gibianskii, Leonid. 'Sekretnaya sovetsko-yugoslavskaya perepiska 1948 (II)' *Voprosy istorii* 6–7 (1992), 158.
Gibianskii, Leonid. 'Sekretnaya sovetsko-yugoslavskaya perepiska 1948 (III)' *Voprosy istorii* 10 (1992), 141.
Gibianskii, Leonid (ed.) *U istokov 'sotsialisticheskogo sodruzhestva' : SSSR i vostochnoevropeiskie strany v 1944–1949*. Moscow: Nauka, 1995.
Gibianskii, Leonid. 'Report of Milovan Djilas about a Secret Soviet-Bulgarian – Yugoslav Meeting 10 February 1948,' *Cold War International History Project Bulletin*, 10 (March 1998), 128.
Gibianskii, Leonid. 'Ideya balkanskogo ob'edineniya I plany ee osushchestyleniya y 40-e gody XX Veka' *Voprosy istorii*, 11 (2001), 43.
Gibianskii, Leonid. 'Tretskii vopros v kontse vtoroi mirovoi voiny (1944-1945),' *Slayanovedenie* 4 (2001), 3.
Girenko, Yuri. *Stalin-Tito*. Moscow: Politizdat, 1991.
Grose, Peter. *Gentleman Spy: A life of Allen Dulles*. Boston: Houghton Mifflin, 1994.
Hauser, Beatrice. *Western 'Containment' Policies in the Cold War: The Case of Yugoslavia, 1948–1953*. London: Routledge, 1989.
Holloway, David. *Stalin and the Bomb: The Soviet Union and Atomic Energy 1939-1954*. New Haven, Conn.: Yale University Press, 1994.
Iatrides, John. *Revolt in Athens: The Greek Communist 'Second Round' 1944–1945*. New Jersey: Princeton University Press, 1972.
Jakobson, Max. *Finland: Myth and Reality*. Helsinki: Otava, 1987.
Jakovina, Tvrtko. *Američki komunistički saveznik; Hrvati, Titova Jugoslavija i Sjedinjene Američke Države 1945–1955*. Zagreb: Srednja Europa, 2003.
Jović, Dejan. *Yugoslavia: A State that Withered Away*. West Lafayette, Indiana: Purdue University Press, 2009.
Kaganovich, L.M. *Pamiatnye zapiski rabochego kommunista-bol'shevika, profsouznogo, partiinogo i sovetsko-gosudartsvennogo rabotnika*. Moscow: Vagrius, 1996.
Kardelj, Edvard. *Istorijski koreni nesvrstavanja*. Belgrade: Komunist, 1975.
Kardelj, Edvard. *Nations and Socialism*. Belgrade: STP, 1981.
Kardelj, Edvard. *Reminiscences: The Struggle for Recognition and Independence: The New Yugoslavia, 1944–1957*. London: Blond & Briggs, Summerfield Press, 1982.
Kardelj, Edvard. *Sećanja. Borba za priznanje I nezavisnost nove Jugoslavije, 1944–1957*. Ljubljana; Belgrade: Državna založba Slovenije—Radnicka štampa, 1980.

Keep, John, and Alter Litvin. *Stalinism: Russian and Western Views at the Turn of the Millennium.* London: Routledge, 2006.
Kekkonen, Urho Kaleva. *Urho Kekkosen Päiväkirjat I.* Juhani Suomi: Helsinki: Otava, 2001.
Kolanović, Nada Kisić. *Andrija Hebrang: iluzije i otrežnjenja.* Zagreb: Institut za Suvremneu Povijest, 1996.
Kramer, Mark. '"The Malin Notes" on the Crises in Hungary and Poland, 1956.' *Bulletin of the Cold War International History Project,* 8–9, (1996–97).
Krivosheev, G.A., (ed.) *Grif sekretnosti snyat: Poteri Vooruzhenykh Sil SSSR v Voinakh, Boevykh Deistviyakh I Voennykh konfliktakh: Statisticheskoe issledovanie.* Moskva: Voenizdat, 1993.
Lampe, John R.; Prickett, Russell O. and Adamović, Ljubiša (eds.) *Yugoslav-American Economic Relations Since World War II.* Durham: Duke University Press, 1990.
Lampe, John R. *Yugoslavia as History: Twice There Was a Country* 2nd ed. Cambridge: Cambridge University Press, 2000.
Lane, Ann and Temperley, Howard (eds.) *The Rise and Fall of the Grand Alliance, 1941–1945.* Basingstoke: Macmillan, 1995.
Laqueur, Walter. *The Political Psychology of Appeasement: Finlandization and Other Unpopular Essays.* New Brunswick, N.J.: Transaction Books, 1980.
Leffler, Melvyn P. *The Specter of Communism: The United States and the Origins of the Cold War, 1917–1953.* New York: Harper Collins, 1995.
Leffler, Melvyn P. 'The Cold War: What Do "We Now Know"'? *The American Historical Review,* 104 (2) (1999), 501.
Leffler, Melvyn P., and Painter, David S. (eds.) *Origins of the Cold War: An International History* 2nd edition. New York: Routledge, 2005.
Mates, Leo. *Medjunarodni odnosi socijalističke Jugoslavije.* Belgrade: Nolit, 1976.
McNeill, William H. *America, Britain and Russia: Their Cooperation and Conflict.* Oxford: Oxford University Press, 1953.
Mićunović, Veljko. *Moscow Diary,* translated by David Floyd. New York, Garden City: Doubleday and Company, 1980.
Mikoian, A.I. *Tak bylo: Razmyshleniia o minuvshem.* Moscow: Vagrius, 1999.
Milatović, Arso. *Pet Diplomatskih Misija: Bukurešt – Varšava.* Ljubljana and Zagreb: Cankareva Založba, 1986.
Milivojević, Marko, Allcock, John B. and Maurer, Pierre (eds.) *Yugoslavia's Security Dilemmas: Armed Forces, National Defense and Foreign Policy.* Oxford: Berg Press, 1988.
Miljković, Mita. *Burne Diplomatske Godine iz Sofijskog Dnevnika 1953–1956.* Belgrade: Službeni list SRJ, 1995.
Murashko, Galina. *Vlast i tserkov v SSSR i stranakh Vostochnoii Evropy, 1939–1958: diskussionnye aspekty.* Moscow: RAN, 2003.
Naimark, Norman. 'Cold War Studies and New Archival Materials on Stalin.' *The Russian Review* 61 January 2002, 1.
Naimark, Norman. 'Post-Soviet Russian Historiography on the Emergence of the Soviet Bloc' *Kritika 5: 3 2004,* 561.
Naimark, Norman and Gibianski, Leonid (eds.) *The Establishment of Communist Regimes in Eastern Europe, 1944–49.* Boulder, Co: Westview Press, 1997.

Nevakivi, Jukka. 'Finland and the Cold War,' *Scandinavian Journal of History*, 10:3, (1985).
Nevakivi, Jukka. *Ulkoasiainhallinnon historia.1: 1918–1956*. Helsinki: Ulkoaisiainministerio, 1988.
Novak, Bogdan C. *Trieste 1941–1954: The Ethnic, Political and Ideological Struggle*. Chicago: Chicago University Press, 1970.
Paxton, Robert. *Europe in the Twentieth Century*. Fourth edition. Forth Worth, Texas: Harcourt College Publishing, 2002.
Perović, Jeronim. 'The Tito-Stalin Split: A Reassessment in Light of New Evidence' *Journal of Cold War Studies* 9 (2) (2007): 34.
Petković, Ranko. *Subjektivna Istorija Jugoslovenske Diplomatije 1943–1991*. Belgrade: Službeni list SRJ, 1995.
Petković, Ranko. *1948: Jugoslavija I Kominform – pedeset godina kasnije*. Belgrade: Medjunarodna Politika, 1998.
Petranović, Branco. *Balkanska Federacija 1943–1948*. Belgrade: IKP, 1991.
Pijade, Moša. *Priča o Sovjetskoj Pomoći za Diranje Ustanka u Jugoslaviji*. Belgrade: Borba, 1950.
Pons, Silvio and Gori, Francesca (eds.) *The Soviet Union and Europe 1943-1953*. New York: St. Martin's Press, 1996.
Pons, Silvio. 'The Papers on Foreign and International Policy in the Russian Archives: The Stalin Years' Cahiers du Monde russe, 40/1–2, Janvier-juin 1999, 235.
Popović, Nikola. *Jugoslavensko-sovjetski odnosi u drugom svetskom ratu (1941–1945)*. Belgrade: Institute za savremenu Istoriju, 1988.
Procacci, Giuliano et. al. *The Cominform: Minutes of the Three Conferences 1947/1948/1949*. Milan: Feltrinelli, 1994.
Radonić, Radovan. *Izgubljena Orijentacija*. Belgrade: Radnička Štampa, 1985.
Ramet, Sabrina. *The Three Yugoslavias: State-Building and Legitimation, 1918–2004*. Indiana: Indiana University Press, 2007.
Reiss, Albert. 'The Churchill-Stalin Secret "Percentages" Agreement on the Balkans, Moscow, October 1944,' *American Historical Review*, 83 (1978): 368.
Rieber, Alfred J. *Zhdanov in Finland*. Pittsburgh, Pennsylvania: Center for Russian and East European Studies, University of Pittsburgh, 1995.
Reynolds, David (ed.) *The Origins of the Cold War in Europe: International Perspectives*. New Haven, Conn.: Yale University Press, 1994.
The Royal Institute of International Affairs. *Documents on International Affairs 1956*. Oxford: Oxford University Press, 1959.
The Royal Institute of International Affairs. *The Soviet-Yugoslav Dispute: Text of the Published Correspondence*. London: RIIA, 1948.
Rubinstein, Alvin. *Yugoslavia and the Nonaligned World*. Princeton: University Press, 1970.
Rusinow, Dennison. *The Yugoslav Experiment 1948–1974*. Berkeley: Published for the Royal Institute of International Affairs, London, by the University of California Press, 1977.
Sakwa, Richard. *The Rise and Fall of the Soviet Union 1917–1991*. London: Routledge, 1999.
Savez Komunista Jugoslavije. *Centralni Komitet: Pisma C.K.K.P.J.* Belgrade: Jugoslovenska Knjiga, 1948.

Selinić, Slobodan et.al. *Spoljna politika Jugoslavije 1950-1961*. Belgrade: Institut a Savremenu Istoriju, 2008.
Seppinen, Jukka. *Urho Kekkonen—Suomen Johtaja: Poliittinen elämänkerta*. Jyväskylä: Gummerus, 2004.
Service, Robert. *A History of Modern Russia: From Nicholas II to Vladimir Putin*. Cambridge: Harvard University Press, 2005.
Simola, Matti and Tuula Sirviö. *Isänmaan puolesta - Suojeluspoliisi 50 vuotta*. Helsinki: Gummerus, 1999.
Singleton, Fred. *Twentieth Century Yugoslavia*. New York: Columbia University Press, 1976.
Stavrakis, Peter J. *Moscow and Greek Communism, 1944–1949* (New York: Cornell University Press, 1989.
Štrbac, Čedomir. *Jugoslavija I Odnosi Izmedju Socijalističkih Zemalja: Sukob KPJ I Informbiroa*. Belgrade: Instituta za Medjunarodnu Politiku I Privredu, 1975.
Suomi, Juhani. *Urho Kekkonen 1972–1976: Liennytyksen akanvirrassa*. Helsinki: Otava, 1998.
Taubmann, William. *Khrushchev, The Man of his Era*. New York, New York: W.W. Norton, 2003.
Ulam, Adam. *Titoism and the Cominform*. Cambridge: Harvard University Press, 1952.
Ulam, Adam. *The New Face of Soviet Totalitarianism*. Cambridge, Mass., 1963.
Ulam, Adam. *Understanding the Cold War: A Historians Personal Reflections*, 2nd ed. New Brunswick, N.J., 2002.
Vihavainen, Timo. *Kansakunta Rähmällään: Suomettumisen lyhyt historia*. Helsinki: Otava, 1991.
Volgokonov, Dmitri. *The Rise and Fall of the Soviet Empire: Political Leaders From Lenin to Gorbachev*. London: HarperCollins, 1991.
Volkogonov, Dmitri. *Stalin: Triumph and Tragedy*. Edited and translated by Harold Shukman. New York, New York: Grove Weidenfeld, 1991.
Volokitina, T.V. Vostochnaia Evropa v dokumentakh rossiiskikh arkhivov: 1944–1953: Tom I 1944–1948. Moscow: Novosibirsk: Sibirskii khronograf, 1997–1998.
Volokitina, T.V. *Kholodnaia voina i sotsial-demokratiia Vostochnoi Evropy, 1944–1948 gg.: ocherki istorii*. Moskva : Rossiiskaia akademiia nauk, In-t slavianovedeniia, 1998.
Volokitina, T.V. et al. *Moskva i Vostochnaia Evropa : Stanovlenie Politicheskikh Rezhimov Sovetskogo Tipa : 1949–1953*. Moscow: Rosspen, 2002.
Volokitina, T.V. et. al. *Sovietskii factor v Vostochnoi Evrope 1944–1953: dokumenty*. Moscow: Rosspen, 1999–2002.
Volokitina, T.V. et. al. *Moskva i Vostochnaia Evropa: Stanovlenie politicheskikh rezhimov sovetskogo tipa, 1949–1953*. Moscow: Rosspen, 2002.
Vucinich, Wayne S. (ed.) *At the Brink of War and Peace: The Tito-Stalin Split in a Historic Perspective*. New York: Columbia University Press, East European Monographs, 1982.
Willets, Peter. *The Non-Aligned Movement: The Origins of a Third World Alliance*. London: Frances Pinter Ltd., 1978.
Williams, William Appleman. *The Tragedy of American Diplomacy*, 3rd edition. New York: W. Norton & Company, 1972.
Wilson, Duncan. *Tito's Yugoslavia*. Cambridge: Cambridge University Press, 1979.

Wuorinen, John H. 'The Finnish Treaty,' *Annals of the American Academy of Political and Social Science* 257–87 (1948).
Woodhouse, C. M. *The Struggle for Greece 1940–1949*. New York: Beekman-Esanu Press, 1976.
Zubok, Vladislav and Constantine Pleshakov. *Inside the Kremlin's Cold War: from Stalin to Khrushchev*. Cambridge: Harvard University Press, 1996.

INDEX

A

Albania, 10, 32–34, 40–41, 43, 89, 152, 185
   Plan for Balkan Federation 32–34
   Criticism of Yugoslavia 89–90
   Greek Civil War 40–43
Anikeev, Anatolii, 10–11, 14
Anti-Facist National Committee for the Liberation of Yugoslavia (AVNOJ), 28, 36
Australian and New Zealand Army Corps (Anzac), 35

B

Balkan Pact, 88, 90, 93, 100, 104, 151, 169, 174
   Koča Popović 90, 93, 104, 151, 174
Banac, Ivo, 6–7
Bandung Conference of Asian and African states (1955), 3, 12, 16
Belgrade Agreement, 115, 174
   Khrushchev, Nikita 113–115
Beria, Lavrenty, 83, 85, 114
Bled Agreement, 30–32, 88
Bogetić, Dragan, 6, 14
Broz, Josip 'Tito', 3–16, 20–22, 25–28, 30–50, 57–60, 62, 68, 71, 73–74, 77–79, 87–94, 96, 100–103, 105–107, 110–123, 125–126, 131–139, 142–143, 145–148, 150–152, 158, 170–171, 173–179, 181

Bulganin, Nikolai, 44, 85, 115–116, 122, 142
Bulgaria, 2, 26, 28, 30–34, 42, 50, 79, 90, 103, 115, 122–123
   Plan for Balkan Federation 32–34
   Bulgarian Communist Party, 29

C

Chetniks, 28, 36, 59
Cold War, 1–3, 6–10, 16, 18–20, 35, 69, 72, 106, 111–112, 150, 178–179
Cominform, 1, 5–9, 15, 22, 25–26, 30, 32, 35, 38–39, 45, 47–49, 79, 84, 92, 95–96, 105, 113–115, 123, 132, 135–136, 139, 147, 173
Communist Party of Greece, 8, 29
Communist Party of Yugoslavia, 5, 9, 26–27, 36, 47–48, 50, 90, 92, 188
Crnobrnja, Bogdan, 40–43, 100
Czechoslovakia, 7, 31–33. 35, 54–56, 62, 75, 84, 90, 123
   Criticism of Yugoslavia 90, 123
   Czechoslovak-Soviet Treaty 54–56

D

Dedijer, Vladimir, 5, 7, 14–15, 26, 120
Denmark, 75, 117–118, 202
   Scandinavian regionalism of Nikita Khrushchev 117–118

Dimitrov, Georgi, 30, 32–34, 71
Djilas, Milovan, 6–9, 26, 34–36, 39–41, 47–48, 62, 74, 89, 91, 105, 126, 137–138

E
East Berlin, 107
Egypt, 3, 12–13, 16, 177
   Suez crisis 3, 13, 16, 123
   Non-Aligned Movement 13, 16, 177
European Free Trade Association, 4
European Recovery Program, 75

F
Finnish- Soviet Agreement on Friendship, Cooperation and Mutual Assistance, 3, 18, 21, 26, 51, 54–56, 58–71, 76–79, 81, 84–85, 95, 101, 112, 127, 174, 179
Free Territory of Trieste (FTT), 35

G
Gibianskii, Leonid, 10
Greece, 5, 8, 2–29, 32–33, 41, 88, 93, 123, 169, 188–190
Greek Civil War, 8, 11, 26, 29
   Yugoslav support of 10–11, 29, 31, 34, 41
   National Popular Liberation Army (ELAS) 29

H
Hungary, 3, 22, 28, 32–34, 53, 64, 69, 75, 98, 109–112, 115, 120–123, 129–130, 133–139, 141–143, 145–146, 155, 164, 167, 175, 180
Hungarian Revolution (1956), 4, 14, 77, 96, 107, 110–112, 120, 130, 137, 147, 159, 175, 180
   Josip Broz 'Tito' 4, 112–113, 118–120, 136–138, 143, 146, 148
   Urho Kaleva Kekkonen 110, 112, 129, 147, 159, 180

I
Iceland, 117–118, 142, 202
   Scandinavian regionalism of Nikita Khrushchev 117–118, 142
India, 12–13, 15–16, 177
Italy, 5, 12–13, 34–35, 56, 93–94, 97, 150–151, 160
   Sovereignty over Trieste 34–35, 93, 97, 151

K
Kardelj, Edvard, 1, 4, 6–7, 9, 14–15, 20–22, 26, 30, 34–41, 43, 46, 48, 50, 53, 55, 57, 60, 62, 68, 74, 77–78, 83, 83, 87–92, 96, 100–101, 103, 106, 111, 113–114, 116, 120–121, 125–126, 134–139, 143, 145–146, 148, 150–151, 170–171, 173–177
Kekkonen, Urho Kaleva, 2, 18–20, 23, 56–63, 66, 68–69, 71, 78–79, 83, 85–86, 96, 100, 110–112, 116, 118–119, 125–127, 129–130, 141–142, 146–147, 158–165, 167–171, 176–181
Khrushchev, Nikita, 3, 22, 83, 85, 104, 107, 110–123, 125–126, 131–133, 135, 142, 146–153, 156–157, 163, 167, 170, 174–176, 179
   Policy of Scandinavian regionalism 113, 117–119, 131, 142, 147–148, 157
Kidrič, Boris, 45, 47
Korean War, 12, 14, 38, 81

L
Lavrentev, Anatolii, 10, 31
Lavrishchev, Aleksandr, 10
League of Communists of Yugoslavia (LCY), 89, 105, 117, 151, 157

M
Malenkov, Georgi, 83, 85, 104, 149, 168

Mannerheim, Carl Gustav Emil, 54–56, 193
　Andrei Zhdanov 54–56
Marshall Plan, 76
Mediterranean, 3, 11, 30, 34, 57, 88, 188
Mićunović, Veljko, 91–92, 100, 104, 120, 134–135, 146, 150–152, 154–155, 158, 167, 173, 175, 177
Mikoyan, Anastas, 70, 85, 122
Molotov, Vyacheslav, 10, 21, 28, 34, 37, 40, 45–46, 49–50, 54–57, 69, 71, 81, 83–88, 101, 103–104, 113, 119, 149, 168, 170, 198–199, 202, 209
Moscow Declaration, 115, 121–125, 131–132, 135, 137, 139, 143, 145–148, 174

N
Naimark, Norman, 9, 185
Nasser, Gamal Abdel, 12–13, 16, 123, 177
　Non-Aligned Movement 12–13, 16
National Popular Liberation Army (ELAS), 29
Nehru, Jawaharlal, 12–13, 15–16, 116, 123, 177
Neutralism, 1–4, 8, 17–20, 22, 50–51, 53, 56, 58–59, 62, 64, 71–72, 74–76, 79–80, 83, 94, 98, 100, 103, 106–107, 109–110, 112, 114, 117, 119, 121, 127, 131–132, 143, 146, 151–154, 158–159, 168, 171, 173–174, 176, 178–181
Neutrality, 65–66, 73, 109–111, 143, 178
Niskanen, Ville, 77–78, 140–141, 199
Night Frost Crisis, 159, 162–163, 176–177
Non-Aligned Movement, 2–6, 12–17, 21, 94, 177–178
　Founding conference (1961), 2, 4, 13, 15–16, 177–178
Non-alignment, 4, 11 – 16, 18, 20, 74, 94, 178
Nordic Council, 116–117, 121, 126, 142
North Atlantic Treaty Organization (NATO), 3, 5, 17, 75, 82, 88, 104, 107, 117–118, 150, 156–157, 174–175
Norway, 75, 82, 117–118, 202
　Scandinavian regionalism of Nikita Khrushchev 117–118

O
Organization on Security and Cooperation in Europe (OSCE), 17

P
Paasikivi, Juho Kusti, 2, 19, 21, 53–64, 66–70, 74, 78–79, 83, 94, 96, 116–118, 126–130, 162, 171, 178–180
Paasikivi–Kekkonen Line, 2, 4, 18–19, 22, 58–59, 66, 69, 72, 74–76, 79, 85, 100, 103, 106, 119, 121, 125–127, 129–131, 139, 142–143, 147–148, 158–160, 162–163, 170–171, 174–176, 206
Partisans (Yugoslav), 7–8, 27–28, 35–36, 59, 93
Percentages Agreement, 28, 34
Pleshakov, Constantine, 9, 55
Poland, 7, 32–35, 42, 50, 84, 110, 122–123, 149, 167
Popović, Koča, 15, 20, 22, 40–42, 46–47, 49, 83, 87, 90–94, 97, 100, 102, 104, 114, 117, 120–121, 146, 151–152, 15, 169, 171, 173–175, 177–178, 180
　Yugoslav Foreign Ministry 22, 40, 87, 90–93, 97, 100, 104, 121, 146, 151, 171, 173, 175, 178
Porkkala, 54, 58, 116, 120, 129, 142, 179

R

Ramet, Sabrina, 13
Ranković, Aleksandar, 26, 39–40, 47, 92–94, 100, 151, 155, 206
Rapprochement, 11, 17, 22, 83, 87, 89, 100–103, 110–113, 115, 119, 126–127, 130–131, 136, 142, 148
Red Army, 27, 56, 136, 176, 188, 197, 201
Romania, 28, 32–34, 42–44, 53, 64, 69, 75, 79, 90, 98, 105, 120, 123–124, 148
Rubinstein, Alvin, 6, 12–13
Rusinow, Dennison, 7

S

Simić, Stanoje, 36–37, 49, 53, 77–78
Singleton, Fred, 13, 15
Split (Tito-Stalin), 2–11, 13, 20, 22, 25–26, 37, 39, 45, 48–49, 72–73, 75, 78, 83, 86, 88–89, 92, 98, 100–102, 104, 111, 115, 134, 136, 138, 145, 173, 176–177, 179
Stalin, Josef, 1, 3–11, 21–22, 25–35, 37, 39. 40, 43, 45, 47–50, 53, 55–56, 59, 62, 65, 68, 70, 74–75, 78, 81–90, 93, 96–97, 100, 102–107, 109, 113–114, 117–119, 146, 148, 153, 168, 174, 176
    Death of, 4, 22, 34, 50, 79, 81–84, 86–90, 93–94, 96–97, 100–103, 105–107, 113–114, 117, 174
Stalinism, 111, 113, 147–148, 152
Suez Crisis, 3, 13, 15–16, 123, 142, 151
    Non-Aligned Movement 3, 13, 15–16
Suslov, Mikhail, 32, 122
Sweden, 18, 59–60, 75–76, 82, 84, 117–118, 202
    Scandinavian regionalism of Nikita Khrushchev 117–118

T

Third World, 3, 13–15
Tito *please see* Broz, Josip 'Tito'
Titoism, 127
Turkey, 16, 29, 88, 93, 150, 169
    Balkan Pact 88, 93, 169

U

Ulam, Adam, 6–8
United Nations (UN), 16, 38, 84, 109, 117, 121, 129, 142, 169, 177, 180, 200
    United Nations Relief and Rehabilitation Aid (UNRRA), 177, 210

W

Warsaw Pact, 3, 14, 95, 109, 111, 112, 119, 121, 133, 142, 169
West Berlin, 175, 178
Wilson, Duncan, 11, 14, 178

Y

Yugoslav Administration for State Security (UDBa), 8, 38–40, 48, 92–93, 100, 155, 175
Yugoslav Foreign Ministry, 2–4, 10, 14–17, 20–23, 37, 39, 41–42, 44, 47, 50, 71–72, 74, 77, 79, 82–83, 86–96, 100–101, 103–107, 110–111, 113–114, 117, 121–132, 134, 138–143, 146, 150–151, 153–158, 165, 169–181
Yugoslav Peoples' Army, 40, 93

Z

Zhdanov, Andrei, 8, 54–56, 69, 85, 193
Zubok, Vladislav, 9, 55

Lightning Source UK Ltd.
Milton Keynes UK
UKHW021909280520
363987UK00010B/645